Yocto Project Development Manual

A catalogue record for this book is available from the Hong Kong Public Libraries.

Published in Hong Kong by Samurai Media Limited.

Email: info@samuraimedia.org

ISBN 978-988-8381-97-5

Table of Contents

1. The Yocto Project Development Manual 1
    1.1. Introduction 1
    1.2. What This Manual Provides 1
    1.3. What this Manual Does Not Provide 1
    1.4. Other Information 2
2. Getting Started with the Yocto Project 4
    2.1. Introducing the Yocto Project 4
    2.2. Getting Set Up 4
    2.3. Building Images 7
    2.4. Using Pre-Built Binaries and QEMU 7
3. The Yocto Project Open Source Development Environment 9
    3.1. Open Source Philosophy 9
    3.2. Using the Yocto Project in a Team Environment 9
        3.2.1. System Configurations 9
        3.2.2. Source Control Management (SCM) 10
        3.2.3. Autobuilders 11
        3.2.4. Policies and Change Flow 11
        3.2.5. Summary 12
    3.3. Yocto Project Source Repositories 12
    3.4. Yocto Project Terms 14
    3.5. Licensing 17
    3.6. Git 18
        3.6.1. Repositories, Tags, and Branches 18
        3.6.2. Basic Commands 19
    3.7. Workflows 20
    3.8. Tracking Bugs 22
    3.9. How to Submit a Change 23
        3.9.1. Using Scripts to Push a Change Upstream and Request a Pull 25
        3.9.2. Using Email to Submit a Patch 25
4. Common Development Models 27
    4.1. System Development Workflow 27
        4.1.1. Developing a Board Support Package (BSP) 27
        4.1.2. Modifying the Kernel 30
    4.2. Application Development Workflow 34
        4.2.1. Workflow Using the ADT and Eclipse™ 34
        4.2.2. Working Within Eclipse 37
        4.2.3. Workflow Using Stand-Alone Cross-Development Toolchains 45
    4.3. Modifying Temporary Source Code 46
        4.3.1. Finding the Temporary Source Code 46
        4.3.2. Using a Quilt Workflow 47
        4.3.3. Using a Git Workflow 48
    4.4. Image Development Using Hob 50
    4.5. Using a Development Shell 50
5. Common Tasks 52
    5.1. Understanding and Creating Layers 52
        5.1.1. Layers 52
        5.1.2. Creating Your Own Layer 52
        5.1.3. Best Practices to Follow When Creating Layers 54
        5.1.4. Enabling Your Layer 55
        5.1.5. Using .bbappend Files 56
        5.1.6. Prioritizing Your Layer 57
        5.1.7. Managing Layers 58
        5.1.8. Creating a General Layer Using the yocto-layer Script 59
    5.2. Customizing Images 60
        5.2.1. Customizing Images Using local.conf 60
        5.2.2. Customizing Images Using Custom IMAGE_FEATURES and
        EXTRA_IMAGE_FEATURES 61
        5.2.3. Customizing Images Using Custom .bb Files 61
        5.2.4. Customizing Images Using Custom Package Groups 62
    5.3. Writing a New Recipe 62
        5.3.1. Overview 63

5.3.2. Locate a Base Recipe 63
5.3.3. Storing and Naming the Recipe 64
5.3.4. Understanding Recipe Syntax 65
5.3.5. Running a Build on the Recipe 68
5.3.6. Fetching Code 69
5.3.7. Unpacking Code 70
5.3.8. Patching Code 71
5.3.9. Licensing 71
5.3.10. Configuring the Recipe 72
5.3.11. Compilation 73
5.3.12. Installing 73
5.3.13. Enabling System Services 74
5.3.14. Packaging 75
5.3.15. Properly Versioning Pre-Release Recipes 76
5.3.16. Post-Installation Scripts 76
5.3.17. Testing 77
5.3.18. Examples 77
5.4. Adding a New Machine 80
5.4.1. Adding the Machine Configuration File 80
5.4.2. Adding a Kernel for the Machine 81
5.4.3. Adding a Formfactor Configuration File 81
5.5. Working With Libraries 82
5.5.1. Including Static Library Files 82
5.5.2. Combining Multiple Versions of Library Files into One Image 83
5.5.3. Installing Multiple Versions of the Same Library 84
5.6. Creating Partitioned Images 85
5.6.1. Background 85
5.6.2. Requirements 86
5.6.3. Getting Help 86
5.6.4. Operational Modes 86
5.6.5. Using an Existing Kickstart File 88
5.6.6. Examples 88
5.6.7. Plugins 91
5.6.8. OpenEmbedded Kickstart (.wks) Reference 92
5.7. Configuring the Kernel 94
5.7.1. Using menuconfig 94
5.7.2. Creating Configuration Fragments 95
5.7.3. Fine-Tuning the Kernel Configuration File 96
5.8. Patching the Kernel 96
5.8.1. Create a Layer for your Changes 97
5.8.2. Finding the Kernel Source Code 97
5.8.3. Creating the Patch 97
5.8.4. Set Up Your Layer for the Build 98
5.8.5. Set Up for the Build 99
5.8.6. Build the Modified QEMU Kernel Image 100
5.8.7. Boot the Image and Verify Your Changes 100
5.9. Making Images More Secure 100
5.9.1. General Considerations 101
5.9.2. Security Flags 101
5.9.3. Considerations Specific to the OpenEmbedded Build System 102
5.9.4. Tools for Hardening Your Image 102
5.10. Creating Your Own Distribution 102
5.11. Creating a Custom Template Configuration Directory 104
5.12. Building a Tiny System 105
5.12.1. Overview 105
5.12.2. Goals and Guiding Principles 105
5.12.3. Understand What Contributes to Your Image Size 105
5.12.4. Trim the Root Filesystem 106
5.12.5. Trim the Kernel 107
5.12.6. Remove Package Management Requirements 107
5.12.7. Look for Other Ways to Minimize Size 108
5.12.8. Iterate on the Process 108
5.13. Working with Packages 108
5.13.1. Excluding Packages from an Image 108

5.13.2. Incrementing a Package Revision Number 109
5.13.3. Handling a Package Name Alias 111
5.13.4. Handling Optional Module Packaging 111
5.13.5. Using Runtime Package Management 114
5.13.6. Testing Packages With ptest 117
5.14. Working with Source Files 119
5.14.1. Setting up Effective Mirrors 119
5.14.2. Getting Source Files and Suppressing the Build 119
5.15. Building Software from an External Source 120
5.16. Selecting an Initialization Manager 120
5.16.1. Using systemd Exclusively 120
5.16.2. Using systemd for the Main Image and Using SysVinit for the Rescue Image .. 121
5.17. Using an External SCM 121
5.18. Creating a Read-Only Root Filesystem 122
5.18.1. Creating the Root Filesystem 122
5.18.2. Post-Installation Scripts 123
5.18.3. Areas With Write Access 123
5.19. Performing Automated Runtime Testing 123
5.19.1. Enabling Tests 123
5.19.2. Running Tests 127
5.19.3. Exporting Tests 128
5.19.4. Writing New Tests 129
5.20. Debugging With the GNU Project Debugger (GDB) Remotely 130
5.20.1. Set Up the Cross-Development Debugging Environment 131
5.20.2. Launch Gdbserver on the Target 131
5.20.3. Launch GDB on the Host Computer 131
5.20.4. Connect to the Remote GDB Server 132
5.20.5. Use the Debugger 132
5.21. Debugging Parallel Make Races 133
5.21.1. The Failure 133
5.21.2. Reproducing the Error 134
5.21.3. Creating a Patch for the Fix 135
5.21.4. Testing the Build 135
5.22. Examining Builds Using the Toaster API 136
5.22.1. Starting Toaster 136
5.22.2. Using Toaster 137
5.22.3. Examining Toaster Data 137
5.22.4. Stopping Toaster 138
5.23. Profiling with OProfile 138
5.23.1. Profiling on the Target 138
5.23.2. Using OProfileUI 139
5.24. Maintaining Open Source License Compliance During Your Product's Lifecycle 140
5.24.1. Providing the Source Code 141
5.24.2. Providing License Text 142
5.24.3. Providing Compilation Scripts and Source Code Modifications 142
5.25. Using the Error Reporting Tool 143
5.25.1. Enabling and Using the Tool 143
5.25.2. Disabling the Tool 144
5.25.3. Setting Up Your Own Error Reporting Server 144
6. Using the Quick EMUlator (QEMU) 145
6.1. Overview 145
6.2. Running QEMU 145
6.2.1. Setting Up the Environment 145
6.2.2. Using the runqemu Command 145
6.3. Running Under a Network File System (NFS) Server 147
6.3.1. Setting Up to Use NFS 147
6.3.2. Starting and Stopping NFS 148
6.4. Tips and Tricks 148

Chapter 1. The Yocto Project Development Manual

1.1. Introduction

Welcome to the Yocto Project Development Manual! This manual provides information on how to use the Yocto Project to develop embedded Linux images and user-space applications that run on targeted devices. The manual provides an overview of image, kernel, and user-space application development using the Yocto Project. Because much of the information in this manual is general, it contains many references to other sources where you can find more detail. For example, you can find detailed information on Git, repositories, and open source in general in many places on the Internet. Another example specific to the Yocto Project is how to quickly set up your host development system and build an image, which you find in the Yocto Project Quick Start [http://www.yoctoproject.org/docs/1.7.2/yocto-project-qs/yocto-project-qs.html].

The Yocto Project Development Manual does, however, provide guidance and examples on how to change the kernel source code, reconfigure the kernel, and develop an application using the popular Eclipse™ IDE.

Note

By default, using the Yocto Project creates a Poky distribution. However, you can create your own distribution by providing key Metadata [16]. A good example is Angstrom, which has had a distribution based on the Yocto Project since its inception. Other examples include commercial distributions like Wind River Linux [https://www.yoctoproject.org/organization/wind-river-systems], Mentor Embedded Linux [https://www.yoctoproject.org/organization/mentor-graphics], ENEA Linux [https://www.yoctoproject.org/organization/enea-ab] and others [https://www.yoctoproject.org/ecosystem/member-organizations]. See the "Creating Your Own Distribution" section for more information.

1.2. What This Manual Provides

The following list describes what you can get from this manual:

- Information that lets you get set up to develop using the Yocto Project.

- Information to help developers who are new to the open source environment and to the distributed revision control system Git, which the Yocto Project uses.

- An understanding of common end-to-end development models and tasks.

- Information about common development tasks generally used during image development for embedded devices.

- Information on using the Yocto Project integration of the QuickEMUlator (QEMU), which lets you simulate running on hardware an image you have built using the OpenEmbedded build system.

- Many references to other sources of related information.

1.3. What this Manual Does Not Provide

This manual will not give you the following:

- Step-by-step instructions when those instructions exist in other Yocto Project documentation: For example, the Yocto Project Application Developer's Guide contains detailed instructions on how to run the ADT Installer [http://www.yoctoproject.org/docs/1.7.2/adt-manual/adt-manual.html#installing-the-adt], which is used to set up a cross-development environment.

- Reference material: This type of material resides in an appropriate reference manual. For example, system variables are documented in the Yocto Project Reference Manual [http://www.yoctoproject.org/docs/1.7.2/ref-manual/ref-manual.html].

• Detailed public information that is not specific to the Yocto Project: For example, exhaustive information on how to use Git is covered better through the Internet than in this manual.

1.4. Other Information

Because this manual presents overview information for many different topics, supplemental information is recommended for full comprehension. The following list presents other sources of information you might find helpful:

• Yocto Project Website [http://www.yoctoproject.org]: The home page for the Yocto Project provides lots of information on the project as well as links to software and documentation.

• Yocto Project Quick Start [http://www.yoctoproject.org/docs/1.7.2/yocto-project-qs/yocto-project-qs.html]: This short document lets you get started with the Yocto Project and quickly begin building an image.

• Yocto Project Reference Manual [http://www.yoctoproject.org/docs/1.7.2/ref-manual/ref-manual.html]: This manual is a reference guide to the OpenEmbedded build system, which is based on BitBake. The build system is sometimes referred to as "Poky".

• Yocto Project Application Developer's Guide [http://www.yoctoproject.org/docs/1.7.2/adt-manual/adt-manual.html]: This guide provides information that lets you get going with the Application Development Toolkit (ADT) and stand-alone cross-development toolchains to develop projects using the Yocto Project.

• Yocto Project Board Support Package (BSP) Developer's Guide [http://www.yoctoproject.org/docs/1.7.2/bsp-guide/bsp-guide.html]: This guide defines the structure for BSP components. Having a commonly understood structure encourages standardization.

• Yocto Project Linux Kernel Development Manual [http://www.yoctoproject.org/docs/1.7.2/kernel-dev/kernel-dev.html]: This manual describes how to work with Linux Yocto kernels as well as provides a bit of conceptual information on the construction of the Yocto Linux kernel tree.

• Yocto Project Profiling and Tracing Manual [http://www.yoctoproject.org/docs/1.7.2/profile-manual/profile-manual.html]: This manual presents a set of common and generally useful tracing and profiling schemes along with their applications (as appropriate) to each tool.

• Eclipse IDE Yocto Plug-in [http://www.youtube.com/watch?v=3ZlOu-gLsh0]: A step-by-step instructional video that demonstrates how an application developer uses Yocto Plug-in features within the Eclipse IDE.

• FAQ [https://wiki.yoctoproject.org/wiki/FAQ]: A list of commonly asked questions and their answers.

• Release Notes [http://www.yoctoproject.org/downloads/core/dizzy172]: Features, updates and known issues for the current release of the Yocto Project.

• Hob [http://www.yoctoproject.org/tools-resources/projects/hob]: A graphical user interface for BitBake. Hob's primary goal is to enable a user to perform common tasks more easily.

• Toaster [http://www.yoctoproject.org/tools-resources/projects/toaster]: An Application Programming Interface (API) and web-based interface to the OpenEmbedded build system, which uses BitBake, that reports build information.

• Build Appliance [http://www.yoctoproject.org/tools-resources/projects/build-appliance]: A virtual machine that enables you to build and boot a custom embedded Linux image with the Yocto Project using a non-Linux development system.

• Bugzilla [http://bugzilla.yoctoproject.org]: The bug tracking application the Yocto Project uses. If you find problems with the Yocto Project, you should report them using this application.

• Yocto Project Mailing Lists: To subscribe to the Yocto Project mailing lists, click on the following URLs and follow the instructions:

    • http://lists.yoctoproject.org/listinfo/yocto for a Yocto Project Discussions mailing list.

    • http://lists.yoctoproject.org/listinfo/poky for a Yocto Project Discussions mailing list about the OpenEmbedded build system (Poky).

- http://lists.yoctoproject.org/listinfo/yocto-announce for a mailing list to receive official Yocto Project announcements as well as Yocto Project milestones.

- http://lists.yoctoproject.org/listinfo for a listing of all public mailing lists on lists.yoctoproject.org.

- Internet Relay Chat (IRC): Two IRC channels on freenode are available for Yocto Project and Poky discussions: #yocto and #poky, respectively.

- OpenEmbedded [http://www.openembedded.org]: The build system used by the Yocto Project. This project is the upstream, generic, embedded distribution from which the Yocto Project derives its build system (Poky) and to which it contributes.

- BitBake [http://www.openembedded.org/wiki/BitBake]: The tool used by the OpenEmbedded build system to process project metadata.

- BitBake User Manual: [http://www.yoctoproject.org/docs/1.7.2/bitbake-user-manual/bitbake-user-manual.html] A comprehensive guide to the BitBake tool. If you want information on BitBake, see this manual.

- Quick EMUlator (QEMU) [http://wiki.qemu.org/Index.html]: An open-source machine emulator and virtualizer.

Chapter 2. Getting Started with the Yocto Project

This chapter introduces the Yocto Project and gives you an idea of what you need to get started. You can find enough information to set up your development host and build or use images for hardware supported by the Yocto Project by reading the Yocto Project Quick Start [http://www.yoctoproject.org/docs/1.7.2/yocto-project-qs/yocto-project-qs.html].

The remainder of this chapter summarizes what is in the Yocto Project Quick Start and provides some higher-level concepts you might want to consider.

2.1. Introducing the Yocto Project

The Yocto Project is an open-source collaboration project focused on embedded Linux development. The project currently provides a build system that is referred to as the OpenEmbedded build system [15] in the Yocto Project documentation. The Yocto Project provides various ancillary tools for the embedded developer and also features the Sato reference User Interface, which is optimized for stylus driven, low-resolution screens.

You can use the OpenEmbedded build system, which uses BitBake [14], to develop complete Linux images and associated user-space applications for architectures based on ARM, MIPS, PowerPC, x86 and x86-64.

Note

By default, using the Yocto Project creates a Poky distribution. However, you can create your own distribution by providing key Metadata [16]. See the "Creating Your Own Distribution" section for more information.

While the Yocto Project does not provide a strict testing framework, it does provide or generate for you artifacts that let you perform target-level and emulated testing and debugging. Additionally, if you are an Eclipse™ IDE user, you can install an Eclipse Yocto Plug-in to allow you to develop within that familiar environment.

2.2. Getting Set Up

Here is what you need to use the Yocto Project:

- Host System: You should have a reasonably current Linux-based host system. You will have the best results with a recent release of Fedora, openSUSE, Debian, Ubuntu, or CentOS as these releases are frequently tested against the Yocto Project and officially supported. For a list of the distributions under validation and their status, see the "Supported Linux Distributions [http://www.yoctoproject.org/docs/1.7.2/ref-manual/ref-manual.html#detailed-supported-distros]" section in the Yocto Project Reference Manual and the wiki page at Distribution Support [https://wiki.yoctoproject.org/wiki/Distribution_Support].

  You should also have about 50 Gbytes of free disk space for building images.

- Packages: The OpenEmbedded build system requires that certain packages exist on your development system (e.g. Python 2.6 or 2.7). See "The Packages [http://www.yoctoproject.org/docs/1.7.2/yocto-project-qs/yocto-project-qs.html#packages]" section in the Yocto Project Quick Start and the "Required Packages for the Host Development System [http://www.yoctoproject.org/docs/1.7.2/ref-manual/ref-manual.html#required-packages-for-the-host-development-system]" section in the Yocto Project Reference Manual for the exact package requirements and the installation commands to install them for the supported distributions.

- Yocto Project Release: You need a release of the Yocto Project locally installed on your development system. The documentation refers to this set of locally installed files as the Source Directory [16]. You create your Source Directory by using Git to clone a local copy of the upstream poky repository, or by downloading and unpacking a tarball of an official Yocto Project release. The preferred method is to create a clone of the repository.

Working from a copy of the upstream repository allows you to contribute back into the Yocto Project or simply work with the latest software on a development branch. Because Git maintains and creates an upstream repository with a complete history of changes and you are working with a local clone of that repository, you have access to all the Yocto Project development branches and tag names used in the upstream repository.

Note

You can view the Yocto Project Source Repositories at http://git.yoctoproject.org/cgit.cgi

The following transcript shows how to clone the poky Git repository into the current working directory. The command creates the local repository in a directory named poky. For information on Git used within the Yocto Project, see the "Git" section.

```
$ git clone git://git.yoctoproject.org/poky
Cloning into 'poky'...
remote: Counting objects: 226790, done.
remote: Compressing objects: 100% (57465/57465), done.
remote: Total 226790 (delta 165212), reused 225887 (delta 164327)
Receiving objects: 100% (226790/226790), 100.98 MiB | 263 KiB/s, done.
Resolving deltas: 100% (165212/165212), done.
```

For another example of how to set up your own local Git repositories, see this wiki page [https://wiki.yoctoproject.org/wiki/Transcript:_from_git_checkout_to_meta-intel_BSP], which describes how to create local Git repositories for both poky and meta-intel.

• Yocto Project Kernel: If you are going to be making modifications to a supported Yocto Project kernel, you need to establish local copies of the source. You can find Git repositories of supported Yocto Project kernels organized under "Yocto Linux Kernel" in the Yocto Project Source Repositories at http://git.yoctoproject.org/cgit.cgi.

This setup can involve creating a bare clone of the Yocto Project kernel and then copying that cloned repository. You can create the bare clone and the copy of the bare clone anywhere you like. For simplicity, it is recommended that you create these structures outside of the Source Directory, which is usually named poky.

As an example, the following transcript shows how to create the bare clone of the linux-yocto-3.10 kernel and then create a copy of that clone.

Note

When you have a local Yocto Project kernel Git repository, you can reference that repository rather than the upstream Git repository as part of the clone command. Doing so can speed up the process.

In the following example, the bare clone is named linux-yocto-3.10.git, while the copy is named my-linux-yocto-3.10-work:

```
$ git clone --bare git://git.yoctoproject.org/linux-yocto-3.10 linux-yocto-3.10.git
Cloning into bare repository 'linux-yocto-3.10.git'...
remote: Counting objects: 3364487, done.
remote: Compressing objects: 100% (507178/507178), done.
remote: Total 3364487 (delta 2827715), reused 3364481 (delta 2827709)
Receiving objects: 100% (3364487/3364487), 722.95 MiB | 423 KiB/s, done.
Resolving deltas: 100% (2827715/2827715), done.
```

Now create a clone of the bare clone just created:

```
$ git clone linux-yocto-3.10.git my-linux-yocto-3.10-work
Cloning into 'my-linux-yocto-3.10-work'...
done.
```

- The `meta-yocto-kernel-extras` Git Repository: The `meta-yocto-kernel-extras` Git repository contains Metadata needed only if you are modifying and building the kernel image. In particular, it contains the kernel BitBake append (`.bbappend`) files that you edit to point to your locally modified kernel source files and to build the kernel image. Pointing to these local files is much more efficient than requiring a download of the kernel's source files from upstream each time you make changes to the kernel.

  You can find the `meta-yocto-kernel-extras` Git Repository in the "Yocto Metadata Layers" area of the Yocto Project Source Repositories at http://git.yoctoproject.org/cgit.cgi. It is good practice to create this Git repository inside the Source Directory.

  Following is an example that creates the `meta-yocto-kernel-extras` Git repository inside the Source Directory, which is named poky in this case:

  ```
  $ cd ~/poky
  $ git clone git://git.yoctoproject.org/meta-yocto-kernel-extras meta-yocto-kernel-extras
  Cloning into 'meta-yocto-kernel-extras'...
  remote: Counting objects: 727, done.
  remote: Compressing objects: 100% (452/452), done.
  remote: Total 727 (delta 260), reused 719 (delta 252)
  Receiving objects: 100% (727/727), 536.36 KiB | 240 KiB/s, done.
  Resolving deltas: 100% (260/260), done.
  ```

- Supported Board Support Packages (BSPs): The Yocto Project supports many BSPs, which are maintained in their own layers or in layers designed to contain several BSPs. To get an idea of machine support through BSP layers, you can look at the index of machines [http://downloads.yoctoproject.org/releases/yocto/yocto-1.7.2/machines] for the release.

  The Yocto Project uses the following BSP layer naming scheme:

  ```
  meta-bsp_name
  ```

  where bsp_name is the recognized BSP name. Here are some examples:

  ```
  meta-crownbay
  meta-emenlow
  meta-n450
  ```

  See the "BSP Layers [http://www.yoctoproject.org/docs/1.7.2/bsp-guide/bsp-guide.html#bsp-layers]" section in the Yocto Project Board Support Package (BSP) Developer's Guide for more information on BSP Layers.

  A useful Git repository released with the Yocto Project is `meta-intel`, which is a parent layer that contains many supported BSP Layers [http://www.yoctoproject.org/docs/1.7.2/bsp-guide/bsp-guide.html#bsp-layers]. You can locate the `meta-intel` Git repository in the "Yocto Metadata Layers" area of the Yocto Project Source Repositories at http://git.yoctoproject.org/cgit.cgi.

  Using Git to create a local clone of the upstream repository can be helpful if you are working with BSPs. Typically, you set up the `meta-intel` Git repository inside the Source Directory. For example, the following transcript shows the steps to clone `meta-intel`.

  ## Note
  Be sure to work in the `meta-intel` branch that matches your Source Directory [16] (i.e. poky) branch. For example, if you have checked out the "master" branch of poky and you are going to use `meta-intel`, be sure to checkout the "master" branch of `meta-intel`.

  ```
  $ cd ~/poky
  ```

```
$ git clone git://git.yoctoproject.org/meta-intel.git
Cloning into 'meta-intel'...
remote: Counting objects: 8844, done.
remote: Compressing objects: 100% (2864/2864), done.
remote: Total 8844 (delta 4931), reused 8780 (delta 4867)
Receiving objects: 100% (8844/8844), 2.48 MiB | 264 KiB/s, done.
Resolving deltas: 100% (4931/4931), done.
```

The same wiki page [https://wiki.yoctoproject.org/wiki/Transcript:_from_git_checkout_to_meta-intel_BSP] referenced earlier covers how to set up the meta-intel Git repository.

• Eclipse Yocto Plug-in: If you are developing applications using the Eclipse Integrated Development Environment (IDE), you will need this plug-in. See the "Setting up the Eclipse IDE" section for more information.

2.3. Building Images

The build process creates an entire Linux distribution, including the toolchain, from source. For more information on this topic, see the "Building an Image [http://www.yoctoproject.org/docs/1.7.2/yocto-project-qs/yocto-project-qs.html#building-image]" section in the Yocto Project Quick Start.

The build process is as follows:

1. Make sure you have set up the Source Directory described in the previous section.

2. Initialize the build environment by sourcing a build environment script (i.e. oe-init-build-env [http://www.yoctoproject.org/docs/1.7.2/ref-manual/ref-manual.html#structure-core-script] or oe-init-build-env-memres [http://www.yoctoproject.org/docs/1.7.2/ref-manual/ref-manual.html#structure-memres-core-script]).

3. Optionally ensure the conf/local.conf configuration file, which is found in the Build Directory [14], is set up how you want it. This file defines many aspects of the build environment including the target machine architecture through the MACHINE [http://www.yoctoproject.org/docs/1.7.2/ref-manual/ref-manual.html#var-MACHINE] variable, the development machine's processor use through the BB_NUMBER_THREADS [http://www.yoctoproject.org/docs/1.7.2/ref-manual/ref-manual.html#var-BB_NUMBER_THREADS] and PARALLEL_MAKE [http://www.yoctoproject.org/docs/1.7.2/ref-manual/ref-manual.html#var-PARALLEL_MAKE] variables, and a centralized tarball download directory through the DL_DIR [http://www.yoctoproject.org/docs/1.7.2/ref-manual/ref-manual.html#var-DL_DIR] variable.

4. Build the image using the bitbake command. If you want information on BitBake, see the BitBake User Manual [http://www.yoctoproject.org/docs/1.7.2/bitbake-user-manual/bitbake-user-manual.html].

5. Run the image either on the actual hardware or using the QEMU emulator.

2.4. Using Pre-Built Binaries and QEMU

Another option you have to get started is to use pre-built binaries. The Yocto Project provides many types of binaries with each release. See the "Images [http://www.yoctoproject.org/docs/1.7.2/ref-manual/ref-manual.html#ref-images]" chapter in the Yocto Project Reference Manual for descriptions of the types of binaries that ship with a Yocto Project release.

Using a pre-built binary is ideal for developing software applications to run on your target hardware. To do this, you need to be able to access the appropriate cross-toolchain tarball for the architecture on which you are developing. If you are using an SDK type image, the image ships with the complete toolchain native to the architecture. If you are not using an SDK type image, you need to separately download and install the stand-alone Yocto Project cross-toolchain tarball.

Regardless of the type of image you are using, you need to download the pre-built kernel that you will boot in the QEMU emulator and then download and extract the target root filesystem for your target machine's architecture. You can get architecture-specific binaries and file systems from machines [http://downloads.yoctoproject.org/releases/yocto/yocto-1.7.2/machines]. You can get installation scripts for stand-alone toolchains from toolchains [http://downloads.yoctoproject.org/releases/yocto/yocto-1.7.2/toolchain/]. Once you have all your files, you set up the environment to emulate the hardware by sourcing an environment setup script. Finally, you start the QEMU emulator. You can find details on all these steps in the "Using Pre-Built Binaries and QEMU [http://www.yoctoproject.org/docs/1.7.2/yocto-project-qs/yocto-project-qs.html#using-pre-built]" section of the Yocto Project Quick Start. You can learn more about using QEMU with the Yocto Project in the "Using the Quick EMUlator (QEMU)" section.

Using QEMU to emulate your hardware can result in speed issues depending on the target and host architecture mix. For example, using the qemux86 image in the emulator on an Intel-based 32-bit (x86) host machine is fast because the target and host architectures match. On the other hand, using the qemuarm image on the same Intel-based host can be slower. But, you still achieve faithful emulation of ARM-specific issues.

To speed things up, the QEMU images support using `distcc` to call a cross-compiler outside the emulated system. If you used runqemu to start QEMU, and the `distccd` application is present on the host system, any BitBake cross-compiling toolchain available from the build system is automatically used from within QEMU simply by calling `distcc`. You can accomplish this by defining the cross-compiler variable (e.g. export `CC="distcc"`). Alternatively, if you are using a suitable SDK image or the appropriate stand-alone toolchain is present, the toolchain is also automatically used.

Note
Several mechanisms exist that let you connect to the system running on the QEMU emulator:

- QEMU provides a framebuffer interface that makes standard consoles available.

- Generally, headless embedded devices have a serial port. If so, you can configure the operating system of the running image to use that port to run a console. The connection uses standard IP networking.

- SSH servers exist in some QEMU images. The `core-image-sato` QEMU image has a Dropbear secure shell (SSH) server that runs with the root password disabled. The `core-image-full-cmdline` and `core-image-lsb` QEMU images have OpenSSH instead of Dropbear. Including these SSH servers allow you to use standard `ssh` and `scp` commands. The `core-image-minimal` QEMU image, however, contains no SSH server.

- You can use a provided, user-space NFS server to boot the QEMU session using a local copy of the root filesystem on the host. In order to make this connection, you must extract a root filesystem tarball by using the `runqemu-extract-sdk` command. After running the command, you must then point the runqemu script to the extracted directory instead of a root filesystem image file.

Chapter 3. The Yocto Project Open Source Development Environment

This chapter helps you understand the Yocto Project as an open source development project. In general, working in an open source environment is very different from working in a closed, proprietary environment. Additionally, the Yocto Project uses specific tools and constructs as part of its development environment. This chapter specifically addresses open source philosophy, using the Yocto Project in a team environment, source repositories, Yocto Project terms, licensing, the open source distributed version control system Git, workflows, bug tracking, and how to submit changes.

3.1. Open Source Philosophy

Open source philosophy is characterized by software development directed by peer production and collaboration through an active community of developers. Contrast this to the more standard centralized development models used by commercial software companies where a finite set of developers produces a product for sale using a defined set of procedures that ultimately result in an end product whose architecture and source material are closed to the public.

Open source projects conceptually have differing concurrent agendas, approaches, and production. These facets of the development process can come from anyone in the public (community) that has a stake in the software project. The open source environment contains new copyright, licensing, domain, and consumer issues that differ from the more traditional development environment. In an open source environment, the end product, source material, and documentation are all available to the public at no cost.

A benchmark example of an open source project is the Linux kernel, which was initially conceived and created by Finnish computer science student Linus Torvalds in 1991. Conversely, a good example of a non-open source project is the Windows® family of operating systems developed by Microsoft® Corporation.

Wikipedia has a good historical description of the Open Source Philosophy here [http://en.wikipedia.org/wiki/Open_source]. You can also find helpful information on how to participate in the Linux Community here [http://ldn.linuxfoundation.org/book/how-participate-linux-community].

3.2. Using the Yocto Project in a Team Environment

It might not be immediately clear how you can use the Yocto Project in a team environment, or scale it for a large team of developers. One of the strengths of the Yocto Project is that it is extremely flexible. Thus, you can adapt it to many different use cases and scenarios. However, these characteristics can cause a struggle if you are trying to create a working setup that scales across a large team.

To help with these types of situations, this section presents some of the project's most successful experiences, practices, solutions, and available technologies that work well. Keep in mind, the information here is a starting point. You can build off it and customize it to fit any particular working environment and set of practices.

3.2.1. System Configurations

Systems across a large team should meet the needs of two types of developers: those working on the contents of the operating system image itself and those developing applications. Regardless of the type of developer, their workstations must be both reasonably powerful and run Linux.

3.2.1.1. Application Development

For developers who mainly do application level work on top of an existing software stack, here are some practices that work best:

- Use a pre-built toolchain that contains the software stack itself. Then, develop the application code on top of the stack. This method works well for small numbers of relatively isolated applications.

- When possible, use the Yocto Project plug-in for the Eclipse™ IDE and other pieces of Application Development Technology (ADT). For more information, see the "Application Development Workflow" section as well as the Yocto Project Application Developer's Guide [http://www.yoctoproject.org/docs/1.7.2/adt-manual/adt-manual.html].

- Keep your cross-development toolchains updated. You can do this through provisioning either as new toolchain downloads or as updates through a package update mechanism using opkg to provide updates to an existing toolchain. The exact mechanics of how and when to do this are a question for local policy.

- Use multiple toolchains installed locally into different locations to allow development across versions.

3.2.1.2. Core System Development

For core system development, it is often best to have the build system itself available on the developer workstations so developers can run their own builds and directly rebuild the software stack. You should keep the core system unchanged as much as possible and do your work in layers on top of the core system. Doing so gives you a greater level of portability when upgrading to new versions of the core system or Board Support Packages (BSPs). You can share layers amongst the developers of a particular project and contain the policy configuration that defines the project.

Aside from the previous best practices, there exists a number of tips and tricks that can help speed up core development projects:

- Use a Shared State Cache [http://www.yoctoproject.org/docs/1.7.2/ref-manual/ref-manual.html#shared-state-cache] (sstate) among groups of developers who are on a fast network. The best way to share sstate is through a Network File System (NFS) share. The first user to build a given component for the first time contributes that object to the sstate, while subsequent builds from other developers then reuse the object rather than rebuild it themselves.

  Although it is possible to use other protocols for the sstate such as HTTP and FTP, you should avoid these. Using HTTP limits the sstate to read-only and FTP provides poor performance.

- Have autobuilders contribute to the sstate pool similarly to how the developer workstations contribute. For information, see the "Autobuilders" section.

- Build stand-alone tarballs that contain "missing" system requirements if for some reason developer workstations do not meet minimum system requirements such as latest Python versions, chrpath, or other tools. You can install and relocate the tarball exactly as you would the usual cross-development toolchain so that all developers can meet minimum version requirements on most distributions.

- Use a small number of shared, high performance systems for testing purposes (e.g. dual, six-core Xeons with 24 Gbytes of RAM and plenty of disk space). Developers can use these systems for wider, more extensive testing while they continue to develop locally using their primary development system.

- Enable the PR Service when package feeds need to be incremental with continually increasing PR [http://www.yoctoproject.org/docs/1.7.2/ref-manual/ref-manual.html#var-PR] values. Typically, this situation occurs when you use or publish package feeds and use a shared state. You should enable the PR Service for all users who use the shared state pool. For more information on the PR Service, see the "Working With a PR Service".

3.2.2. Source Control Management (SCM)

Keeping your Metadata [http://www.yoctoproject.org/docs/1.7.2/dev-manual/dev-manual.html#metadata] and any software you are developing under the control of an SCM system that is compatible with the OpenEmbedded build system is advisable. Of the SCMs BitBake supports, the Yocto Project team strongly recommends using Git. Git is a distributed system that is easy to backup, allows you to work remotely, and then connects back to the infrastructure.

Note

For information about BitBake, see the BitBake User Manual [http://www.yoctoproject.org/docs/1.7.2/bitbake-user-manual/bitbake-user-manual.html].

It is relatively easy to set up Git services and create infrastructure like http://git.yoctoproject.org, which is based on server software called gitolite with cgit being used to generate the web interface that lets you view the repositories. The gitolite software identifies users using SSH keys and allows branch-based access controls to repositories that you can control as little or as much as necessary.

Note
The setup of these services is beyond the scope of this manual. However, sites such as these exist that describe how to perform setup:

- Git documentation [http://git-scm.com/book/ch4-8.html]: Describes how to install gitolite on the server.

- The gitolite master index [http://sitaramc.github.com/gitolite/master-toc.html]: All topics for gitolite.

- Interfaces, frontends, and tools [https://git.wiki.kernel.org/index.php/Interfaces,_frontends,_and_tools]: Documentation on how to create interfaces and frontends for Git.

3.2.3. Autobuilders

Autobuilders are often the core of a development project. It is here that changes from individual developers are brought together and centrally tested and subsequent decisions about releases can be made. Autobuilders also allow for "continuous integration" style testing of software components and regression identification and tracking.

See "Yocto Project Autobuilder [http://autobuilder.yoctoproject.org]" for more information and links to buildbot. The Yocto Project team has found this implementation works well in this role. A public example of this is the Yocto Project Autobuilders, which we use to test the overall health of the project.

The features of this system are:

- Highlights when commits break the build.

- Populates an sstate cache from which developers can pull rather than requiring local builds.

- Allows commit hook triggers, which trigger builds when commits are made.

- Allows triggering of automated image booting and testing under the QuickEMUlator (QEMU).

- Supports incremental build testing and from-scratch builds.

- Shares output that allows developer testing and historical regression investigation.

- Creates output that can be used for releases.

- Allows scheduling of builds so that resources can be used efficiently.

3.2.4. Policies and Change Flow

The Yocto Project itself uses a hierarchical structure and a pull model. Scripts exist to create and send pull requests (i.e. create-pull-request and send-pull-request). This model is in line with other open source projects where maintainers are responsible for specific areas of the project and a single maintainer handles the final "top-of-tree" merges.

Note
You can also use a more collective push model. The gitolite software supports both the push and pull models quite easily.

As with any development environment, it is important to document the policy used as well as any main project guidelines so they are understood by everyone. It is also a good idea to have well structured commit messages, which are usually a part of a project's guidelines. Good commit messages are essential when looking back in time and trying to understand why changes were made.

If you discover that changes are needed to the core layer of the project, it is worth sharing those with the community as soon as possible. Chances are if you have discovered the need for changes, someone else in the community needs them also.

3.2.5. Summary

This section summarizes the key recommendations described in the previous sections:

• Use Git as the source control system.

• Maintain your Metadata in layers that make sense for your situation. See the "Understanding and Creating Layers" section for more information on layers.

• Separate the project's Metadata and code by using separate Git repositories. See the "Yocto Project Source Repositories" section for information on these repositories. See the "Getting Set Up" section for information on how to set up local Git repositories for related upstream Yocto Project Git repositories.

• Set up the directory for the shared state cache (SSTATE_DIR [http://www.yoctoproject.org/docs/1.7.2/ref-manual/ref-manual.html#var-SSTATE_DIR]) where it makes sense. For example, set up the sstate cache on a system used by developers in the same organization and share the same source directories on their machines.

• Set up an Autobuilder and have it populate the sstate cache and source directories.

• The Yocto Project community encourages you to send patches to the project to fix bugs or add features. If you do submit patches, follow the project commit guidelines for writing good commit messages. See the "How to Submit a Change" section.

• Send changes to the core sooner than later as others are likely to run into the same issues. For some guidance on mailing lists to use, see the list in the "How to Submit a Change" section. For a description of the available mailing lists, see the "Mailing Lists [http://www.yoctoproject.org/docs/1.7.2/ref-manual/ref-manual.html#resources-mailinglist]" section in the Yocto Project Reference Manual.

3.3. Yocto Project Source Repositories

The Yocto Project team maintains complete source repositories for all Yocto Project files at http://git.yoctoproject.org/cgit/cgit.cgi. This web-based source code browser is organized into categories by function such as IDE Plugins, Matchbox, Poky, Yocto Linux Kernel, and so forth. From the interface, you can click on any particular item in the "Name" column and see the URL at the bottom of the page that you need to clone a Git repository for that particular item. Having a local Git repository of the Source Directory [16], which is usually named "poky", allows you to make changes, contribute to the history, and ultimately enhance the Yocto Project's tools, Board Support Packages, and so forth.

For any supported release of Yocto Project, you can also go to the Yocto Project Website [http://www.yoctoproject.org] and select the "Downloads" tab and get a released tarball of the poky repository or any supported BSP tarballs. Unpacking these tarballs gives you a snapshot of the released files.

Notes

• The recommended method for setting up the Yocto Project Source Directory [16] and the files for supported BSPs (e.g., meta-intel) is to use Git to create a local copy of the upstream repositories.

• Be sure to always work in matching branches for both the selected BSP repository and the Source Directory [16] (i.e. poky) repository. For example, if you have checked out the "master" branch of poky and you are going to use meta-intel, be sure to checkout the "master" branch of meta-intel.

In summary, here is where you can get the project files needed for development:

• Source Repositories: [http://git.yoctoproject.org/cgit/cgit.cgi] This area contains IDE Plugins, Matchbox, Poky, Poky Support, Tools, Yocto Linux Kernel, and Yocto Metadata Layers. You can create local copies of Git repositories for each of these areas.

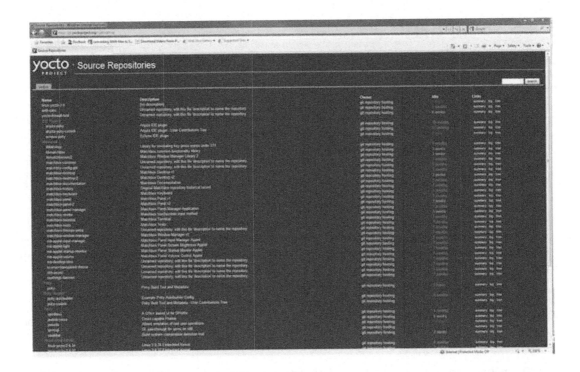

- Index of /releases: [http://downloads.yoctoproject.org/releases/] This is an index of releases such as the Eclipse™ Yocto Plug-in, miscellaneous support, Poky, Pseudo, installers for cross-development toolchains, and all released versions of Yocto Project in the form of images or tarballs. Downloading and extracting these files does not produce a local copy of the Git repository but rather a snapshot of a particular release or image.

Index of /releases

Name	Last modified	Size	Description
Parent Directory			
anjuta-plugin-sdk/	08-May-2012 19:40	-	
bitbake/	08-May-2012 19:40	-	
eclipse-plugin/	19-Jan-2013 02:02	-	
eglibc/	15-Jan-2013 17:43	-	
exmap-console/	08-May-2012 19:40	-	
gnu-config/	03-Oct-2012 17:23	-	
libgconf-bridge/	08-May-2012 21:11	-	
libowl-av/	08-May-2012 19:40	-	
matchbox/	08-May-2012 19:40	-	
media/	08-May-2012 19:40	-	
miscsupport/	08-May-2012 21:11	-	
oprofileui/	08-May-2012 19:40	-	
poky-archive-images/	08-May-2012 21:11	-	
poky/	08-May-2012 19:40	-	
pseudo/	28-Feb-2013 19:31	-	
psplash/	08-May-2012 21:11	-	
sato/	08-May-2012 21:11	-	
xoo/	08-May-2012 21:11	-	
xresponse/	08-May-2012 21:11	-	
xrestop/	08-May-2012 21:11	-	
yocto/	05-Apr-2013 21:53	-	

Apache/2 Server at downloads.yoctoproject.org Port 80

- "Downloads" page for the Yocto Project Website [http://www.yoctoproject.org]: Access this page by going to the website and then selecting the "Downloads" tab. This page allows you to download any Yocto Project release or Board Support Package (BSP) in tarball form. The tarballs are similar to those found in the Index of /releases: [http://downloads.yoctoproject.org/releases/] area.

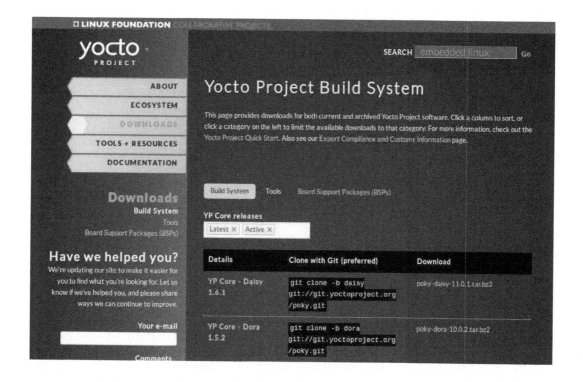

3.4. Yocto Project Terms

Following is a list of terms and definitions users new to the Yocto Project development environment might find helpful. While some of these terms are universal, the list includes them just in case:

- Append Files: Files that append build information to a recipe file. Append files are known as BitBake append files and .bbappend files. The OpenEmbedded build system expects every append file to have a corresponding recipe (.bb) file. Furthermore, the append file and corresponding recipe file must use the same root filename. The filenames can differ only in the file type suffix used (e.g. formfactor_0.0.bb and formfactor_0.0.bbappend).

  Information in append files extends or overrides the information in the similarly-named recipe file. For an example of an append file in use, see the "Using .bbappend Files" section.

  ### Note
  Append files can also use wildcard patterns in their version numbers so they can be applied to more than one version of the underlying recipe file.

- BitBake: The task executor and scheduler used by the OpenEmbedded build system to build images. For more information on BitBake, see the BitBake User Manual [http://www.yoctoproject.org/docs/1.7.2/bitbake-user-manual/bitbake-user-manual.html].

- Build Directory: This term refers to the area used by the OpenEmbedded build system for builds. The area is created when you source the setup environment script that is found in the Source Directory (i.e. oe-init-build-env [http://www.yoctoproject.org/docs/1.7.2/ref-manual/ref-manual.html#structure-core-script] or oe-init-build-env-memres [http://www.yoctoproject.org/docs/1.7.2/ref-manual/ref-manual.html#structure-memres-core-script]). The TOPDIR [http://www.yoctoproject.org/docs/1.7.2/ref-manual/ref-manual.html#var-TOPDIR] variable points to the Build Directory.

  You have a lot of flexibility when creating the Build Directory. Following are some examples that show how to create the directory. The examples assume your Source Directory [16] is named poky:

  - Create the Build Directory inside your Source Directory and let the name of the Build Directory default to build:

```
$ cd $HOME/poky
$ source oe-init-build-env
```

- Create the Build Directory inside your home directory and specifically name it test-builds:

```
$ cd $HOME
$ source poky/oe-init-build-env test-builds
```

- Provide a directory path and specifically name the Build Directory. Any intermediate folders in the pathname must exist. This next example creates a Build Directory named YP-12.0.2 in your home directory within the existing directory mybuilds:

```
$cd $HOME
$ source $HOME/poky/oe-init-build-env $HOME/mybuilds/YP-12.0.2
```

Note

By default, the Build Directory contains TMPDIR [http://www.yoctoproject.org/docs/1.7.2/ ref-manual/ref-manual.html#var-TMPDIR], which is a temporary directory the build system uses for its work. TMPDIR cannot be under NFS. Thus, by default, the Build Directory cannot be under NFS. However, if you need the Build Directory to be under NFS, you can set this up by setting TMPDIR in your local.conf file to use a local drive. Doing so effectively separates TMPDIR from TOPDIR, which is the Build Directory.

- Build System: In the context of the Yocto Project, this term refers to the OpenEmbedded build system used by the project. This build system is based on the project known as "Poky." For some historical information about Poky, see the Poky [16] term.

- Classes: Files that provide for logic encapsulation and inheritance so that commonly used patterns can be defined once and then easily used in multiple recipes. For reference information on the Yocto Project classes, see the "Classes [http://www.yoctoproject.org/docs/1.7.2/ref-manual/ref-manual.html#ref-classes]" chapter of the Yocto Project Reference Manual. Class files end with the .bbclass filename extension.

- Configuration File: Configuration information in various .conf files provides global definitions of variables. The conf/local.conf configuration file in the Build Directory [14] contains user-defined variables that affect every build. The meta-yocto/conf/distro/poky.conf configuration file defines Yocto "distro" configuration variables used only when building with this policy. Machine configuration files, which are located throughout the Source Directory [16], define variables for specific hardware and are only used when building for that target (e.g. the machine/beaglebone.conf configuration file defines variables for the Texas Instruments ARM Cortex-A8 development board). Configuration files end with a .conf filename extension.

- Cross-Development Toolchain: In general, a cross-development toolchain is a collection of software development tools and utilities that run on one architecture and allow you to develop software for a different, or targeted, architecture. These toolchains contain cross-compilers, linkers, and debuggers that are specific to the target architecture.

The Yocto Project supports two different cross-development toolchains:

- A toolchain only used by and within BitBake when building an image for a target architecture.

- A relocatable toolchain used outside of BitBake by developers when developing applications that will run on a targeted device. Sometimes this relocatable cross-development toolchain is referred to as the meta-toolchain.

Creation of these toolchains is simple and automated. For information on toolchain concepts as they apply to the Yocto Project, see the "Cross-Development Toolchain Generation [http://www.yoctoproject.org/docs/1.7.2/ref-manual/ref-manual.html#cross-development-toolchain-generation]" section in the Yocto Project Reference Manual. You can also find more information on using the relocatable toolchain in the Yocto Project Application Developer's Guide [http://www.yoctoproject.org/docs/1.7.2/adt-manual/adt-manual.html].

- Image: An image is an artifact of the BitBake build process given a collection of recipes and related Metadata. Images are the binary output that run on specific hardware or QEMU and are used for specific use-cases. For a list of the supported image types that the Yocto Project provides, see the "Images [http://www.yoctoproject.org/docs/1.7.2/ref-manual/ref-manual.html#ref-images]" chapter in the Yocto Project Reference Manual.

- Layer: A collection of recipes representing the core, a BSP, or an application stack. For a discussion specifically on BSP Layers, see the "BSP Layers [http://www.yoctoproject.org/docs/1.7.2/bsp-guide/bsp-guide.html#bsp-layers]" section in the Yocto Project Board Support Packages (BSP) Developer's Guide.

- Meta-Toolchain: A term sometimes used for Cross-Development Toolchain [15].

- Metadata: The files that BitBake parses when building an image. In general, Metadata includes recipes, classes, and configuration files. In the context of the kernel ("kernel Metadata"), it refers to Metadata in the meta branches of the kernel source Git repositories.

- OE-Core: A core set of Metadata originating with OpenEmbedded (OE) that is shared between OE and the Yocto Project. This Metadata is found in the meta directory of the Source Directory [16].

- Package: In the context of the Yocto Project, this term refers to a recipe's packaged output produced by BitBake (i.e. a "baked recipe"). A package is generally the compiled binaries produced from the recipe's sources. You "bake" something by running it through BitBake.

  It is worth noting that the term "package" can, in general, have subtle meanings. For example, the packages referred to in the "The Packages [http://www.yoctoproject.org/docs/1.7.2/yocto-project-qs/yocto-project-qs.html#packages]" section are compiled binaries that, when installed, add functionality to your Linux distribution.

  Another point worth noting is that historically within the Yocto Project, recipes were referred to as packages - thus, the existence of several BitBake variables that are seemingly mis-named, (e.g. PR [http://www.yoctoproject.org/docs/1.7.2/ref-manual/ref-manual.html#var-PR], PV [http://www.yoctoproject.org/docs/1.7.2/ref-manual/ref-manual.html#var-PV], and PE [http://www.yoctoproject.org/docs/1.7.2/ref-manual/ref-manual.html#var-PE]).

- Package Groups: Arbitrary groups of software Recipes. You use package groups to hold recipes that, when built, usually accomplish a single task. For example, a package group could contain the recipes for a company's proprietary or value-add software. Or, the package group could contain the recipes that enable graphics. A package group is really just another recipe. Because package group files are recipes, they end with the .bb filename extension.

- Poky: The term "poky" can mean several things. In its most general sense, it is an open-source project that was initially developed by OpenedHand. With OpenedHand, poky was developed off of the existing OpenEmbedded build system becoming a build system for embedded images. After Intel Corporation acquired OpenedHand, the project poky became the basis for the Yocto Project's build system.

  Within the Yocto Project source repositories, poky exists as a separate Git repository that can be cloned to yield a local copy on the host system. Thus, "poky" can refer to the local copy of the Source Directory used to develop within the Yocto Project.

- Recipe: A set of instructions for building packages. A recipe describes where you get source code, which patches to apply, how to configure the source, how to compile it and so on. Recipes also describe dependencies for libraries or for other recipes. Recipes represent the logical unit of execution, the software to build, the images to build, and use the .bb file extension.

- Source Directory: This term refers to the directory structure created as a result of creating a local copy of the poky Git repository git://git.yoctoproject.org/poky or expanding a released poky tarball.

Note

Creating a local copy of the poky Git repository is the recommended method for setting up your Source Directory.

Sometimes you might hear the term "poky directory" used to refer to this directory structure.

Note

The OpenEmbedded build system does not support file or directory names that contain spaces. Be sure that the Source Directory you use does not contain these types of names.

The Source Directory contains BitBake, Documentation, Metadata and other files that all support the Yocto Project. Consequently, you must have the Source Directory in place on your development system in order to do any development using the Yocto Project.

When you create a local copy of the Git repository, you can name the repository anything you like. Throughout much of the documentation, "poky" is used as the name of the top-level folder of the local copy of the poky Git repository. So, for example, cloning the poky Git repository results in a local Git repository whose top-level folder is also named "poky".

While it is not recommended that you use tarball expansion to set up the Source Directory, if you do, the top-level directory name of the Source Directory is derived from the Yocto Project release tarball. For example, downloading and unpacking poky-dizzy-12.0.2.tar.bz2 results in a Source Directory whose root folder is named poky-dizzy-12.0.2.

It is important to understand the differences between the Source Directory created by unpacking a released tarball as compared to cloning git://git.yoctoproject.org/poky. When you unpack a tarball, you have an exact copy of the files based on the time of release - a fixed release point. Any changes you make to your local files in the Source Directory are on top of the release and will remain local only. On the other hand, when you clone the poky Git repository, you have an active development repository with access to the upstream repository's branches and tags. In this case, any local changes you make to the local Source Directory can be later applied to active development branches of the upstream poky Git repository.

For more information on concepts related to Git repositories, branches, and tags, see the "Repositories, Tags, and Branches" section.

- Task: A unit of execution for BitBake (e.g. do_compile [http://www.yoctoproject.org/docs/1.7.2/ref-manual/ref-manual.html#ref-tasks-compile], do_fetch [http://www.yoctoproject.org/docs/1.7.2/ref-manual/ref-manual.html#ref-tasks-fetch], do_patch [http://www.yoctoproject.org/docs/1.7.2/ref-manual/ref-manual.html#ref-tasks-patch], and so forth).

- Upstream: A reference to source code or repositories that are not local to the development system but located in a master area that is controlled by the maintainer of the source code. For example, in order for a developer to work on a particular piece of code, they need to first get a copy of it from an "upstream" source.

3.5. Licensing

Because open source projects are open to the public, they have different licensing structures in place. License evolution for both Open Source and Free Software has an interesting history. If you are interested in this history, you can find basic information here:

- Open source license history [http://en.wikipedia.org/wiki/Open-source_license]

- Free software license history [http://en.wikipedia.org/wiki/Free_software_license]

In general, the Yocto Project is broadly licensed under the Massachusetts Institute of Technology (MIT) License. MIT licensing permits the reuse of software within proprietary software as long as the license is distributed with that software. MIT is also compatible with the GNU General Public License (GPL). Patches to the Yocto Project follow the upstream licensing scheme. You can find information on the MIT license here [http://www.opensource.org/licenses/mit-license.php]. You can find information on the GNU GPL here [http://www.opensource.org/licenses/LGPL-3.0].

When you build an image using the Yocto Project, the build process uses a known list of licenses to ensure compliance. You can find this list in the Source Directory [16] at meta/files/common-licenses. Once the build completes, the list of all licenses found and used during that build are kept in the Build Directory [14] at tmp/deploy/licenses.

If a module requires a license that is not in the base list, the build process generates a warning during the build. These tools make it easier for a developer to be certain of the licenses with which their shipped products must comply. However, even with these tools it is still up to the developer to resolve potential licensing issues.

The base list of licenses used by the build process is a combination of the Software Package Data Exchange (SPDX) list and the Open Source Initiative (OSI) projects. SPDX Group [http://spdx.org] is a working group of the Linux Foundation that maintains a specification for a standard format for communicating the components, licenses, and copyrights associated with a software package. OSI [http://opensource.org] is a corporation dedicated to the Open Source Definition and the effort for reviewing and approving licenses that conform to the Open Source Definition (OSD).

You can find a list of the combined SPDX and OSI licenses that the Yocto Project uses in the meta/files/common-licenses directory in your Source Directory [16].

For information that can help you maintain compliance with various open source licensing during the lifecycle of a product created using the Yocto Project, see the "Maintaining Open Source License Compliance During Your Product's Lifecycle" section.

3.6. Git

The Yocto Project makes extensive use of Git, which is a free, open source distributed version control system. Git supports distributed development, non-linear development, and can handle large projects. It is best that you have some fundamental understanding of how Git tracks projects and how to work with Git if you are going to use the Yocto Project for development. This section provides a quick overview of how Git works and provides you with a summary of some essential Git commands.

For more information on Git, see http://git-scm.com/documentation. If you need to download Git, go to http://git-scm.com/download.

3.6.1. Repositories, Tags, and Branches

As mentioned earlier in the section "Yocto Project Source Repositories", the Yocto Project maintains source repositories at http://git.yoctoproject.org/cgit.cgi. If you look at this web-interface of the repositories, each item is a separate Git repository.

Git repositories use branching techniques that track content change (not files) within a project (e.g. a new feature or updated documentation). Creating a tree-like structure based on project divergence allows for excellent historical information over the life of a project. This methodology also allows for an environment from which you can do lots of local experimentation on projects as you develop changes or new features.

A Git repository represents all development efforts for a given project. For example, the Git repository poky contains all changes and developments for Poky over the course of its entire life. That means that all changes that make up all releases are captured. The repository maintains a complete history of changes.

You can create a local copy of any repository by "cloning" it with the Git clone command. When you clone a Git repository, you end up with an identical copy of the repository on your development system. Once you have a local copy of a repository, you can take steps to develop locally. For examples on how to clone Git repositories, see the "Getting Set Up" section.

It is important to understand that Git tracks content change and not files. Git uses "branches" to organize different development efforts. For example, the poky repository has denzil, danny, dylan, dora, daisy, and master branches among others. You can see all the branches by going to http://git.yoctoproject.org/cgit.cgi/poky/ and clicking on the [...] [http://git.yoctoproject.org/cgit.cgi/poky/refs/heads] link beneath the "Branch" heading.

Each of these branches represents a specific area of development. The master branch represents the current or most recent development. All other branches represent offshoots of the master branch.

When you create a local copy of a Git repository, the copy has the same set of branches as the original. This means you can use Git to create a local working area (also called a branch) that tracks a specific development branch from the source Git repository. in other words, you can define your local Git environment to work on any development branch in the repository. To help illustrate, here is a set of commands that creates a local copy of the poky Git repository and then creates and checks out a local Git branch that tracks the Yocto Project 1.7.2 Release (dizzy) development:

```
$ cd ~
$ git clone git://git.yoctoproject.org/poky
$ cd poky
$ git checkout -b dizzy origin/dizzy
```

In this example, the name of the top-level directory of your local Source Directory [16] is "poky" and the name of that local working area (local branch) you just created and checked out is "dizzy". The files in your local repository now reflect the same files that are in the "dizzy" development branch of the Yocto Project's "poky" upstream repository. It is important to understand that when you create and checkout a local working branch based on a branch name, your local environment matches the "tip" of that development branch at the time you created your local branch, which could be different from the files at the time of a similarly named release. In other words, creating and checking out a local branch based on the "dizzy" branch name is not the same as cloning and checking out the "master" branch. Keep reading to see how you create a local snapshot of a Yocto Project Release.

Git uses "tags" to mark specific changes in a repository. Typically, a tag is used to mark a special point such as the final change before a project is released. You can see the tags used with the poky Git repository by going to http://git.yoctoproject.org/cgit.cgi/poky/ and clicking on the [...] [http://git.yoctoproject.org/cgit.cgi/poky/refs/tags] link beneath the "Tag" heading.

Some key tags are dylan-9.0.0, dora-10.0.0, daisy-11.0.0, and dizzy-12.0.2. These tags represent Yocto Project releases.

When you create a local copy of the Git repository, you also have access to all the tags. Similar to branches, you can create and checkout a local working Git branch based on a tag name. When you do this, you get a snapshot of the Git repository that reflects the state of the files when the change was made associated with that tag. The most common use is to checkout a working branch that matches a specific Yocto Project release. Here is an example:

```
$ cd ~
$ git clone git://git.yoctoproject.org/poky
$ cd poky
$ git checkout -b my-dizzy-12.0.2 dizzy-12.0.2
```

In this example, the name of the top-level directory of your local Yocto Project Files Git repository is poky. And, the name of the local branch you have created and checked out is my-dizzy-12.0.2. The files in your repository now exactly match the Yocto Project 1.7.2 Release tag (dizzy-12.0.2). It is important to understand that when you create and checkout a local working branch based on a tag, your environment matches a specific point in time and not the entire development branch.

3.6.2. Basic Commands

Git has an extensive set of commands that lets you manage changes and perform collaboration over the life of a project. Conveniently though, you can manage with a small set of basic operations and workflows once you understand the basic philosophy behind Git. You do not have to be an expert in Git to be functional. A good place to look for instruction on a minimal set of Git commands is here [http://git-scm.com/documentation]. If you need to download Git, you can do so here [http://git-scm.com/download].

If you do not know much about Git, you should educate yourself by visiting the links previously mentioned.

The following list briefly describes some basic Git operations as a way to get started. As with any set of commands, this list (in most cases) simply shows the base command and omits the many arguments they support. See the Git documentation for complete descriptions and strategies on how to use these commands:

- git init: Initializes an empty Git repository. You cannot use Git commands unless you have a .git repository.

- git clone: Creates a local clone of a Git repository. During collaboration, this command allows you to create a local Git repository that is on equal footing with a fellow developer's Git repository.

- `git add`: Stages updated file contents to the index that Git uses to track changes. You must stage all files that have changed before you can commit them.

- `git commit`: Creates a "commit" that documents the changes you made. Commits are used for historical purposes, for determining if a maintainer of a project will allow the change, and for ultimately pushing the change from your local Git repository into the project's upstream (or master) repository.

- `git status`: Reports any modified files that possibly need to be staged and committed.

- `git checkout <branch-name>`: Changes your working branch. This command is analogous to "cd".

- `git checkout —b <working-branch>`: Creates a working branch on your local machine where you can isolate work. It is a good idea to use local branches when adding specific features or changes. This way if you do not like what you have done you can easily get rid of the work.

- `git branch`: Reports existing local branches and tells you the branch in which you are currently working.

- `git branch -D <branch-name>`: Deletes an existing local branch. You need to be in a local branch other than the one you are deleting in order to delete <branch-name>.

- `git pull`: Retrieves information from an upstream Git repository and places it in your local Git repository. You use this command to make sure you are synchronized with the repository from which you are basing changes (.e.g. the master branch).

- `git push`: Sends all your committed local changes to an upstream Git repository (e.g. a contribution repository). The maintainer of the project draws from these repositories when adding changes to the project's master repository or other development branch.

- `git merge`: Combines or adds changes from one local branch of your repository with another branch. When you create a local Git repository, the default branch is named "master". A typical workflow is to create a temporary branch for isolated work, make and commit your changes, switch to your local master branch, merge the changes from the temporary branch into the local master branch, and then delete the temporary branch.

- `git cherry-pick`: Choose and apply specific commits from one branch into another branch. There are times when you might not be able to merge all the changes in one branch with another but need to pick out certain ones.

- `gitk`: Provides a GUI view of the branches and changes in your local Git repository. This command is a good way to graphically see where things have diverged in your local repository.

- `git log`: Reports a history of your changes to the repository.

- `git diff`: Displays line-by-line differences between your local working files and the same files in the upstream Git repository that your branch currently tracks.

3.7. Workflows

This section provides some overview on workflows using Git. In particular, the information covers basic practices that describe roles and actions in a collaborative development environment. Again, if you are familiar with this type of development environment, you might want to just skip this section.

The Yocto Project files are maintained using Git in a "master" branch whose Git history tracks every change and whose structure provides branches for all diverging functionality. Although there is no need to use Git, many open source projects do so. For the Yocto Project, a key individual called the "maintainer" is responsible for the "master" branch of a given Git repository. The "master" branch is the "upstream" repository where the final builds of the project occur. The maintainer is responsible for accepting changes from other developers and for organizing the underlying branch structure to reflect release strategies and so forth.

Note

For information on finding out who is responsible for (maintains) a particular area of code, see the "How to Submit a Change" section.

The project also has an upstream contribution Git repository named poky-contrib. You can see all the branches in this repository using the web interface of the Source Repositories [http://git.yoctoproject.org] organized within the "Poky Support" area. These branches temporarily hold changes to the project that have been submitted or committed by the Yocto Project development team and by community members who contribute to the project. The maintainer determines if the changes are qualified to be moved from the "contrib" branches into the "master" branch of the Git repository.

Developers (including contributing community members) create and maintain cloned repositories of the upstream "master" branch. These repositories are local to their development platforms and are used to develop changes. When a developer is satisfied with a particular feature or change, they "push" the changes to the appropriate "contrib" repository.

Developers are responsible for keeping their local repository up-to-date with "master". They are also responsible for straightening out any conflicts that might arise within files that are being worked on simultaneously by more than one person. All this work is done locally on the developer's machines before anything is pushed to a "contrib" area and examined at the maintainer's level.

A somewhat formal method exists by which developers commit changes and push them into the "contrib" area and subsequently request that the maintainer include them into "master" This process is called "submitting a patch" or "submitting a change." For information on submitting patches and changes, see the "How to Submit a Change" section.

To summarize the environment: a single point of entry exists for changes into the project's "master" branch of the Git repository, which is controlled by the project's maintainer. And, a set of developers exist who independently develop, test, and submit changes to "contrib" areas for the maintainer to examine. The maintainer then chooses which changes are going to become a permanent part of the project.

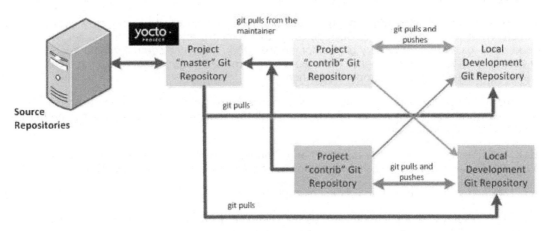

While each development environment is unique, there are some best practices or methods that help development run smoothly. The following list describes some of these practices. For more information about Git workflows, see the workflow topics in the Git Community Book [http://book.git-scm.com].

• Make Small Changes: It is best to keep the changes you commit small as compared to bundling many disparate changes into a single commit. This practice not only keeps things manageable but also allows the maintainer to more easily include or refuse changes.

   It is also good practice to leave the repository in a state that allows you to still successfully build your project. In other words, do not commit half of a feature, then add the other half as a separate, later commit. Each commit should take you from one buildable project state to another buildable state.

• Use Branches Liberally: It is very easy to create, use, and delete local branches in your working Git repository. You can name these branches anything you like. It is helpful to give them names associated with the particular feature or change on which you are working. Once you are done with a feature or change and have merged it into your local master branch, simply discard the temporary branch.

- Merge Changes: The `git merge` command allows you to take the changes from one branch and fold them into another branch. This process is especially helpful when more than a single developer might be working on different parts of the same feature. Merging changes also automatically identifies any collisions or "conflicts" that might happen as a result of the same lines of code being altered by two different developers.

- Manage Branches: Because branches are easy to use, you should use a system where branches indicate varying levels of code readiness. For example, you can have a "work" branch to develop in, a "test" branch where the code or change is tested, a "stage" branch where changes are ready to be committed, and so forth. As your project develops, you can merge code across the branches to reflect ever-increasing stable states of the development.

- Use Push and Pull: The push-pull workflow is based on the concept of developers "pushing" local commits to a remote repository, which is usually a contribution repository. This workflow is also based on developers "pulling" known states of the project down into their local development repositories. The workflow easily allows you to pull changes submitted by other developers from the upstream repository into your work area ensuring that you have the most recent software on which to develop. The Yocto Project has two scripts named `create-pull-request` and `send-pull-request` that ship with the release to facilitate this workflow. You can find these scripts in the `scripts` folder of the Source Directory [16]. For information on how to use these scripts, see the "Using Scripts to Push a Change Upstream and Request a Pull" section.

- Patch Workflow: This workflow allows you to notify the maintainer through an email that you have a change (or patch) you would like considered for the "master" branch of the Git repository. To send this type of change, you format the patch and then send the email using the Git commands `git format-patch` and `git send-email`. For information on how to use these scripts, see the "How to Submit a Change" section.

3.8. Tracking Bugs

The Yocto Project uses its own implementation of Bugzilla [http://www.bugzilla.org/about/] to track bugs. Implementations of Bugzilla work well for group development because they track bugs and code changes, can be used to communicate changes and problems with developers, can be used to submit and review patches, and can be used to manage quality assurance. The home page for the Yocto Project implementation of Bugzilla is http://bugzilla.yoctoproject.org.

Sometimes it is helpful to submit, investigate, or track a bug against the Yocto Project itself such as when discovering an issue with some component of the build system that acts contrary to the documentation or your expectations. Following is the general procedure for submitting a new bug using the Yocto Project Bugzilla. You can find more information on defect management, bug tracking, and feature request processes all accomplished through the Yocto Project Bugzilla on the wiki page here [https://wiki.yoctoproject.org/wiki/Bugzilla_Configuration_and_Bug_Tracking].

1. Always use the Yocto Project implementation of Bugzilla to submit a bug.

2. When submitting a new bug, be sure to choose the appropriate Classification, Product, and Component for which the issue was found. Defects for the Yocto Project fall into one of seven classifications: Yocto Project Components, Infrastructure, Build System & Metadata, Documentation, QA/Testing, Runtime and Hardware. Each of these Classifications break down into multiple Products and, in some cases, multiple Components.

3. Use the bug form to choose the correct Hardware and Architecture for which the bug applies.

4. Indicate the Yocto Project version you were using when the issue occurred.

5. Be sure to indicate the Severity of the bug. Severity communicates how the bug impacted your work.

6. Select the appropriate "Documentation change" item for the bug. Fixing a bug may or may not affect the Yocto Project documentation.

7. Provide a brief summary of the issue. Try to limit your summary to just a line or two and be sure to capture the essence of the issue.

8. Provide a detailed description of the issue. You should provide as much detail as you can about the context, behavior, output, and so forth that surrounds the issue. You can even attach supporting files for output from logs by using the "Add an attachment" button.

9. Be sure to copy the appropriate people in the "CC List" for the bug. See the "How to Submit a Change" section for information about finding out who is responsible for code.

10 Submit the bug by clicking the "Submit Bug" button.

3.9. How to Submit a Change

Contributions to the Yocto Project and OpenEmbedded are very welcome. Because the system is extremely configurable and flexible, we recognize that developers will want to extend, configure or optimize it for their specific uses. You should send patches to the appropriate mailing list so that they can be reviewed and merged by the appropriate maintainer.

Before submitting any change, be sure to find out who you should be notifying. Several methods exist through which you find out who you should be copying or notifying:

- Maintenance File: Examine the `maintainers.inc` file, which is located in the Source Directory [16] at `meta-yocto/conf/distro/include`, to see who is responsible for code.

- Board Support Package (BSP) README Files: For BSP maintainers of supported BSPs, you can examine individual BSP README files. In addition, some layers (such as the `meta-intel` layer), include a MAINTAINERS file which contains a list of all supported BSP maintainers for that layer.

- Search by File: Using Git, you can enter the following command to bring up a short list of all commits against a specific file:

```
git shortlog -- filename
```

Just provide the name of the file for which you are interested. The information returned is not ordered by history but does include a list of all committers grouped by name. From the list, you can see who is responsible for the bulk of the changes against the file.

For a list of the Yocto Project and related mailing lists, see the "Mailing lists [http://www.yoctoproject.org/docs/1.7.2/ref-manual/ref-manual.html#resources-mailinglist]" section in the Yocto Project Reference Manual.

Here is some guidance on which mailing list to use for what type of change:

- For changes to the core Metadata [16], send your patch to the openembedded-core [http://lists.openembedded.org/mailman/listinfo/openembedded-core] mailing list. For example, a change to anything under the `meta` or `scripts` directories should be sent to this mailing list.

- For changes to BitBake (anything under the `bitbake` directory), send your patch to the bitbake-devel [http://lists.openembedded.org/mailman/listinfo/bitbake-devel] mailing list.

- For changes to `meta-yocto`, send your patch to the poky [http://lists.yoctoproject.org/listinfo/poky] mailing list.

- For changes to other layers hosted on `yoctoproject.org` (unless the layer's documentation specifies otherwise), tools, and Yocto Project documentation, use the yocto [http://lists.yoctoproject.org/listinfo/yocto] mailing list.

- For additional recipes that do not fit into the core Metadata, you should determine which layer the recipe should go into and submit the change in the manner recommended by the documentation (e.g. README) supplied with the layer. If in doubt, please ask on the yocto [http://lists.yoctoproject.org/listinfo/yocto] or openembedded-devel [http://lists.openembedded.org/mailman/listinfo/openembedded-devel] mailing lists.

When you send a patch, be sure to include a "Signed-off-by:" line in the same style as required by the Linux kernel. Adding this line signifies that you, the submitter, have agreed to the Developer's Certificate of Origin 1.1 as follows:

```
Developer's Certificate of Origin 1.1

By making a contribution to this project, I certify that:

(a) The contribution was created in whole or in part by me and I
    have the right to submit it under the open source license
    indicated in the file; or

(b) The contribution is based upon previous work that, to the best
    of my knowledge, is covered under an appropriate open source
    license and I have the right under that license to submit that
    work with modifications, whether created in whole or in part
    by me, under the same open source license (unless I am
    permitted to submit under a different license), as indicated
    in the file; or

(c) The contribution was provided directly to me by some other
    person who certified (a), (b) or (c) and I have not modified
    it.

(d) I understand and agree that this project and the contribution
    are public and that a record of the contribution (including all
    personal information I submit with it, including my sign-off) is
    maintained indefinitely and may be redistributed consistent with
    this project or the open source license(s) involved.
```

In a collaborative environment, it is necessary to have some sort of standard or method through which you submit changes. Otherwise, things could get quite chaotic. One general practice to follow is to make small, controlled changes. Keeping changes small and isolated aids review, makes merging/rebasing easier and keeps the change history clean when anyone needs to refer to it in future.

When you make a commit, you must follow certain standards established by the OpenEmbedded and Yocto Project development teams. For each commit, you must provide a single-line summary of the change and you should almost always provide a more detailed description of what you did (i.e. the body of the commit message). The only exceptions for not providing a detailed description would be if your change is a simple, self-explanatory change that needs no further description beyond the summary. Here are the guidelines for composing a commit message: bug-id

• Provide a single-line, short summary of the change. This summary is typically viewable in the "shortlist" of changes. Thus, providing something short and descriptive that gives the reader a summary of the change is useful when viewing a list of many commits. This short description should be prefixed by the recipe name (if changing a recipe), or else the short form path to the file being changed.

• For the body of the commit message, provide detailed information that describes what you changed, why you made the change, and the approach you used. It may also be helpful if you mention how you tested the change. Provide as much detail as you can in the body of the commit message.

• If the change addresses a specific bug or issue that is associated with a bug-tracking ID, include a reference to that ID in your detailed description. For example, the Yocto Project uses a specific convention for bug references - any commit that addresses a specific bug should use the following form for the detailed description:

```
Fixes [YOCTO #bug-id]

detailed description of change
```

You can find more guidance on creating well-formed commit messages at this OpenEmbedded wiki page: http://www.openembedded.org/wiki/Commit_Patch_Message_Guidelines.

The next two sections describe general instructions for both pushing changes upstream and for submitting changes as patches.

3.9.1. Using Scripts to Push a Change Upstream and Request a Pull

The basic flow for pushing a change to an upstream "contrib" Git repository is as follows:

* Make your changes in your local Git repository.

* Stage your changes by using the git add command on each file you changed.

* Commit the change by using the git commit command. Be sure to provide a commit message that follows the project's commit message standards as described earlier.

* Push the change to the upstream "contrib" repository by using the git push command.

* Notify the maintainer that you have pushed a change by making a pull request. The Yocto Project provides two scripts that conveniently let you generate and send pull requests to the Yocto Project. These scripts are create-pull-request and send-pull-request. You can find these scripts in the scripts directory within the Source Directory [16].

  Using these scripts correctly formats the requests without introducing any whitespace or HTML formatting. The maintainer that receives your patches needs to be able to save and apply them directly from your emails. Using these scripts is the preferred method for sending patches.

  For help on using these scripts, simply provide the -h argument as follows:

  ```
  $ poky/scripts/create-pull-request -h
  $ poky/scripts/send-pull-request -h
  ```

You can find general Git information on how to push a change upstream in the Git Community Book [http://book.git-scm.com/3_distributed_workflows.html].

3.9.2. Using Email to Submit a Patch

You can submit patches without using the create-pull-request and send-pull-request scripts described in the previous section. However, keep in mind, the preferred method is to use the scripts.

Depending on the components changed, you need to submit the email to a specific mailing list. For some guidance on which mailing list to use, see the list in the "How to Submit a Change" section. For a description of the available mailing lists, see the "Mailing Lists [http://www.yoctoproject.org/docs/1.7.2/ref-manual/ref-manual.html#resources-mailinglist]" section in the Yocto Project Reference Manual.

Here is the general procedure on how to submit a patch through email without using the scripts:

* Make your changes in your local Git repository.

* Stage your changes by using the git add command on each file you changed.

* Commit the change by using the git commit --signoff command. Using the --signoff option identifies you as the person making the change and also satisfies the Developer's Certificate of Origin (DCO) shown earlier.

  When you form a commit, you must follow certain standards established by the Yocto Project development team. See the earlier section "How to Submit a Change" for Yocto Project commit message standards.

* Format the commit into an email message. To format commits, use the git format-patch command. When you provide the command, you must include a revision list or a number of patches as part of the command. For example, either of these two commands takes your most recent single commit and formats it as an email message in the current directory:

  ```
  $ git format-patch -1
  ```

or

```
$ git format-patch HEAD~
```

After the command is run, the current directory contains a numbered .patch file for the commit.

If you provide several commits as part of the command, the git format-patch command produces a series of numbered files in the current directory – one for each commit. If you have more than one patch, you should also use the --cover option with the command, which generates a cover letter as the first "patch" in the series. You can then edit the cover letter to provide a description for the series of patches. For information on the git format-patch command, see GIT_FORMAT_PATCH(1) displayed using the man git-format-patch command.

Note

If you are or will be a frequent contributor to the Yocto Project or to OpenEmbedded, you might consider requesting a contrib area and the necessary associated rights.

• Import the files into your mail client by using the git send-email command.

Note

In order to use git send-email, you must have the the proper Git packages installed. For Ubuntu, Debian, and Fedora the package is git-email.

The git send-email command sends email by using a local or remote Mail Transport Agent (MTA) such as msmtp, sendmail, or through a direct smtp configuration in your Git config file. If you are submitting patches through email only, it is very important that you submit them without any whitespace or HTML formatting that either you or your mailer introduces. The maintainer that receives your patches needs to be able to save and apply them directly from your emails. A good way to verify that what you are sending will be applicable by the maintainer is to do a dry run and send them to yourself and then save and apply them as the maintainer would.

The git send-email command is the preferred method for sending your patches since there is no risk of compromising whitespace in the body of the message, which can occur when you use your own mail client. The command also has several options that let you specify recipients and perform further editing of the email message. For information on how to use the git send-email command, see GIT-SEND-EMAIL(1) displayed using the man git-send-email command.

Chapter 4. Common Development Models

Many development models exist for which you can use the Yocto Project. This chapter overviews simple methods that use tools provided by the Yocto Project:

- System Development: System Development covers Board Support Package (BSP) development and kernel modification or configuration. For an example on how to create a BSP, see the "Creating a New BSP Layer Using the yocto-bsp Script [http://www.yoctoproject.org/docs/1.7.2/bsp-guide/bsp-guide.html#creating-a-new-bsp-layer-using-the-yocto-bsp-script]" section in the Yocto Project Board Support Package (BSP) Developer's Guide. For more complete information on how to work with the kernel, see the Yocto Project Linux Kernel Development Manual [http://www.yoctoproject.org/docs/1.7.2/kernel-dev/kernel-dev.html].

- User Application Development: User Application Development covers development of applications that you intend to run on target hardware. For information on how to set up your host development system for user-space application development, see the Yocto Project Application Developer's Guide [http://www.yoctoproject.org/docs/1.7.2/adt-manual/adt-manual.html]. For a simple example of user-space application development using the Eclipse™ IDE, see the "Application Development Workflow" section.

- Temporary Source Code Modification: Direct modification of temporary source code is a convenient development model to quickly iterate and develop towards a solution. Once you implement the solution, you should of course take steps to get the changes upstream and applied in the affected recipes.

- Image Development using Hob: You can use the Hob [http://www.yoctoproject.org/tools-resources/projects/hob] to build custom operating system images within the build environment. Hob provides an efficient interface to the OpenEmbedded build system.

- Using a Development Shell: You can use a devshell to efficiently debug commands or simply edit packages. Working inside a development shell is a quick way to set up the OpenEmbedded build environment to work on parts of a project.

4.1. System Development Workflow

System development involves modification or creation of an image that you want to run on a specific hardware target. Usually, when you want to create an image that runs on embedded hardware, the image does not require the same number of features that a full-fledged Linux distribution provides. Thus, you can create a much smaller image that is designed to use only the features for your particular hardware.

To help you understand how system development works in the Yocto Project, this section covers two types of image development: BSP creation and kernel modification or configuration.

4.1.1. Developing a Board Support Package (BSP)

A BSP is a collection of recipes that, when applied during a build, results in an image that you can run on a particular board. Thus, the package when compiled into the new image, supports the operation of the board.

Note
For a brief list of terms used when describing the development process in the Yocto Project, see the "Yocto Project Terms" section.

The remainder of this section presents the basic steps used to create a BSP using the Yocto Project's BSP Tools [http://www.yoctoproject.org/docs/1.7.2/bsp-guide/bsp-guide.html#using-the-yocto-projects-bsp-tools]. Although not required for BSP creation, the meta-intel repository, which contains many BSPs supported by the Yocto Project, is part of the example.

For an example that shows how to create a new layer using the tools, see the "Creating a New BSP Layer Using the yocto-bsp Script [http://www.yoctoproject.org/docs/1.7.2/bsp-guide/bsp-guide.html#creating-a-new-bsp-layer-using-the-yocto-bsp-script]" section in the Yocto Project Board Support Package (BSP) Developer's Guide.

The following illustration and list summarize the BSP creation general workflow.

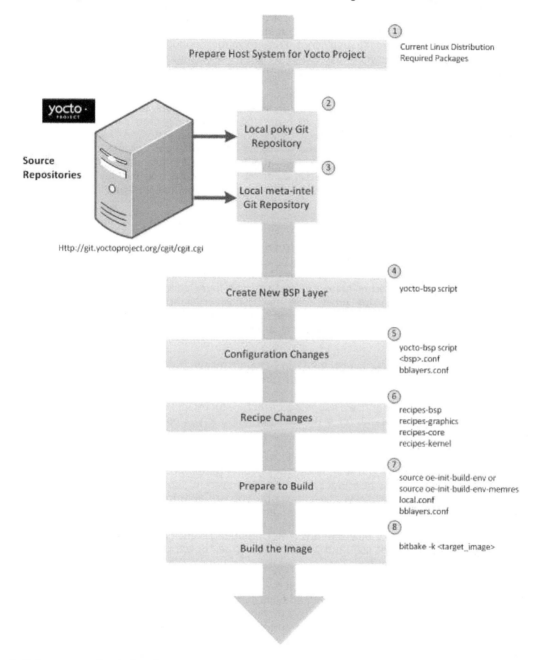

1. Set up your host development system to support development using the Yocto Project: See the "The Linux Distribution [http://www.yoctoproject.org/docs/1.7.2/yocto-project-qs/yocto-project-qs.html#the-linux-distro]" and the "The Packages [http://www.yoctoproject.org/docs/1.7.2/yocto-project-qs/yocto-project-qs.html#packages]" sections both in the Yocto Project Quick Start for requirements.

2. Establish a local copy of the project files on your system: You need this Source Directory [16] available on your host system. Having these files on your system gives you access to the build process and to the tools you need. For information on how to set up the Source Directory, see the "Getting Set Up" section.

3. Establish the meta-intel repository on your system: Having local copies of these supported BSP layers on your system gives you access to layers you might be able to build on or modify to create your BSP. For information on how to get these files, see the "Getting Set Up" section.

4. Create your own BSP layer using the yocto-bsp [http://www.yoctoproject.org/docs/1.7.2/bsp-guide/bsp-guide.html#creating-a-new-bsp-layer-using-the-yocto-bsp-script] script: Layers are ideal for isolating and storing work for a given piece of hardware. A layer is really just a location or area in which you place the recipes and configurations for your BSP. In fact, a BSP is, in itself, a special type of layer. The simplest way to create a new BSP layer that is compliant with the Yocto Project is to use the yocto-bsp script. For information about that script, see the "Creating a New BSP Layer Using the yocto-bsp Script [http://www.yoctoproject.org/docs/1.7.2/bsp-guide/bsp-guide.html#creating-a-new-bsp-layer-using-the-yocto-bsp-script]" section in the Yocto Project Board Support (BSP) Developer's Guide.

Another example that illustrates a layer is an application. Suppose you are creating an application that has library or other dependencies in order for it to compile and run. The layer, in this case, would be where all the recipes that define those dependencies are kept. The key point for a layer is that it is an isolated area that contains all the relevant information for the project that the OpenEmbedded build system knows about. For more information on layers, see the "Understanding and Creating Layers" section. For more information on BSP layers, see the "BSP Layers [http://www.yoctoproject.org/docs/1.7.2/bsp-guide/bsp-guide.html#bsp-layers]" section in the Yocto Project Board Support Package (BSP) Developer's Guide.

Note

Five BSPs exist that are part of the Yocto Project release: genericx86, genericx86-64, beaglebone (ARM), mpc8315e (PowerPC), and edgerouter (MIPS). The recipes and configurations for these five BSPs are located and dispersed within the Source Directory [16]. On the other hand, the meta-intel layer contains BSP layers for many supported BSPs (e.g. Crystal Forest, Emenlow, Fish River Island 2, Haswell, Jasper Forest, and so forth). Aside from the BSPs in the meta-intel layer, the Source Repositories [http://git.yoctoproject.org] contain additional BSP layers such as meta-minnow and meta-raspberrypi.

When you set up a layer for a new BSP, you should follow a standard layout. This layout is described in the "Example Filesystem Layout [http://www.yoctoproject.org/docs/1.7.2/bsp-guide/bsp-guide.html#bsp-filelayout]" section of the Board Support Package (BSP) Development Guide. In the standard layout, you will notice a suggested structure for recipes and configuration information. You can see the standard layout for a BSP by examining any supported BSP found in the meta-intel layer inside the Source Directory.

5. Make configuration changes to your new BSP layer: The standard BSP layer structure organizes the files you need to edit in conf and several recipes-* directories within the BSP layer. Configuration changes identify where your new layer is on the local system and identify which kernel you are going to use. When you run the yocto-bsp script, you are able to interactively configure many things for the BSP (e.g. keyboard, touchscreen, and so forth).

6. Make recipe changes to your new BSP layer: Recipe changes include altering recipes (.bb files), removing recipes you do not use, and adding new recipes or append files (.bbappend) that you need to support your hardware.

7. Prepare for the build: Once you have made all the changes to your BSP layer, there remains a few things you need to do for the OpenEmbedded build system in order for it to create your image. You need to get the build environment ready by sourcing an environment setup script (i.e. oe-init-build-env or oe-init-build-env-memres) and you need to be sure two key configuration files are configured appropriately: the conf/local.conf and the conf/bblayers.conf file. You must make the OpenEmbedded build system aware of your new layer. See the "Enabling Your Layer" section for information on how to let the build system know about your new layer.

The entire process for building an image is overviewed in the section "Building an Image [http://www.yoctoproject.org/docs/1.7.2/yocto-project-qs/yocto-project-qs.html#building-image]" section of the Yocto Project Quick Start. You might want to reference this information.

8. Build the image: The OpenEmbedded build system uses the BitBake tool to build images based on the type of image you want to create. You can find more information about BitBake in the BitBake User Manual [http://www.yoctoproject.org/docs/1.7.2/bitbake-user-manual/bitbake-user-manual.html].

The build process supports several types of images to satisfy different needs. See the "Images [http://www.yoctoproject.org/docs/1.7.2/ref-manual/ref-manual.html#ref-images]" chapter in the Yocto Project Reference Manual for information on supported images.

You can view a video presentation on "Building Custom Embedded Images with Yocto" at Free Electrons [http://free-electrons.com/blog/elc-2011-videos]. After going to the page, just search for "Embedded". You can also find supplemental information in the Yocto Project Board Support Package (BSP) Developer's Guide [http://www.yoctoproject.org/docs/1.7.2/bsp-guide/bsp-guide.html]. Finally, there is a wiki page write up of the example also located here [https://wiki.yoctoproject.org/wiki/Transcript:_creating_one_generic_Atom_BSP_from_another] that you might find helpful.

4.1.2. Modifying the Kernel

Kernel modification involves changing the Yocto Project kernel, which could involve changing configuration options as well as adding new kernel recipes. Configuration changes can be added in the form of configuration fragments, while recipe modification comes through the kernel's recipes-kernel area in a kernel layer you create.

The remainder of this section presents a high-level overview of the Yocto Project kernel architecture and the steps to modify the kernel. You can reference the "Patching the Kernel" section for an example that changes the source code of the kernel. For information on how to configure the kernel, see the "Configuring the Kernel" section. For more information on the kernel and on modifying the kernel, see the Yocto Project Linux Kernel Development Manual [http://www.yoctoproject.org/docs/1.7.2/kernel-dev/kernel-dev.html].

4.1.2.1. Kernel Overview

Traditionally, when one thinks of a patched kernel, they think of a base kernel source tree and a fixed structure that contains kernel patches. The Yocto Project, however, employs mechanisms that, in a sense, result in a kernel source generator. By the end of this section, this analogy will become clearer.

You can find a web interface to the Yocto Project kernel source repositories at http://git.yoctoproject.org. If you look at the interface, you will see to the left a grouping of Git repositories titled "Yocto Linux Kernel." Within this group, you will find several kernels supported by the Yocto Project:

- linux-yocto-3.8 - The stable Yocto Project kernel to use with the Yocto Project Release 1.4. This kernel is based on the Linux 3.8 released kernel.

- linux-yocto-3.10 - The stable Yocto Project kernel to use with the Yocto Project Release 1.5. This kernel is based on the Linux 3.10 released kernel.

- linux-yocto-3.14 - The stable Yocto Project kernel to use with the Yocto Project Releases 1.6 and 1.7. This kernel is based on the Linux 3.14 released kernel.

- linux-yocto-3.17 - An additional Yocto Project kernel used with the Yocto Project Release 1.7. This kernel is based on the Linux 3.17 released kernel.

- linux-yocto-dev - A development kernel based on the latest upstream release candidate available.

The kernels are maintained using the Git revision control system that structures them using the familiar "tree", "branch", and "leaf" scheme. Branches represent diversions from general code to more specific code, while leaves represent the end-points for a complete and unique kernel whose source files, when gathered from the root of the tree to the leaf, accumulate to create the files necessary for a specific piece of hardware and its features. The following figure displays this concept:

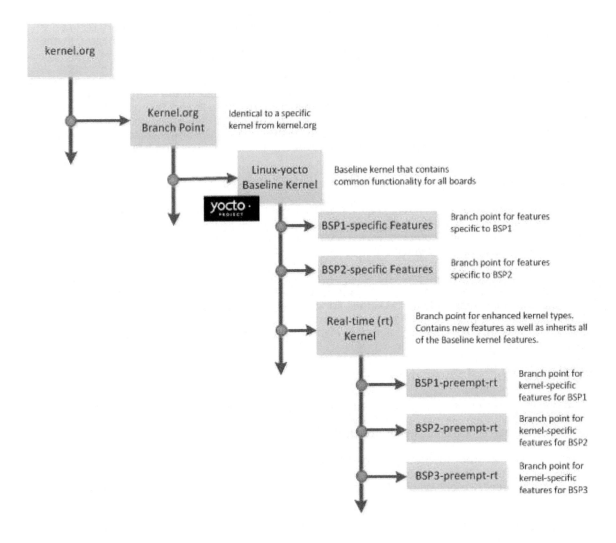

Within the figure, the "Kernel.org Branch Point" represents the point in the tree where a supported base kernel is modified from the Linux kernel. For example, this could be the branch point for the linux-yocto-3.4 kernel. Thus, everything further to the right in the structure is based on the linux-yocto-3.4 kernel. Branch points to the right in the figure represent where the linux-yocto-3.4 kernel is modified for specific hardware or types of kernels, such as real-time kernels. Each leaf thus represents the end-point for a kernel designed to run on a specific targeted device.

The overall result is a Git-maintained repository from which all the supported kernel types can be derived for all the supported devices. A big advantage to this scheme is the sharing of common features by keeping them in "larger" branches within the tree. This practice eliminates redundant storage of similar features shared among kernels.

Note

Keep in mind the figure does not take into account all the supported Yocto Project kernel types, but rather shows a single generic kernel just for conceptual purposes. Also keep in mind that this structure represents the Yocto Project source repositories that are either pulled from during the build or established on the host development system prior to the build by either cloning a particular kernel's Git repository or by downloading and unpacking a tarball.

Upstream storage of all the available kernel source code is one thing, while representing and using the code on your host development system is another. Conceptually, you can think of the kernel source repositories as all the source files necessary for all the supported kernels. As a developer, you are just interested in the source files for the kernel on which you are working. And, furthermore, you need them available on your host system.

Kernel source code is available on your host system a couple of different ways. If you are working in the kernel all the time, you probably would want to set up your own local Git repository of the kernel tree. If you just need to make some patches to the kernel, you can access temporary kernel source files that were extracted and used during a build. We will just talk about working with the temporary source code. For more information on how to get kernel source code onto your host system, see the "Yocto Project Kernel" bulleted item earlier in the manual.

What happens during the build? When you build the kernel on your development system, all files needed for the build are taken from the source repositories pointed to by the SRC_URI [http://www.yoctoproject.org/docs/1.7.2/ref-manual/ref-manual.html#var-SRC_URI] variable and gathered in a temporary work area where they are subsequently used to create the unique kernel. Thus, in a sense, the process constructs a local source tree specific to your kernel to generate the new kernel image - a source generator if you will.

The following figure shows the temporary file structure created on your host system when the build occurs. This Build Directory [14] contains all the source files used during the build.

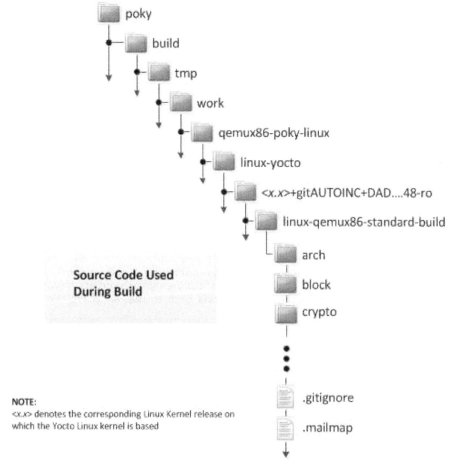

Again, for additional information on the Yocto Project kernel's architecture and its branching strategy, see the Yocto Project Linux Kernel Development Manual [http://www.yoctoproject.org/docs/1.7.2/kernel-dev/kernel-dev.html]. You can also reference the "Patching the Kernel" section for a detailed example that modifies the kernel.

4.1.2.2. Kernel Modification Workflow

This illustration and the following list summarizes the kernel modification general workflow.

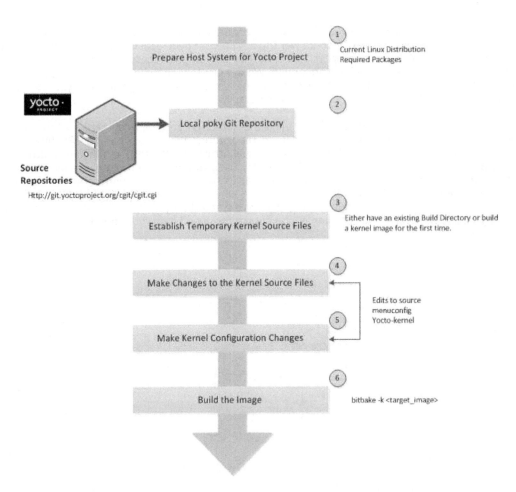

1. Set up your host development system to support development using the Yocto Project: See "The Linux Distribution [http://www.yoctoproject.org/docs/1.7.2/yocto-project-qs/yocto-project-qs.html#the-linux-distro]" and "The Packages [http://www.yoctoproject.org/docs/1.7.2/yocto-project-qs/yocto-project-qs.html#packages]" sections both in the Yocto Project Quick Start for requirements.

2. Establish a local copy of project files on your system: Having the Source Directory [16] on your system gives you access to the build process and tools you need. For information on how to get these files, see the bulleted item "Yocto Project Release" earlier in this manual.

3. Establish the temporary kernel source files: Temporary kernel source files are kept in the Build Directory [14] created by the OpenEmbedded build system when you run BitBake. If you have never built the kernel in which you are interested, you need to run an initial build to establish local kernel source files.

   If you are building an image for the first time, you need to get the build environment ready by sourcing an environment setup script (i.e. oe-init-build-env or oe-init-build-env-memres). You also need to be sure two key configuration files (local.conf and bblayers.conf) are configured appropriately.

   The entire process for building an image is overviewed in the "Building an Image [http://www.yoctoproject.org/docs/1.7.2/yocto-project-qs/yocto-project-qs.html#building-image]" section of the Yocto Project Quick Start. You might want to reference this information. You can find more information on BitBake in the BitBake User Manual [http://www.yoctoproject.org/docs/1.7.2/bitbake-user-manual/bitbake-user-manual.html].

   The build process supports several types of images to satisfy different needs. See the "Images [http://www.yoctoproject.org/docs/1.7.2/ref-manual/ref-manual.html#ref-images]" chapter in the Yocto Project Reference Manual for information on supported images.

4. Make changes to the kernel source code if applicable: Modifying the kernel does not always mean directly changing source files. However, if you have to do this, you make the changes to the files in the Build Directory.

5. Make kernel configuration changes if applicable: If your situation calls for changing the kernel's configuration, you can use the yocto-kernel script or menuconfig to enable and disable kernel configurations. Using the script lets you interactively set up kernel configurations. Using menuconfig allows you to interactively develop and test the configuration changes you are making to the kernel. When saved, changes using menuconfig update the kernel's .config file. Try to resist the temptation of directly editing the .config file found in the Build Directory at tmp/sysroots/ <machine-name>/kernel. Doing so, can produce unexpected results when the OpenEmbedded build system regenerates the configuration file.

Once you are satisfied with the configuration changes made using menuconfig, you can directly compare the .config file against a saved original and gather those changes into a config fragment to be referenced from within the kernel's .bbappend file.

6. Rebuild the kernel image with your changes: Rebuilding the kernel image applies your changes.

4.2. Application Development Workflow

Application development involves creating an application that you want to run on your target hardware, which is running a kernel image created using the OpenEmbedded build system. The Yocto Project provides an Application Development Toolkit (ADT) [http:// www.yoctoproject.org/docs/1.7.2/adt-manual/adt-manual.html#adt-intro] and stand-alone cross-development toolchains [http://www.yoctoproject.org/docs/1.7.2/adt-manual/adt-manual.html#the-cross-development-toolchain] that facilitate quick development and integration of your application into its runtime environment. Using the ADT and toolchains, you can compile and link your application. You can then deploy your application to the actual hardware or to the QEMU emulator for testing. If you are familiar with the popular Eclipse™ IDE, you can use an Eclipse Yocto Plug-in to allow you to develop, deploy, and test your application all from within Eclipse.

While we strongly suggest using the ADT to develop your application, this option might not be best for you. If this is the case, you can still use pieces of the Yocto Project for your development process. However, because the process can vary greatly, this manual does not provide detail on the process.

4.2.1. Workflow Using the ADT and Eclipse™

To help you understand how application development works using the ADT, this section provides an overview of the general development process and a detailed example of the process as it is used from within the Eclipse IDE.

The following illustration and list summarize the application development general workflow.

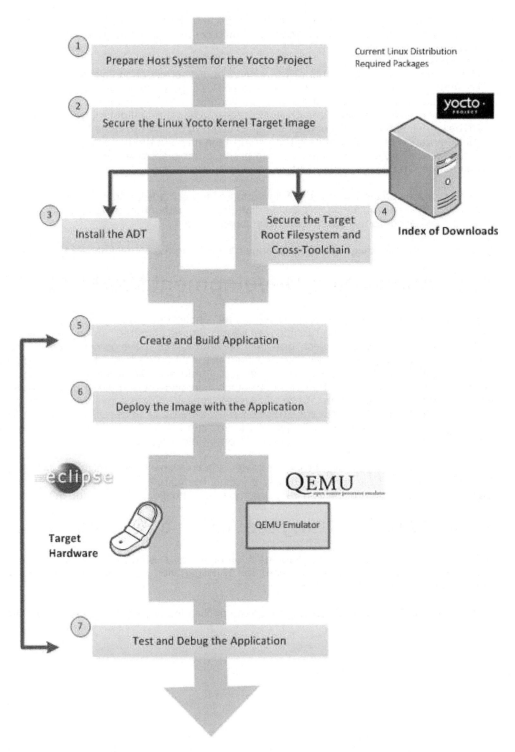

1. Prepare the host system for the Yocto Project: See "Supported Linux Distributions [http://www.yoctoproject.org/docs/1.7.2/ref-manual/ref-manual.html#detailed-supported-distros]" and "Required Packages for the Host Development System [http://www.yoctoproject.org/docs/1.7.2/ref-manual/ref-manual.html#required-packages-for-the-host-development-system]" sections both in the Yocto Project Reference Manual for requirements. In particular, be sure your host system has the xterm package installed.

2. Secure the Yocto Project kernel target image: You must have a target kernel image that has been built using the OpenEmbedded build system.

Depending on whether the Yocto Project has a pre-built image that matches your target architecture and where you are going to run the image while you develop your application (QEMU or real hardware), the area from which you get the image differs.

- Download the image from machines [http://downloads.yoctoproject.org/releases/yocto/yocto-1.7.2/machines] if your target architecture is supported and you are going to develop and test your application on actual hardware.

- Download the image from machines/qemu [http://downloads.yoctoproject.org/releases/yocto/yocto-1.7.2/machines/qemu] if your target architecture is supported and you are going to develop and test your application using the QEMU emulator.

- Build your image if you cannot find a pre-built image that matches your target architecture. If your target architecture is similar to a supported architecture, you can modify the kernel image before you build it. See the "Patching the Kernel" section for an example.

For information on pre-built kernel image naming schemes for images that can run on the QEMU emulator, see the "Downloading the Pre-Built Linux Kernel [http://www.yoctoproject.org/docs/1.7.2/yocto-project-qs/yocto-project-qs.html#downloading-the-pre-built-linux-kernel]" section in the Yocto Project Quick Start.

3. Install the ADT: The ADT provides a target-specific cross-development toolchain, the root filesystem, the QEMU emulator, and other tools that can help you develop your application. While it is possible to get these pieces separately, the ADT Installer provides an easy, inclusive method. You can get these pieces by running an ADT installer script, which is configurable. For information on how to install the ADT, see the "Using the ADT Installer [http://www.yoctoproject.org/docs/1.7.2/adt-manual/adt-manual.html#using-the-adt-installer]" section in the Yocto Project Application Developer's Guide.

4. If applicable, secure the target root filesystem and the Cross-development toolchain: If you choose not to install the ADT using the ADT Installer, you need to find and download the appropriate root filesystem and the cross-development toolchain.

You can find the tarballs for the root filesystem in the same area used for the kernel image. Depending on the type of image you are running, the root filesystem you need differs. For example, if you are developing an application that runs on an image that supports Sato, you need to get a root filesystem that supports Sato.

You can find the cross-development toolchains at toolchains [http://downloads.yoctoproject.org/releases/yocto/yocto-1.7.2/toolchain/]. Be sure to get the correct toolchain for your development host and your target architecture. See the "Using a Cross-Toolchain Tarball [http://www.yoctoproject.org/docs/1.7.2/adt-manual/adt-manual.html#using-an-existing-toolchain-tarball]" section in the Yocto Project Application Developer's Guide for information and the "Installing the Toolchain [http://www.yoctoproject.org/docs/1.7.2/yocto-project-qs/yocto-project-qs.html#installing-the-toolchain]" in the Yocto Project Quick Start for information on finding and installing the correct toolchain based on your host development system and your target architecture.

5. Create and build your application: At this point, you need to have source files for your application. Once you have the files, you can use the Eclipse IDE to import them and build the project. If you are not using Eclipse, you need to use the cross-development tools you have installed to create the image.

6. Deploy the image with the application: If you are using the Eclipse IDE, you can deploy your image to the hardware or to QEMU through the project's preferences. If you are not using the Eclipse IDE, then you need to deploy the application to the hardware using other methods. Or, if you are using QEMU, you need to use that tool and load your image in for testing. See the "Using the Quick EMUlator (QEMU)" chapter for information on using QEMU.

7. Test and debug the application: Once your application is deployed, you need to test it. Within the Eclipse IDE, you can use the debugging environment along with the set of user-space tools installed along with the ADT to debug your application. Of course, the same user-space tools are available separately if you choose not to use the Eclipse IDE.

4.2.2. Working Within Eclipse

The Eclipse IDE is a popular development environment and it fully supports development using the Yocto Project.

Note
This release of the Yocto Project supports both the Kepler and Juno versions of the Eclipse IDE. Thus, the following information provides setup information for both versions.

When you install and configure the Eclipse Yocto Project Plug-in into the Eclipse IDE, you maximize your Yocto Project experience. Installing and configuring the Plug-in results in an environment that has extensions specifically designed to let you more easily develop software. These extensions allow for cross-compilation, deployment, and execution of your output into a QEMU emulation session as well as actual target hardware. You can also perform cross-debugging and profiling. The environment also supports a suite of tools that allows you to perform remote profiling, tracing, collection of power data, collection of latency data, and collection of performance data.

This section describes how to install and configure the Eclipse IDE Yocto Plug-in and how to use it to develop your application.

4.2.2.1. Setting Up the Eclipse IDE

To develop within the Eclipse IDE, you need to do the following:

1. Install the optimal version of the Eclipse IDE.

2. Configure the Eclipse IDE.

3. Install the Eclipse Yocto Plug-in.

4. Configure the Eclipse Yocto Plug-in.

Note
Do not install Eclipse from your distribution's package repository. Be sure to install Eclipse from the official Eclipse download site as directed in the next section.

4.2.2.1.1. Installing the Eclipse IDE

It is recommended that you have the Kepler 4.3.2 version of the Eclipse IDE installed on your development system. However, if you currently have the Juno 4.2 version installed and you do not want to upgrade the IDE, you can configure Juno to work with the Yocto Project.

If you do not have the Kepler 4.3.2 Eclipse IDE installed, you can find the tarball at http://www.eclipse.org/downloads. From that site, choose the Eclipse Standard 4.3.2 version particular to your development host. This version contains the Eclipse Platform, the Java Development Tools (JDT), and the Plug-in Development Environment.

Once you have downloaded the tarball, extract it into a clean directory. For example, the following commands unpack and install the downloaded Eclipse IDE tarball into a clean directory using the default name eclipse:

```
$ cd ~
$ tar -xzvf ~/Downloads/eclipse-standard-kepler-SR2-linux-gtk-x86_64.tar.gz
```

4.2.2.1.2. Configuring the Eclipse IDE

This section presents the steps needed to configure the Eclipse IDE.

Before installing and configuring the Eclipse Yocto Plug-in, you need to configure the Eclipse IDE. Follow these general steps:

1. Start the Eclipse IDE.

2. Make sure you are in your Workbench and select "Install New Software" from the "Help" pull-down menu.

3. Select Kepler - `http://download.eclipse.org/releases/kepler` from the "Work with:" pull-down menu.

> ## Note
> For Juno, select Juno - `http://download.eclipse.org/releases/juno`

4. Expand the box next to "Linux Tools" and select the LTTng - Linux Tracing Toolkit boxes.

5. Expand the box next to "Mobile and Device Development" and select the following boxes:

   - C/C++ Remote Launch (Requires RSE Remote System Explorer)

   - Remote System Explorer End-user Runtime

   - Remote System Explorer User Actions

   - Target Management Terminal

   - TCF Remote System Explorer add-in

   - TCF Target Explorer

6. Expand the box next to "Programming Languages" and select the C/C++ Autotools Support and C/C++ Development Tools boxes.

7. Complete the installation and restart the Eclipse IDE.

4.2.2.1.3. Installing or Accessing the Eclipse Yocto Plug-in

You can install the Eclipse Yocto Plug-in into the Eclipse IDE one of two ways: use the Yocto Project's Eclipse Update site to install the pre-built plug-in or build and install the plug-in from the latest source code.

4.2.2.1.3.1. Installing the Pre-built Plug-in from the Yocto Project Eclipse Update Site

To install the Eclipse Yocto Plug-in from the update site, follow these steps:

1. Start up the Eclipse IDE.

2. In Eclipse, select "Install New Software" from the "Help" menu.

3. Click "Add..." in the "Work with:" area.

4. Enter `http://downloads.yoctoproject.org/releases/eclipse-plugin/1.7.2/kepler` in the URL field and provide a meaningful name in the "Name" field.

> ## Note
> If you are using Juno, use `http://downloads.yoctoproject.org/releases/eclipse-plugin/1.7.2/juno` in the URL field.

5. Click "OK" to have the entry added to the "Work with:" drop-down list.

6. Select the entry for the plug-in from the "Work with:" drop-down list.

7. Check the boxes next to Yocto Project ADT Plug-in, Yocto Project Bitbake Commander Plug-in, and Yocto Project Documentation plug-in.

8. Complete the remaining software installation steps and then restart the Eclipse IDE to finish the installation of the plug-in.

4.2.2.1.3.2. Installing the Plug-in Using the Latest Source Code

To install the Eclipse Yocto Plug-in from the latest source code, follow these steps:

1. Be sure your development system is not using OpenJDK to build the plug-in by doing the following:

a. Use the Oracle JDK. If you don't have that, go to http://www.oracle.com/technetwork/java/javase/downloads/jdk7-downloads-1880260.html and download the appropriate tarball for your development system and extract it into your home directory.

b. In the shell you are going to do your work, export the location of the Oracle Java as follows:

```
export PATH=~/jdk1.7.0_40/bin:$PATH
```

2. In the same shell, create a Git repository with:

```
$ cd ~
$ git clone git://git.yoctoproject.org/eclipse-poky-kepler
```

Note

If you are using Juno, the repository is located at `git://git.yoctoproject.org/eclipse-poky-juno`.
For this example, the repository is named `~/eclipse-poky-kepler`.

3. Change to the directory where you set up the Git repository:

```
$ cd ~/eclipse-poky-kepler
```

4. Be sure you are in the right branch for your Git repository. For this release set the branch to dizzy:

```
$ git checkout dizzy
```

5. Change to the `scripts` directory within the Git repository:

```
$ cd scripts
```

6. Set up the local build environment by running the setup script:

```
$ ./setup.sh
```

7. When the script finishes execution, it prompts you with instructions on how to run the `build.sh` script, which is also in the `scripts` directory of the Git repository created earlier.

8. Run the `build.sh` script as directed. Be sure to provide the name of the Git branch along with the Yocto Project release you are using. Here is an example that uses the `dizzy` branch:

```
$ ECLIPSE_HOME=/home/scottrif/eclipse-poky-kepler/scripts/eclipse ./build.sh dizzy dizzy
```

After running the script, the file `org.yocto.sdk-<release>-<date>-archive.zip` is in the current directory.

9. If necessary, start the Eclipse IDE and be sure you are in the Workbench.

10 Select "Install New Software" from the "Help" pull-down menu.

11 Click "Add".

12 Provide anything you want in the "Name" field.

13Click "Archive" and browse to the ZIP file you built in step eight. This ZIP file should not be "unzipped", and must be the *archive.zip file created by running the build.sh script.

14Click through the "Okay" buttons.

15Check the boxes in the installation window and complete the installation.

16Restart the Eclipse IDE if necessary.

At this point you should be able to configure the Eclipse Yocto Plug-in as described in the "Configuring the Eclipse Yocto Plug-in" section.

4.2.2.1.4. Configuring the Eclipse Yocto Plug-in

Configuring the Eclipse Yocto Plug-in involves setting the Cross Compiler options and the Target options. The configurations you choose become the default settings for all projects. You do have opportunities to change them later when you configure the project (see the following section).

To start, you need to do the following from within the Eclipse IDE:

• Choose "Preferences" from the "Windows" menu to display the Preferences Dialog.

• Click "Yocto Project ADT".

4.2.2.1.4.1. Configuring the Cross-Compiler Options

To configure the Cross Compiler Options, you must select the type of toolchain, point to the toolchain, specify the sysroot location, and select the target architecture.

• Selecting the Toolchain Type: Choose between Standalone pre-built toolchain and Build system derived toolchain for Cross Compiler Options.

  • Standalone Pre-built Toolchain: Select this mode when you are using a stand-alone cross-toolchain. For example, suppose you are an application developer and do not need to build a target image. Instead, you just want to use an architecture-specific toolchain on an existing kernel and target root filesystem.

  • Build System Derived Toolchain: Select this mode if the cross-toolchain has been installed and built as part of the Build Directory [14]. When you select Build system derived toolchain, you are using the toolchain bundled inside the Build Directory.

• Point to the Toolchain: If you are using a stand-alone pre-built toolchain, you should be pointing to where it is installed. If you used the ADT Installer script and accepted the default installation directory, the toolchain will be installed in the /opt/poky/1.7.2 directory. Sections "Configuring and Running the ADT Installer Script [http://www.yoctoproject.org/docs/1.7.2/adt-manual/adt-manual.html#configuring-and-running-the-adt-installer-script]" and "Using a Cross-Toolchain Tarball [http://www.yoctoproject.org/docs/1.7.2/adt-manual/adt-manual.html#using-an-existing-toolchain-tarball]" in the Yocto Project Application Developer's Guide describe how to install a stand-alone cross-toolchain.

  If you are using a system-derived toolchain, the path you provide for the Toolchain Root Location field is the Build Directory [14]. See the "Using BitBake and the Build Directory [http://www.yoctoproject.org/docs/1.7.2/adt-manual/adt-manual.html#using-the-toolchain-from-within-the-build-tree]" section in the Yocto Project Application Developer's Guide for information on how to install the toolchain into the Build Directory.

• Specify the Sysroot Location: This location is where the root filesystem for the target hardware resides. If you used the ADT Installer script and accepted the default installation directory, then the location is /opt/poky/1.7.2. Additionally, when you use the ADT Installer script, the same location is used for the QEMU user-space tools and the NFS boot process.

  If you used either of the other two methods to install the toolchain or did not accept the ADT Installer script's default installation directory, then the location of the sysroot filesystem depends on where you separately extracted and installed the filesystem.

  For information on how to install the toolchain and on how to extract and install the sysroot filesystem, see the "Installing the ADT and Toolchains [http://www.yoctoproject.org/docs/1.7.2/adt-manual/adt-manual.html#installing-the-adt]" section in the Yocto Project Application Developer's Guide.

- Select the Target Architecture: The target architecture is the type of hardware you are going to use or emulate. Use the pull-down Target Architecture menu to make your selection. The pull-down menu should have the supported architectures. If the architecture you need is not listed in the menu, you will need to build the image. See the "Building an Image [http://www.yoctoproject.org/docs/1.7.2/yocto-project-qs/yocto-project-qs.html#building-image]" section of the Yocto Project Quick Start for more information.

4.2.2.1.4.2. Configuring the Target Options

You can choose to emulate hardware using the QEMU emulator, or you can choose to run your image on actual hardware.

- QEMU: Select this option if you will be using the QEMU emulator. If you are using the emulator, you also need to locate the kernel and specify any custom options.

  If you selected Build system derived toolchain, the target kernel you built will be located in the Build Directory in tmp/deploy/images/machine directory. If you selected Standalone pre-built toolchain, the pre-built image you downloaded is located in the directory you specified when you downloaded the image.

  Most custom options are for advanced QEMU users to further customize their QEMU instance. These options are specified between paired angled brackets. Some options must be specified outside the brackets. In particular, the options serial, nographic, and kvm must all be outside the brackets. Use the man qemu command to get help on all the options and their use. The following is an example:

  ```
  serial '<-m 256 -full-screen>'
  ```

  Regardless of the mode, Sysroot is already defined as part of the Cross-Compiler Options configuration in the Sysroot Location: field.

- External HW: Select this option if you will be using actual hardware.

Click the "OK" to save your plug-in configurations.

4.2.2.2. Creating the Project

You can create two types of projects: Autotools-based, or Makefile-based. This section describes how to create Autotools-based projects from within the Eclipse IDE. For information on creating Makefile-based projects in a terminal window, see the section "Using the Command Line [http://www.yoctoproject.org/docs/1.7.2/adt-manual/adt-manual.html#using-the-command-line]" in the Yocto Project Application Developer's Guide.

Note
Do not use special characters in project names (e.g. spaces, underscores, etc.). Doing so can cause configuration to fail.

To create a project based on a Yocto template and then display the source code, follow these steps:

1. Select "Project" from the "File -> New" menu.

2. Double click CC++.

3. Double click C Project to create the project.

4. Expand Yocto Project ADT Project.

5. Select Hello World ANSI C Autotools Project. This is an Autotools-based project based on a Yocto template.

6. Put a name in the Project name: field. Do not use hyphens as part of the name.

7. Click "Next".

8. Add information in the `Author` and `Copyright notice` fields.

9. Be sure the `License` field is correct.

10Click "Finish".

11If the "open perspective" prompt appears, click "Yes" so that you in the C/C++ perspective.

12The left-hand navigation pane shows your project. You can display your source by double clicking the project's source file.

4.2.2.3. Configuring the Cross-Toolchains

The earlier section, "Configuring the Eclipse Yocto Plug-in", sets up the default project configurations. You can override these settings for a given project by following these steps:

1. Select "Change Yocto Project Settings" from the "Project" menu. This selection brings up the Yocto Project Settings Dialog and allows you to make changes specific to an individual project.

   By default, the Cross Compiler Options and Target Options for a project are inherited from settings you provided using the Preferences Dialog as described earlier in the "Configuring the Eclipse Yocto Plug-in" section. The Yocto Project Settings Dialog allows you to override those default settings for a given project.

2. Make your configurations for the project and click "OK". If you are running the Juno version of Eclipse, you can skip down to the next section where you build the project. If you are not working with Juno, you need to reconfigure the project as described in the next step.

3. Select "Reconfigure Project" from the "Project" menu. This selection reconfigures the project by running `autogen.sh` in the workspace for your project. The script also runs `libtoolize`, `aclocal`, `autoconf`, `autoheader`, `automake --a`, and `./configure`. Click on the "Console" tab beneath your source code to see the results of reconfiguring your project.

4.2.2.4. Building the Project

To build the project in Juno, right click on the project in the navigator pane and select "Build Project". If you are not running Juno, select "Build Project" from the "Project" menu. The console should update and you can note the cross-compiler you are using.

4.2.2.5. Starting QEMU in User-Space NFS Mode

To start the QEMU emulator from within Eclipse, follow these steps:

Note
See the "Using the Quick EMUlator (QEMU)" chapter for more information on using QEMU.

1. Expose and select "External Tools" from the "Run" menu. Your image should appear as a selectable menu item.

2. Select your image from the menu to launch the emulator in a new window.

3. If needed, enter your host root password in the shell window at the prompt. This sets up a Tap `0` connection needed for running in user-space NFS mode.

4. Wait for QEMU to launch.

5. Once QEMU launches, you can begin operating within that environment. For example, you could determine the IP Address for the user-space NFS by using the `ifconfig` command.

4.2.2.6. Deploying and Debugging the Application

Once the QEMU emulator is running the image, you can deploy your application using the Eclipse IDE and then use the emulator to perform debugging. Follow these steps to deploy the application.

1. Select "Debug Configurations..." from the "Run" menu.

2. In the left area, expand `C/C++Remote Application`.

3. Locate your project and select it to bring up a new tabbed view in the Debug Configurations Dialog.

4. Enter the absolute path into which you want to deploy the application. Use the "Remote Absolute File Path for C/C++Application:" field. For example, enter /usr/bin/<programname>.

5. Click on the "Debugger" tab to see the cross-tool debugger you are using.

6. Click on the "Main" tab.

7. Create a new connection to the QEMU instance by clicking on "new".

8. Select TCF, which means Target Communication Framework.

9. Click "Next".

10 Clear out the "host name" field and enter the IP Address determined earlier.

11 Click "Finish" to close the New Connections Dialog.

12 Use the drop-down menu now in the "Connection" field and pick the IP Address you entered.

13 Click "Run" to bring up a login screen and login.

14 Accept the debug perspective.

4.2.2.7. Running User-Space Tools

As mentioned earlier in the manual, several tools exist that enhance your development experience. These tools are aids in developing and debugging applications and images. You can run these user-space tools from within the Eclipse IDE through the "YoctoTools" menu.

Once you pick a tool, you need to configure it for the remote target. Every tool needs to have the connection configured. You must select an existing TCF-based RSE connection to the remote target. If one does not exist, click "New" to create one.

Here are some specifics about the remote tools:

* OProfile: Selecting this tool causes the oprofile-server on the remote target to launch on the local host machine. The oprofile-viewer must be installed on the local host machine and the oprofile-server must be installed on the remote target, respectively, in order to use. You must compile and install the oprofile-viewer from the source code on your local host machine. Furthermore, in order to convert the target's sample format data into a form that the host can use, you must have OProfile version 0.9.4 or greater installed on the host.

  You can locate both the viewer and server from http://git.yoctoproject.org/cgit/cgit.cgi/oprofileui/. You can also find more information on setting up and using this tool in the "oprofile [http://www.yoctoproject.org/docs/1.7.2/profile-manual/profile-manual.html#profile-manual-oprofile]" section of the Yocto Project Profiling and Tracing Manual.

  ### Note
  The oprofile-server is installed by default on the core-image-sato-sdk image.

* Lttng2.0 ust trace import: Selecting this tool transfers the remote target's Lttng tracing data back to the local host machine and uses the Lttng Eclipse plug-in to graphically display the output. For information on how to use Lttng to trace an application, see http://lttng.org/documentation and the "LTTng (Linux Trace Toolkit, next generation) [http://www.yoctoproject.org/docs/1.7.2/profile-manual/profile-manual.html#lttng-linux-trace-toolkit-next-generation]" section, which is in the Yocto Project Profiling and Tracing Manual.

  ### Note
  Do not use Lttng-user space (legacy) tool. This tool no longer has any upstream support.

  Before you use the Lttng2.0 ust trace import tool, you need to setup the Lttng Eclipse plug-in and create a Tracing project. Do the following:

  1. Select "Open Perspective" from the "Window" menu and then select "Tracing".

  2. Click "OK" to change the Eclipse perspective into the Tracing perspective.

3. Create a new Tracing project by selecting "Project" from the "File -> New" menu.

4. Choose "Tracing Project" from the "Tracing" menu.

5. Generate your tracing data on the remote target.

6. Select "Lttng2.0 ust trace import" from the "Yocto Project Tools" menu to start the data import process.

7. Specify your remote connection name.

8. For the Ust directory path, specify the location of your remote tracing data. Make sure the location ends with ust (e.g. /usr/mysession/ust).

9. Click "OK" to complete the import process. The data is now in the local tracing project you created.

10 Right click on the data and then use the menu to Select "Generic CTF Trace" from the "Trace Type... -> Common Trace Format" menu to map the tracing type.

11 Right click the mouse and select "Open" to bring up the Eclipse Lttng Trace Viewer so you view the tracing data.

- PowerTOP: Selecting this tool runs PowerTOP on the remote target machine and displays the results in a new view called PowerTOP.

  The "Time to gather data(sec):" field is the time passed in seconds before data is gathered from the remote target for analysis.

  The "show pids in wakeups list:" field corresponds to the -p argument passed to PowerTOP.

- LatencyTOP and Perf: LatencyTOP identifies system latency, while Perf monitors the system's performance counter registers. Selecting either of these tools causes an RSE terminal view to appear from which you can run the tools. Both tools refresh the entire screen to display results while they run. For more information on setting up and using perf, see the "perf [http://www.yoctoproject.org/docs/1.7.2/profile-manual/profile-manual.html#profile-manual-perf]" section in the Yocto Project Profiling and Tracing Manual.

4.2.2.8. Customizing an Image Using a BitBake Commander Project and Hob

Within the Eclipse IDE, you can create a Yocto BitBake Commander project, edit the Metadata [16], and then use Hob [http://www.yoctoproject.org/tools-resources/projects/hob] to build a customized image all within one IDE.

4.2.2.8.1. Creating the Yocto BitBake Commander Project

To create a Yocto BitBake Commander project, follow these steps:

1. Select "Other" from the "Window -> Open Perspective" menu and then choose "Bitbake Commander".

2. Click "OK" to change the perspective to Bitbake Commander.

3. Select "Project" from the "File -> New" menu to create a new Yocto Bitbake Commander project.

4. Choose "New Yocto Project" from the "Yocto Project Bitbake Commander" menu and click "Next".

5. Enter the Project Name and choose the Project Location. The Yocto project's Metadata files will be put under the directory project_location/project_name. If that directory does not exist, you need to check the "Clone from Yocto Git Repository" box, which would execute a git clone command to get the project's Metadata files.

> ## Note
> Do not specify your BitBake Commander project location as your Eclipse workspace. Doing so causes an error indicating that the current project overlaps the location of another project. This error occurs even if no such project exits.

6. Select Finish to create the project.

4.2.2.8.2. Editing the Metadata

After you create the Yocto Bitbake Commander project, you can modify the Metadata [16] files by opening them in the project. When editing recipe files (.bb files), you can view BitBake variable values and information by hovering the mouse pointer over the variable name and waiting a few seconds.

To edit the Metadata, follow these steps:

1. Select your Yocto Bitbake Commander project.

2. Select "BitBake Recipe" from the "File -> New -> Yocto BitBake Commander" menu to open a new recipe wizard.

3. Point to your source by filling in the "SRC_URL" field. For example, you can add a recipe to your Source Directory [16] by defining "SRC_URL" as follows:

   ```
   ftp://ftp.gnu.org/gnu/m4/m4-1.4.9.tar.gz
   ```

4. Click "Populate" to calculate the archive md5, sha256, license checksum values and to auto-generate the recipe filename.

5. Fill in the "Description" field.

6. Be sure values for all required fields exist.

7. Click "Finish".

4.2.2.8.3. Building and Customizing the Image Using Hob

To build and customize the image using Hob from within the Eclipse IDE, follow these steps:

1. Select your Yocto Bitbake Commander project.

2. Select "Launch Hob" from the "Project" menu.

3. Enter the Build Directory [14] where you want to put your final images.

4. Click "OK" to launch Hob.

5. Use Hob to customize and build your own images. For information on Hob, see the Hob Project Page [http://www.yoctoproject.org/tools-resources/projects/hob] on the Yocto Project website.

4.2.3. Workflow Using Stand-Alone Cross-Development Toolchains

If you want to develop an application without prior installation of the ADT, you still can employ the Cross Development Toolchain [15], the QEMU emulator, and a number of supported target image files. You just need to follow these general steps:

1. Install the cross-development toolchain for your target hardware: For information on how to install the toolchain, see the "Using a Cross-Toolchain Tarball [http://www.yoctoproject.org/docs/1.7.2/adt-manual/adt-manual.html#using-an-existing-toolchain-tarball]" section in the Yocto Project Application Developer's Guide.

2. Download the Target Image: The Yocto Project supports several target architectures and has many pre-built kernel images and root filesystem images.

   If you are going to develop your application on hardware, go to the machines [http://downloads.yoctoproject.org/releases/yocto/yocto-1.7.2/machines] download area and choose a target machine area from which to download the kernel image and root filesystem. This download area could have several files in it that support development using actual hardware. For example, the area might contain .hddimg files that combine the kernel image with the filesystem, boot loaders, and so forth. Be sure to get the files you need for your particular development process.

If you are going to develop your application and then run and test it using the QEMU emulator, go to the machines/qemu [http://downloads.yoctoproject.org/releases/yocto/yocto-1.7.2/machines/qemu] download area. From this area, go down into the directory for your target architecture (e.g. qemux86_64 for an Intel®-based 64-bit architecture). Download kernel, root filesystem, and any other files you need for your process.

Note

In order to use the root filesystem in QEMU, you need to extract it. See the "Extracting the Root Filesystem [http://www.yoctoproject.org/docs/1.7.2/adt-manual/adt-manual.html#extracting-the-root-filesystem]" section for information on how to extract the root filesystem.

3. Develop and Test your Application: At this point, you have the tools to develop your application. If you need to separately install and use the QEMU emulator, you can go to QEMU Home Page [http://wiki.qemu.org/Main_Page] to download and learn about the emulator. You can see the "Using the Quick EMUlator (QEMU)" chapter for information on using QEMU within the Yocto Project.

4.3. Modifying Temporary Source Code

You might find it helpful during development to modify the temporary source code used by recipes to build packages. For example, suppose you are developing a patch and you need to experiment a bit to figure out your solution. After you have initially built the package, you can iteratively tweak the source code, which is located in the Build Directory [14], and then you can force a re-compile and quickly test your altered code. Once you settle on a solution, you can then preserve your changes in the form of patches. You can accomplish these steps all within either a Quilt [http://savannah.nongnu.org/projects/quilt] or Git workflow.

4.3.1. Finding the Temporary Source Code

During a build, the unpacked temporary source code used by recipes to build packages is available in the Build Directory as defined by the S [http://www.yoctoproject.org/docs/1.7.2/ref-manual/ref-manual.html#var-S] variable. Below is the default value for the S variable as defined in the meta/conf/bitbake.conf configuration file in the Source Directory [16]:

```
S = "${WORKDIR}/${BP}"
```

You should be aware that many recipes override the S variable. For example, recipes that fetch their source from Git usually set S to ${WORKDIR}/git.

Note
The BP [http://www.yoctoproject.org/docs/1.7.2/ref-manual/ref-manual.html#var-BP] represents the base recipe name, which consists of the name and version:

```
BP = "${BPN}-${PV}"
```

The path to the work directory for the recipe (WORKDIR [http://www.yoctoproject.org/docs/1.7.2/ref-manual/ref-manual.html#var-WORKDIR]) is defined as follows:

```
${TMPDIR}/work/${MULTIMACH_TARGET_SYS}/${PN}/${EXTENDPE}${PV}-${PR}
```

The actual directory depends on several things:

• TMPDIR [http://www.yoctoproject.org/docs/1.7.2/ref-manual/ref-manual.html#var-TMPDIR]: The top-level build output directory

• MULTIMACH_TARGET_SYS [http://www.yoctoproject.org/docs/1.7.2/ref-manual/ref-manual.html#var-MULTIMACH_TARGET_SYS]: The target system identifier

- PN [http://www.yoctoproject.org/docs/1.7.2/ref-manual/ref-manual.html#var-PN]: The recipe name

- EXTENDPE   [http://www.yoctoproject.org/docs/1.7.2/ref-manual/ref-manual.html#var-EXTENDPE]:
  The epoch - (if PE [http://www.yoctoproject.org/docs/1.7.2/ref-manual/ref-manual.html#var-PE] is
  not specified, which is usually the case for most recipes, then EXTENDPE is blank)

- PV   [http://www.yoctoproject.org/docs/1.7.2/ref-manual/ref-manual.html#var-PV]:   The   recipe
  version

- PR   [http://www.yoctoproject.org/docs/1.7.2/ref-manual/ref-manual.html#var-PR]:   The   recipe
  revision

As an example, assume a Source Directory top-level folder name poky, a default Build Directory at
poky/build, and a qemux86-poky-linux machine target system. Furthermore, suppose your recipe
is named foo_1.3.0.bb. In this case, the work directory the build system uses to build the package
would be as follows:

```
poky/build/tmp/work/qemux86-poky-linux/foo/1.3.0-r0
```

Now that you know where to locate the directory that has the temporary source code, you can use
a Quilt or Git workflow to make your edits, test the changes, and preserve the changes in the form
of patches.

4.3.2. Using a Quilt Workflow

Quilt [http://savannah.nongnu.org/projects/quilt] is a powerful tool that allows you to capture source
code changes without having a clean source tree. This section outlines the typical workflow you can
use to modify temporary source code, test changes, and then preserve the changes in the form of
a patch all using Quilt.

Follow these general steps:

1. Find the Source Code: The temporary source code used by the OpenEmbedded build system is kept
   in the Build Directory. See the "Finding the Temporary Source Code" section to learn how to locate
   the directory that has the temporary source code for a particular package.

2. Change Your Working Directory: You need to be in the directory that has the temporary source
   code. That directory is defined by the S [http://www.yoctoproject.org/docs/1.7.2/ref-manual/ref-
   manual.html#var-S] variable.

3. Create a New Patch: Before modifying source code, you need to create a new patch. To create a
   new patch file, use quilt new as below:

   ```
   $ quilt new my_changes.patch
   ```

4. Notify Quilt and Add Files: After creating the patch, you need to notify Quilt about the files you plan
   to edit. You notify Quilt by adding the files to the patch you just created:

   ```
   $ quilt add file1.c file2.c file3.c
   ```

5. Edit the Files: Make your changes in the temporary source code to the files you added to the patch.

6. Test Your Changes: Once you have modified the source code, the easiest way to your changes is
   by calling the do_compile task as shown in the following example:

   ```
   $ bitbake -c compile -f name_of_package
   ```

   The -f or --force option forces the specified task to execute. If you find problems with your code,
   you can just keep editing and re-testing iteratively until things work as expected.

Note

All the modifications you make to the temporary source code disappear once you run the do_clean [http://www.yoctoproject.org/docs/1.7.2/ref-manual/ref-manual.html#ref-tasks-clean] or do_cleanall [http://www.yoctoproject.org/docs/1.7.2/ref-manual/ref-manual.html#ref-tasks-cleanall] tasks using BitBake (i.e. bitbake -c clean name_of_package and bitbake -c cleanall name_of_package). Modifications will also disappear if you use the rm_work feature as described in the "Building an Image [http://www.yoctoproject.org/docs/1.7.2/yocto-project-qs/yocto-project-qs.html#building-image]" section of the Yocto Project Quick Start.

7. Generate the Patch: Once your changes work as expected, you need to use Quilt to generate the final patch that contains all your modifications.

```
$ quilt refresh
```

At this point, the my_changes.patch file has all your edits made to the file1.c, file2.c, and file3.c files.

You can find the resulting patch file in the patches/ subdirectory of the source (S) directory.

8. Copy the Patch File: For simplicity, copy the patch file into a directory named files, which you can create in the same directory that holds the recipe (.bb) file or the append (.bbappend) file. Placing the patch here guarantees that the OpenEmbedded build system will find the patch. Next, add the patch into the SRC_URI [http://www.yoctoproject.org/docs/1.7.2/ref-manual/ref-manual.html#var-SRC_URI] of the recipe. Here is an example:

```
SRC_URI += "file://my_changes.patch"
```

9. Increment the Recipe Revision Number: Finally, don't forget to 'bump' the PR [http://www.yoctoproject.org/docs/1.7.2/ref-manual/ref-manual.html#var-PR] value in the recipe since the resulting packages have changed.

4.3.3. Using a Git Workflow

Git is an even more powerful tool that allows you to capture source code changes without having a clean source tree. This section outlines the typical workflow you can use to modify temporary source code, test changes, and then preserve the changes in the form of a patch all using Git. For general information on Git as it is used in the Yocto Project, see the "Git" section.

Note

This workflow uses Git only for its ability to manage local changes to the source code and produce patches independent of any version control system used with the Yocto Project.

Follow these general steps:

1. Find the Source Code: The temporary source code used by the OpenEmbedded build system is kept in the Build Directory. See the "Finding the Temporary Source Code" section to learn how to locate the directory that has the temporary source code for a particular package.

2. Change Your Working Directory: You need to be in the directory that has the temporary source code. That directory is defined by the S [http://www.yoctoproject.org/docs/1.7.2/ref-manual/ref-manual.html#var-S] variable.

3. If needed, initialize a Git Repository: If the recipe you are working with does not use a Git fetcher, you need to set up a Git repository as follows:

```
$ git init
$ git add *
$ git commit -m "initial revision"
```

The above Git commands initialize a Git repository that is based on the files in your current working directory, stage all the files, and commit the files. At this point, your Git repository is aware of all the source code files. Any edits you now make to files can be committed later and will be tracked by Git.

4. Edit the Files: Make your changes to the temporary source code.

5. Test Your Changes: Once you have modified the source code, the easiest way to test your changes is by calling the do_compile task as shown in the following example:

```
$ bitbake -c compile -f name_of_package
```

The -f or --force option forces the specified task to execute. If you find problems with your code, you can just keep editing and re-testing iteratively until things work as expected.

Note

All the modifications you make to the temporary source code disappear once you -c clean, -c cleansstate, or -c cleanall with BitBake for the package. Modifications will also disappear if you use the rm_work feature as described in the "Building an Image [http://www.yoctoproject.org/docs/1.7.2/yocto-project-qs/yocto-project-qs.html#building-image]" section of the Yocto Project Quick Start.

6. See the List of Files You Changed: Use the git status command to see what files you have actually edited. The ability to have Git track the files you have changed is an advantage that this workflow has over the Quilt workflow. Here is the Git command to list your changed files:

```
$ git status
```

7. Stage the Modified Files: Use the git add command to stage the changed files so they can be committed as follows:

```
$ git add file1.c file2.c file3.c
```

8. Commit the Staged Files and View Your Changes: Use the git commit command to commit the changes to the local repository. Once you have committed the files, you can use the git log command to see your changes:

```
$ git commit -m "commit-summary-message"
$ git log
```

Note

The name of the patch file created in the next step is based on your commit-summary-message.

9. Generate the Patch: Once the changes are committed, use the git format-patch command to generate a patch file:

```
$ git format-patch -1
```

Specifying "-1" causes Git to generate the patch file for the most recent commit.

At this point, the patch file has all your edits made to the file1.c, file2.c, and file3.c files. You can find the resulting patch file in the current directory and it is named according to the git commit summary line. The patch file ends with .patch.

10 Copy the Patch File: For simplicity, copy the patch file into a directory named files, which you can create in the same directory that holds the recipe (.bb) file or the append (.bbappend) file.

Placing the patch here guarantees that the OpenEmbedded build system will find the patch. Next, add the patch into the SRC_URI [http://www.yoctoproject.org/docs/1.7.2/ref-manual/ref-manual.html#var-SRC_URI] of the recipe. Here is an example:

```
SRC_URI += "file://0001-commit-summary-message.patch"
```

11Increment the Recipe Revision Number: Finally, don't forget to 'bump' the PR [http://www.yoctoproject.org/docs/1.7.2/ref-manual/ref-manual.html#var-PR] value in the recipe since the resulting packages have changed.

4.4. Image Development Using Hob

The Hob [http://www.yoctoproject.org/tools-resources/projects/hob] is a graphical user interface for the OpenEmbedded build system, which is based on BitBake. You can use the Hob to build custom operating system images within the Yocto Project build environment. Hob simply provides a friendly interface over the build system used during development. In other words, building images with the Hob lets you take care of common build tasks more easily.

For a better understanding of Hob, see the project page at http://www.yoctoproject.org/tools-resources/projects/hob on the Yocto Project website. If you follow the "Documentation" link from the Hob page, you will find a short introductory training video on Hob. The following lists some features of Hob:

• You can setup and run Hob using these commands:

```
$ source oe-init-build-env
$ hob
```

• You can set the MACHINE [http://www.yoctoproject.org/docs/1.7.2/ref-manual/ref-manual.html#var-MACHINE] for which you are building the image.

• You can modify various policy settings such as the package format with which to build, the parallelism BitBake uses, whether or not to build an external toolchain, and which host to build against.

• You can manage layers.

• You can select a base image and then add extra packages for your custom build.

• You can launch and monitor the build from within Hob.

4.5. Using a Development Shell

When debugging certain commands or even when just editing packages, devshell can be a useful tool. When you invoke devshell, source files are extracted into your working directory and patches are applied. Then, a new terminal is opened and you are placed in the working directory. In the new terminal, all the OpenEmbedded build-related environment variables are still defined so you can use commands such as configure and make. The commands execute just as if the OpenEmbedded build system were executing them. Consequently, working this way can be helpful when debugging a build or preparing software to be used with the OpenEmbedded build system.

Following is an example that uses devshell on a target named matchbox-desktop:

```
$ bitbake matchbox-desktop -c devshell
```

This command spawns a terminal with a shell prompt within the OpenEmbedded build environment. The OE_TERMINAL [http://www.yoctoproject.org/docs/1.7.2/ref-manual/ref-manual.html#var-OE_TERMINAL] variable controls what type of shell is opened.

For spawned terminals, the following occurs:

- The PATH variable includes the cross-toolchain.

- The pkgconfig variables find the correct .pc files.

- The configure command finds the Yocto Project site files as well as any other necessary files.

Within this environment, you can run configure or compile commands as if they were being run by the OpenEmbedded build system itself. As noted earlier, the working directory also automatically changes to the Source Directory (S [http://www.yoctoproject.org/docs/1.7.2/ref-manual/ref-manual.html#var-S]).

When you are finished, you just exit the shell or close the terminal window.

Note

It is worth remembering that when using devshell you need to use the full compiler name such as arm-poky-linux-gnueabi-gcc instead of just using gcc. The same applies to other applications such as binutils, libtool and so forth. BitBake sets up environment variables such as CC to assist applications, such as make to find the correct tools.

It is also worth noting that devshell still works over X11 forwarding and similar situations.

Chapter 5. Common Tasks

This chapter describes fundamental procedures such as creating layers, adding new software packages, extending or customizing images, porting work to new hardware (adding a new machine), and so forth. You will find that the procedures documented here occur often in the development cycle using the Yocto Project.

5.1. Understanding and Creating Layers

The OpenEmbedded build system supports organizing Metadata [16] into multiple layers. Layers allow you to isolate different types of customizations from each other. You might find it tempting to keep everything in one layer when working on a single project. However, the more modular your Metadata, the easier it is to cope with future changes.

To illustrate how layers are used to keep things modular, consider machine customizations. These types of customizations typically reside in a special layer, rather than a general layer, called a Board Support Package (BSP) Layer. Furthermore, the machine customizations should be isolated from recipes and Metadata that support a new GUI environment, for example. This situation gives you a couple of layers: one for the machine configurations, and one for the GUI environment. It is important to understand, however, that the BSP layer can still make machine-specific additions to recipes within the GUI environment layer without polluting the GUI layer itself with those machine-specific changes. You can accomplish this through a recipe that is a BitBake append (.bbappend) file, which is described later in this section.

5.1.1. Layers

The Source Directory [16] contains both general layers and BSP layers right out of the box. You can easily identify layers that ship with a Yocto Project release in the Source Directory by their folder names. Folders that represent layers typically have names that begin with the string meta-.

> ### Note
> It is not a requirement that a layer name begin with the prefix meta-, but it is a commonly accepted standard in the Yocto Project community.

For example, when you set up the Source Directory structure, you will see several layers: meta, meta-skeleton, meta-selftest, meta-yocto, and meta-yocto-bsp. Each of these folders represents a distinct layer.

As another example, if you set up a local copy of the meta-intel Git repository and then explore the folder of that general layer, you will discover many Intel-specific BSP layers inside. For more information on BSP layers, see the "BSP Layers [http://www.yoctoproject.org/docs/1.7.2/bsp-guide/bsp-guide.html#bsp-layers]" section in the Yocto Project Board Support Package (BSP) Developer's Guide.

5.1.2. Creating Your Own Layer

It is very easy to create your own layers to use with the OpenEmbedded build system. The Yocto Project ships with scripts that speed up creating general layers and BSP layers. This section describes the steps you perform by hand to create a layer so that you can better understand them. For information about the layer-creation scripts, see the "Creating a New BSP Layer Using the yocto-bsp Script [http://www.yoctoproject.org/docs/1.7.2/bsp-guide/bsp-guide.html#creating-a-new-bsp-layer-using-the-yocto-bsp-script]" section in the Yocto Project Board Support Package (BSP) Developer's Guide and the "Creating a General Layer Using the yocto-layer Script" section further down in this manual.

Follow these general steps to create your layer:

1. Check Existing Layers: Before creating a new layer, you should be sure someone has not already created a layer containing the Metadata you need. You can see the OpenEmbedded Metadata Index [http://layers.openembedded.org/layerindex/layers/] for a list of layers from the OpenEmbedded community that can be used in the Yocto Project.

2. Create a Directory: Create the directory for your layer. While not strictly required, prepend the name of the folder with the string meta-. For example:

```
meta-mylayer
meta-GUI_xyz
meta-mymachine
```

3. Create a Layer Configuration File: Inside your new layer folder, you need to create a conf/layer.conf file. It is easiest to take an existing layer configuration file and copy that to your layer's conf directory and then modify the file as needed.

The meta-yocto-bsp/conf/layer.conf file demonstrates the required syntax:

```
# We have a conf and classes directory, add to BBPATH
BBPATH .= ":${LAYERDIR}"

# We have recipes-* directories, add to BBFILES
BBFILES += "${LAYERDIR}/recipes-*/*/*.bb \
            ${LAYERDIR}/recipes-*/*/*.bbappend"

BBFILE_COLLECTIONS += "yoctobsp"
BBFILE_PATTERN_yoctobsp = "^${LAYERDIR}/"
BBFILE_PRIORITY_yoctobsp = "5"
LAYERVERSION_yoctobsp = "3"
```

Here is an explanation of the example:

- The configuration and classes directory is appended to BBPATH [http://www.yoctoproject.org/docs/1.7.2/ref-manual/ref-manual.html#var-BBPATH].

Note

All non-distro layers, which include all BSP layers, are expected to append the layer directory to the BBPATH. On the other hand, distro layers, such as meta-yocto, can choose to enforce their own precedence over BBPATH. For an example of that syntax, see the layer.conf file for the meta-yocto layer.

- The recipes for the layers are appended to BBFILES [http://www.yoctoproject.org/docs/1.7.2/ref-manual/ref-manual.html#var-BBFILES].

- The BBFILE_COLLECTIONS [http://www.yoctoproject.org/docs/1.7.2/ref-manual/ref-manual.html#var-BBFILE_COLLECTIONS] variable is then appended with the layer name.

- The BBFILE_PATTERN [http://www.yoctoproject.org/docs/1.7.2/ref-manual/ref-manual.html#var-BBFILE_PATTERN] variable is set to a regular expression and is used to match files from BBFILES into a particular layer. In this case, LAYERDIR [http://www.yoctoproject.org/docs/1.7.2/ref-manual/ref-manual.html#var-LAYERDIR] is used to make BBFILE_PATTERN match within the layer's path.

- The BBFILE_PRIORITY [http://www.yoctoproject.org/docs/1.7.2/ref-manual/ref-manual.html#var-BBFILE_PRIORITY] variable then assigns a priority to the layer. Applying priorities is useful in situations where the same recipe might appear in multiple layers and allows you to choose the layer that takes precedence.

- The LAYERVERSION [http://www.yoctoproject.org/docs/1.7.2/ref-manual/ref-manual.html#var-LAYERVERSION] variable optionally specifies the version of a layer as a single number.

Note the use of the LAYERDIR [http://www.yoctoproject.org/docs/1.7.2/ref-manual/ref-manual.html#var-LAYERDIR] variable, which expands to the directory of the current layer.

Through the use of the BBPATH variable, BitBake locates class files (.bbclass), configuration files, and files that are included with include and require statements. For these cases, BitBake uses the first file that matches the name found in BBPATH. This is similar to the way the PATH variable is used for binaries. It is recommended, therefore, that you use unique class and configuration filenames in your custom layer.

4. Add Content: Depending on the type of layer, add the content. If the layer adds support for a machine, add the machine configuration in a conf/machine/ file within the layer. If the layer adds distro policy, add the distro configuration in a conf/distro/ file within the layer. If the layer introduces new recipes, put the recipes you need in recipes-* subdirectories within the layer.

Note

In order to be compliant with the Yocto Project, a layer must contain a README file. [http://www.yoctoproject.org/docs/1.7.2/bsp-guide/bsp-guide.html#bsp-filelayout-readme]

5.1.3. Best Practices to Follow When Creating Layers

To create layers that are easier to maintain and that will not impact builds for other machines, you should consider the information in the following sections.

5.1.3.1. Avoid "Overlaying" Entire Recipes

Avoid "overlaying" entire recipes from other layers in your configuration. In other words, do not copy an entire recipe into your layer and then modify it. Rather, use an append file (.bbappend) to override only those parts of the original recipe you need to modify.

5.1.3.2. Avoid Duplicating Include Files

Avoid duplicating include files. Use append files (.bbappend) for each recipe that uses an include file. Or, if you are introducing a new recipe that requires the included file, use the path relative to the original layer directory to refer to the file. For example, use require recipes-core/somepackage/somefile.inc instead of require somefile.inc. If you're finding you have to overlay the include file, it could indicate a deficiency in the include file in the layer to which it originally belongs. If this is the case, you need to address that deficiency instead of overlaying the include file.

For example, consider how support plug-ins for the Qt 4 database are configured. The Source Directory does not have MySQL or PostgreSQL. However, OpenEmbedded's layer meta-oe does. Consequently, meta-oe uses append files to modify the QT_SQL_DRIVER_FLAGS variable to enable the appropriate plug-ins. This variable was added to the qt4.inc include file in the Source Directory specifically to allow the meta-oe layer to be able to control which plug-ins are built.

5.1.3.3. Structure Your Layers

Proper use of overrides within append files and placement of machine-specific files within your layer can ensure that a build is not using the wrong Metadata and negatively impacting a build for a different machine. Following are some examples:

- Modifying Variables to Support a Different Machine: Suppose you have a layer named meta-one that adds support for building machine "one". To do so, you use an append file named base-files.bbappend and create a dependency on "foo" by altering the DEPENDS [http://www.yoctoproject.org/docs/1.7.2/ref-manual/ref-manual.html#var-DEPENDS] variable:

```
DEPENDS = "foo"
```

The dependency is created during any build that includes the layer meta-one. However, you might not want this dependency for all machines. For example, suppose you are building for machine "two" but your bblayers.conf file has the meta-one layer included. During the build, the base-files for machine "two" will also have the dependency on foo.

To make sure your changes apply only when building machine "one", use a machine override with the DEPENDS statement:

```
DEPENDS_one = "foo"
```

You should follow the same strategy when using _append and _prepend operations:

```
DEPENDS_append_one = " foo"
DEPENDS_prepend_one = "foo "
```

As an actual example, here's a line from the recipe for the OProfile profiler, which lists an extra build-time dependency when building specifically for 64-bit PowerPC:

```
DEPENDS_append_powerpc64 = " libpfm4"
```

Note
Avoiding "+=" and "=+" and using machine-specific _append and _prepend operations is recommended as well.

• Place Machine-Specific Files in Machine-Specific Locations: When you have a base recipe, such as base-files.bb, that contains a SRC_URI [http://www.yoctoproject.org/docs/1.7.2/ref-manual/ref-manual.html#var-SRC_URI] statement to a file, you can use an append file to cause the build to use your own version of the file. For example, an append file in your layer at meta-one/recipes-core/base-files/base-files.bbappend could extend FILESPATH [http://www.yoctoproject.org/docs/1.7.2/ref-manual/ref-manual.html#var-FILESPATH] using FILESEXTRAPATHS [http://www.yoctoproject.org/docs/1.7.2/ref-manual/ref-manual.html#var-FILESEXTRAPATHS] as follows:

```
FILESEXTRAPATHS_prepend := "${THISDIR}/${BPN}:"
```

The build for machine "one" will pick up your machine-specific file as long as you have the file in meta-one/recipes-core/base-files/base-files/. However, if you are building for a different machine and the bblayers.conf file includes the meta-one layer and the location of your machine-specific file is the first location where that file is found according to FILESPATH, builds for all machines will also use that machine-specific file.

You can make sure that a machine-specific file is used for a particular machine by putting the file in a subdirectory specific to the machine. For example, rather than placing the file in meta-one/recipes-core/base-files/base-files/ as shown above, put it in meta-one/recipes-core/base-files/base-files/one/. Not only does this make sure the file is used only when building for machine "one", but the build process locates the file more quickly.

In summary, you need to place all files referenced from SRC_URI in a machine-specific subdirectory within the layer in order to restrict those files to machine-specific builds.

5.1.3.4. Other Recommendations

We also recommend the following:

• Store custom layers in a Git repository that uses the meta-layer_name format.

• Clone the repository alongside other meta directories in the Source Directory [16].

Following these recommendations keeps your Source Directory and its configuration entirely inside the Yocto Project's core base.

5.1.4. Enabling Your Layer

Before the OpenEmbedded build system can use your new layer, you need to enable it. To enable your layer, simply add your layer's path to the BBLAYERS [http://www.yoctoproject.org/docs/1.7.2/ref-manual/ref-manual.html#var-BBLAYERS] variable in your conf/bblayers.conf file, which is found in the Build Directory [14]. The following example shows how to enable a layer named meta-mylayer:

```
LCONF_VERSION = "6"

BBPATH = "${TOPDIR}"
BBFILES ?= ""

BBLAYERS ?= " \
  $HOME/poky/meta \
  $HOME/poky/meta-yocto \
  $HOME/poky/meta-yocto-bsp \
  $HOME/poky/meta-mylayer \
  "

BBLAYERS_NON_REMOVABLE ?= " \
  $HOME/poky/meta \
  $HOME/poky/meta-yocto \
  "
```

BitBake parses each conf/layer.conf file as specified in the BBLAYERS variable within the conf/bblayers.conf file. During the processing of each conf/layer.conf file, BitBake adds the recipes, classes and configurations contained within the particular layer to the source directory.

5.1.5. Using .bbappend Files

Recipes used to append Metadata to other recipes are called BitBake append files. BitBake append files use the .bbappend file type suffix, while the corresponding recipes to which Metadata is being appended use the .bb file type suffix.

A .bbappend file allows your layer to make additions or changes to the content of another layer's recipe without having to copy the other recipe into your layer. Your .bbappend file resides in your layer, while the main .bb recipe file to which you are appending Metadata resides in a different layer.

Append files must have the same root names as their corresponding recipes. For example, the append file someapp_1.7.2.bbappend must apply to someapp_1.7.2.bb. This means the original recipe and append file names are version number-specific. If the corresponding recipe is renamed to update to a newer version, the corresponding .bbappend file must be renamed (and possibly updated) as well. During the build process, BitBake displays an error on starting if it detects a .bbappend file that does not have a corresponding recipe with a matching name. See the BB_DANGLINGAPPENDS_WARNONLY [http://www.yoctoproject.org/docs/1.7.2/ref-manual/ref-manual.html#var-BB_DANGLINGAPPENDS_WARNONLY] variable for information on how to handle this error.

Being able to append information to an existing recipe not only avoids duplication, but also automatically applies recipe changes in a different layer to your layer. If you were copying recipes, you would have to manually merge changes as they occur.

As an example, consider the main formfactor recipe and a corresponding formfactor append file both from the Source Directory [16]. Here is the main formfactor recipe, which is named formfactor_0.0.bb and located in the "meta" layer at meta/recipes-bsp/formfactor:

```
SUMMARY = "Device formfactor information"
SECTION = "base"
LICENSE = "MIT"
LIC_FILES_CHKSUM = "file://${COREBASE}/LICENSE;md5=4d92cd373abda3937c2bc47fbc49d690 \
            file://${COREBASE}/meta/COPYING.MIT;md5=3da9cfbcb788c80a0384361b4de20420"
PR = "r45"

SRC_URI = "file://config file://machconfig"
S = "${WORKDIR}"
```

```
PACKAGE_ARCH = "${MACHINE_ARCH}"
INHIBIT_DEFAULT_DEPS = "1"

do_install() {
 # Install file only if it has contents
        install -d ${D}${sysconfdir}/formfactor/
        install -m 0644 ${S}/config ${D}${sysconfdir}/formfactor/
 if [ -s "${S}/machconfig" ]; then
        install -m 0644 ${S}/machconfig ${D}${sysconfdir}/formfactor/
 fi
}
```

In the main recipe, note the SRC_URI [http://www.yoctoproject.org/docs/1.7.2/ref-manual/ref-manual.html#var-SRC_URI] variable, which tells the OpenEmbedded build system where to find files during the build.

Following is the append file, which is named formfactor_0.0.bbappend and is from the Crown Bay BSP Layer named meta-intel/meta-crownbay. The file is in recipes-bsp/formfactor:

```
FILESEXTRAPATHS_prepend := "${THISDIR}/${PN}:"
```

By default, the build system uses the FILESPATH [http://www.yoctoproject.org/docs/1.7.2/ref-manual/ref-manual.html#var-FILESPATH] variable to locate files. This append file extends the locations by setting the FILESEXTRAPATHS [http://www.yoctoproject.org/docs/1.7.2/ref-manual/ref-manual.html#var-FILESEXTRAPATHS] variable. Setting this variable in the .bbappend file is the most reliable and recommended method for adding directories to the search path used by the build system to find files.

The statement in this example extends the directories to include ${THISDIR [http://www.yoctoproject.org/docs/1.7.2/ref-manual/ref-manual.html#var-THISDIR]}/${PN [http://www.yoctoproject.org/docs/1.7.2/ref-manual/ref-manual.html#var-PN]}, which resolves to a directory named formfactor in the same directory in which the append file resides (i.e. meta-intel/meta-crownbay/recipes-bsp/formfactor/formfactor. This implies that you must have the supporting directory structure set up that will contain any files or patches you will be including from the layer.

Using the immediate expansion assignment operator := is important because of the reference to THISDIR. The trailing colon character is important as it ensures that items in the list remain colon-separated.

Note

BitBake automatically defines the THISDIR variable. You should never set this variable yourself. Using "_prepend" ensures your path will be searched prior to other paths in the final list.

Also, not all append files add extra files. Many append files simply exist to add build options (e.g. systemd). For these cases, it is not necessary to use the "_prepend" part of the statement.

5.1.6. Prioritizing Your Layer

Each layer is assigned a priority value. Priority values control which layer takes precedence if there are recipe files with the same name in multiple layers. For these cases, the recipe file from the layer with a higher priority number takes precedence. Priority values also affect the order in which multiple .bbappend files for the same recipe are applied. You can either specify the priority manually, or allow the build system to calculate it based on the layer's dependencies.

To specify the layer's priority manually, use the BBFILE_PRIORITY [http://www.yoctoproject.org/docs/1.7.2/ref-manual/ref-manual.html#var-BBFILE_PRIORITY] variable. For example:

```
BBFILE_PRIORITY_mylayer = "1"
```

Note

It is possible for a recipe with a lower version number PV [http://www.yoctoproject.org/docs/1.7.2/ref-manual/ref-manual.html#var-PV] in a layer that has a higher priority to take precedence.

Also, the layer priority does not currently affect the precedence order of .conf or .bbclass files. Future versions of BitBake might address this.

5.1.7. Managing Layers

You can use the BitBake layer management tool to provide a view into the structure of recipes across a multi-layer project. Being able to generate output that reports on configured layers with their paths and priorities and on .bbappend files and their applicable recipes can help to reveal potential problems.

Use the following form when running the layer management tool.

```
$ bitbake-layers command [arguments]
```

The following list describes the available commands:

- help: Displays general help or help on a specified command.

- show-layers: Shows the current configured layers.

- show-recipes: Lists available recipes and the layers that provide them.

- show-overlayed: Lists overlayed recipes. A recipe is overlayed when a recipe with the same name exists in another layer that has a higher layer priority.

- show-appends: Lists .bbappend files and the recipe files to which they apply.

- show-cross-depends: Lists dependency relationships between recipes that cross layer boundaries.

- flatten: Flattens the layer configuration into a separate output directory. Flattening your layer configuration builds a "flattened" directory that contains the contents of all layers, with any overlayed recipes removed and any .bbappend files appended to the corresponding recipes. You might have to perform some manual cleanup of the flattened layer as follows:

  - Non-recipe files (such as patches) are overwritten. The flatten command shows a warning for these files.

  - Anything beyond the normal layer setup has been added to the layer.conf file. Only the lowest priority layer's layer.conf is used.

  - Overridden and appended items from .bbappend files need to be cleaned up. The contents of each .bbappend end up in the flattened recipe. However, if there are appended or changed variable values, you need to tidy these up yourself. Consider the following example. Here, the bitbake-layers command adds the line #### bbappended ... so that you know where the following lines originate:

```
...
DESCRIPTION = "A useful utility"
...
EXTRA_OECONF = "##enable-something"
...

#### bbappended from meta-anotherlayer ####

DESCRIPTION = "Customized utility"
```

```
EXTRA_OECONF += "##enable-somethingelse"
```

Ideally, you would tidy up these utilities as follows:

```
...
DESCRIPTION = "Customized utility"
...
EXTRA_OECONF = "##enable-something ##enable-somethingelse"
...
```

5.1.8. Creating a General Layer Using the yocto-layer Script

The yocto-layer script simplifies creating a new general layer.

Note
For information on BSP layers, see the "BSP Layers [http://www.yoctoproject.org/docs/1.7.2/bsp-guide/bsp-guide.html#bsp-layers]" section in the Yocto Project Board Specific (BSP) Developer's Guide.

The default mode of the script's operation is to prompt you for information needed to generate the layer:

• The layer priority.

• Whether or not to create a sample recipe.

• Whether or not to create a sample append file.

Use the yocto-layer create sub-command to create a new general layer. In its simplest form, you can create a layer as follows:

```
$ yocto-layer create mylayer
```

The previous example creates a layer named meta-mylayer in the current directory.

As the yocto-layer create command runs, default values for the prompts appear in brackets. Pressing enter without supplying anything for the prompts or pressing enter and providing an invalid response causes the script to accept the default value. Once the script completes, the new layer is created in the current working directory. The script names the layer by prepending meta- to the name you provide.

Minimally, the script creates the following within the layer:

• The conf directory: This directory contains the layer's configuration file. The root name for the file is the same as the root name your provided for the layer (e.g. layer.conf).

• The COPYING.MIT file: The copyright and use notice for the software.

• The README file: A file describing the contents of your new layer.

If you choose to generate a sample recipe file, the script prompts you for the name for the recipe and then creates it in layer/recipes-example/example/. The script creates a .bb file and a directory, which contains a sample helloworld.c source file, along with a sample patch file. If you do not provide a recipe name, the script uses "example".

If you choose to generate a sample append file, the script prompts you for the name for the file and then creates it in layer/recipes-example-bbappend/example-bbappend/. The script creates a .bbappend file and a directory, which contains a sample patch file. If you do not provide a recipe name, the script uses "example". The script also prompts you for the version of the append file. The version should match the recipe to which the append file is associated.

The easiest way to see how the yocto-layer script works is to experiment with the script. You can also read the usage information by entering the following:

```
$ yocto-layer help
```

Once you create your general layer, you must add it to your bblayers.conf file. Here is an example where a layer named meta-mylayer is added:

```
BBLAYERS = ?" \
    /usr/local/src/yocto/meta \
    /usr/local/src/yocto/meta-yocto \
    /usr/local/src/yocto/meta-yocto-bsp \
    /usr/local/src/yocto/meta-mylayer \
    "

BBLAYERS_NON_REMOVABLE ?= " \
    /usr/local/src/yocto/meta \
    /usr/local/src/yocto/meta-yocto \
    "
```

Adding the layer to this file enables the build system to locate the layer during the build.

5.2. Customizing Images

You can customize images to satisfy particular requirements. This section describes several methods and provides guidelines for each.

5.2.1. Customizing Images Using`local.conf`

Probably the easiest way to customize an image is to add a package by way of the local.conf configuration file. Because it is limited to local use, this method generally only allows you to add packages and is not as flexible as creating your own customized image. When you add packages using local variables this way, you need to realize that these variable changes are in effect for every build and consequently affect all images, which might not be what you require.

To add a package to your image using the local configuration file, use the IMAGE_INSTALL [http://www.yoctoproject.org/docs/1.7.2/ref-manual/ref-manual.html#var-IMAGE_INSTALL] variable with the _append operator:

```
IMAGE_INSTALL_append = " strace"
```

Use of the syntax is important - specifically, the space between the quote and the package name, which is strace in this example. This space is required since the _append operator does not add the space.

Furthermore, you must use _append instead of the += operator if you want to avoid ordering issues. The reason for this is because doing so unconditionally appends to the variable and avoids ordering problems due to the variable being set in image recipes and .bbclass files with operators like ?=. Using _append ensures the operation takes affect.

As shown in its simplest use, IMAGE_INSTALL_append affects all images. It is possible to extend the syntax so that the variable applies to a specific image only. Here is an example:

```
IMAGE_INSTALL_append_pn-core-image-minimal = " strace"
```

This example adds strace to the core-image-minimal image only.

You can add packages using a similar approach through the CORE_IMAGE_EXTRA_INSTALL [http://www.yoctoproject.org/docs/1.7.2/ref-manual/ref-manual.html#var-CORE_IMAGE_EXTRA_INSTALL] variable. If you use this variable, only core-image-* images are affected.

5.2.2. Customizing Images Using Custom **IMAGE_FEATURES** and **EXTRA_IMAGE_FEATURES**

Another method for customizing your image is to enable or disable high-level image features by using the IMAGE_FEATURES [http://www.yoctoproject.org/docs/1.7.2/ref-manual/ref-manual.html#var-IMAGE_FEATURES] and EXTRA_IMAGE_FEATURES [http://www.yoctoproject.org/docs/1.7.2/ref-manual/ref-manual.html#var-EXTRA_IMAGE_FEATURES] variables. Although the functions for both variables are nearly equivalent, best practices dictate using IMAGE_FEATURES from within a recipe and using EXTRA_IMAGE_FEATURES from within your local.conf file, which is found in the Build Directory [14].

To understand how these features work, the best reference is meta/classes/core-image.bbclass. In summary, the file looks at the contents of the IMAGE_FEATURES variable and then maps those contents into a set of package groups. Based on this information, the build system automatically adds the appropriate packages to the IMAGE_INSTALL [http://www.yoctoproject.org/docs/1.7.2/ref-manual/ref-manual.html#var-IMAGE_INSTALL] variable. Effectively, you are enabling extra features by extending the class or creating a custom class for use with specialized image .bb files.

Use the EXTRA_IMAGE_FEATURES variable from within your local configuration file. Using a separate area from which to enable features with this variable helps you avoid overwriting the features in the image recipe that are enabled with IMAGE_FEATURES. The value of EXTRA_IMAGE_FEATURES is added to IMAGE_FEATURES within meta/conf/bitbake.conf.

To illustrate how you can use these variables to modify your image, consider an example that selects the SSH server. The Yocto Project ships with two SSH servers you can use with your images: Dropbear and OpenSSH. Dropbear is a minimal SSH server appropriate for resource-constrained environments, while OpenSSH is a well-known standard SSH server implementation. By default, the core-image-sato image is configured to use Dropbear. The core-image-full-cmdline and core-image-lsb images both include OpenSSH. The core-image-minimal image does not contain an SSH server.

You can customize your image and change these defaults. Edit the IMAGE_FEATURES variable in your recipe or use the EXTRA_IMAGE_FEATURES in your local.conf file so that it configures the image you are working with to include ssh-server-dropbear or ssh-server-openssh.

Note

See the "Images [http://www.yoctoproject.org/docs/1.7.2/ref-manual/ref-manual.html#ref-images]" section in the Yocto Project Reference Manual for a complete list of image features that ship with the Yocto Project.

5.2.3. Customizing Images Using Custom .bb Files

You can also customize an image by creating a custom recipe that defines additional software as part of the image. The following example shows the form for the two lines you need:

```
IMAGE_INSTALL = "packagegroup-core-x11-base package1 package2"

inherit core-image
```

Defining the software using a custom recipe gives you total control over the contents of the image. It is important to use the correct names of packages in the IMAGE_INSTALL [http://www.yoctoproject.org/docs/1.7.2/ref-manual/ref-manual.html#var-IMAGE_INSTALL] variable. You must use the OpenEmbedded notation and not the Debian notation for the names (e.g. glibc-dev instead of libc6-dev).

The other method for creating a custom image is to base it on an existing image. For example, if you want to create an image based on core-image-sato but add the additional package strace to the image, copy the meta/recipes-sato/images/core-image-sato.bb to a new .bb and add the following line to the end of the copy:

```
IMAGE_INSTALL += "strace"
```

5.2.4. Customizing Images Using Custom Package Groups

For complex custom images, the best approach for customizing an image is to create a custom package group recipe that is used to build the image or images. A good example of a package group recipe is meta/recipes-core/packagegroups/packagegroup-core-boot.bb. The PACKAGES [http://www.yoctoproject.org/docs/1.7.2/ref-manual/ref-manual.html#var-PACKAGES] variable lists the package group packages you wish to produce. inherit packagegroup sets appropriate default values and automatically adds -dev, -dbg, and -ptest complementary packages for every package specified in PACKAGES. Note that the inherit line should be towards the top of the recipe, certainly before you set PACKAGES. For each package you specify in PACKAGES, you can use RDEPENDS [http://www.yoctoproject.org/docs/1.7.2/ref-manual/ref-manual.html#var-RDEPENDS] and RRECOMMENDS [http://www.yoctoproject.org/docs/1.7.2/ref-manual/ref-manual.html#var-RRECOMMENDS] entries to provide a list of packages the parent task package should contain. Following is an example:

```
DESCRIPTION = "My Custom Package Groups"

inherit packagegroup

PACKAGES = "\
    packagegroup-custom-apps \
    packagegroup-custom-tools \
    "

RDEPENDS_packagegroup-custom-apps = "\
    dropbear \
    portmap \
    psplash"

RDEPENDS_packagegroup-custom-tools = "\
    oprofile \
    oprofileui-server \
    lttng-control \
    lttng-viewer"

RRECOMMENDS_packagegroup-custom-tools = "\
    kernel-module-oprofile"
```

In the previous example, two package group packages are created with their dependencies and their recommended package dependencies listed: packagegroup-custom-apps, and packagegroup-custom-tools. To build an image using these package group packages, you need to add packagegroup-custom-apps and/or packagegroup-custom-tools to IMAGE_INSTALL [http://www.yoctoproject.org/docs/1.7.2/ref-manual/ref-manual.html#var-IMAGE_INSTALL]. For other forms of image dependencies see the other areas of this section.

5.3. Writing a New Recipe

Recipes (.bb files) are fundamental components in the Yocto Project environment. Each software component built by the OpenEmbedded build system requires a recipe to define the component. This section describes how to create, write, and test a new recipe.

Note

For information on variables that are useful for recipes and for information about recipe naming issues, see the "Required [http://www.yoctoproject.org/docs/1.7.2/ref-manual/ref-manual.html#ref-varlocality-recipe-required]" section of the Yocto Project Reference Manual.

5.3.1. Overview

The following figure shows the basic process for creating a new recipe. The remainder of the section provides details for the steps.

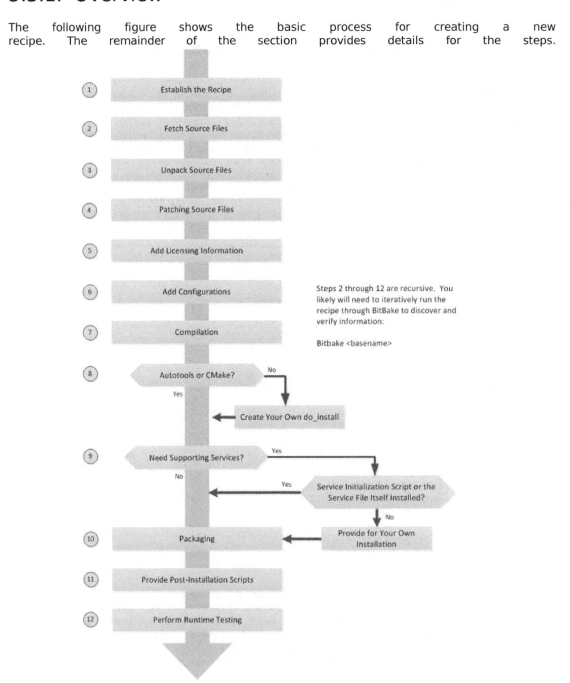

5.3.2. Locate a Base Recipe

Before writing a recipe from scratch, it is often useful to discover whether someone else has already written one that meets (or comes close to meeting) your needs. The Yocto Project and OpenEmbedded communities maintain many recipes that might be candidates for what you are doing. You can find a good central index of these recipes in the OpenEmbedded metadata index [http://layers.openembedded.org].

Working from an existing recipe or a skeleton recipe is the best way to get started. Here are some points on both methods:

- Locate and modify a recipe that is close to what you want to do: This method works when you are familiar with the current recipe space. The method does not work so well for those new to the Yocto Project or writing recipes.

  Some risks associated with this method are using a recipe that has areas totally unrelated to what you are trying to accomplish with your recipe, not recognizing areas of the recipe that you might have to add from scratch, and so forth. All these risks stem from unfamiliarity with the existing recipe space.

- Use and modify the following skeleton recipe:

```
SUMMARY = ""
HOMEPAGE = ""
LICENSE = ""

LIC_FILES_CHKSUM = ""

SRC_URI = ""
SRC_URI[md5sum] = ""
SRC_URI[sha256sum] = ""

S = "${WORKDIR}/${PN}-${PV}"

inherit stuff
```

Modifying this recipe is the recommended method for creating a new recipe. The recipe provides the fundamental areas that you need to include, exclude, or alter to fit your needs.

5.3.3. Storing and Naming the Recipe

Once you have your base recipe, you should put it in your own layer and name it appropriately. Locating it correctly ensures that the OpenEmbedded build system can find it when you use BitBake to process the recipe.

- Storing Your Recipe: The OpenEmbedded build system locates your recipe through the layer's conf/layer.conf file and the BBFILES [http://www.yoctoproject.org/docs/1.7.2/ref-manual/ref-manual.html#var-BBFILES] variable. This variable sets up a path from which the build system can locate recipes. Here is the typical use:

```
BBFILES += "${LAYERDIR}/recipes-*/*/*.bb \
            ${LAYERDIR}/recipes-*/*/*.bbappend"
```

Consequently, you need to be sure you locate your new recipe inside your layer such that it can be found.

You can find more information on how layers are structured in the "Understanding and Creating Layers" section.

- Naming Your Recipe: When you name your recipe, you need to follow this naming convention:

```
basename_version.bb
```

Use lower-cased characters and do not include the reserved suffixes -native, -cross, -initial, or -dev casually (i.e. do not use them as part of your recipe name unless the string applies). Here are some examples:

```
cups_1.7.0.bb
gawk_4.0.2.bb
irssi_0.8.16-rc1.bb
```

5.3.4. Understanding Recipe Syntax

Understanding recipe file syntax is important for writing recipes. The following list overviews the basic items that make up a BitBake recipe file. For more complete BitBake syntax descriptions, see the "Syntax and Operators [http://www.yoctoproject.org/docs/1.7.2/bitbake-user-manual/bitbake-user-manual.html#bitbake-user-manual-metadata]" chapter of the BitBake User Manual.

• Variable Assignments and Manipulations: Variable assignments allow a value to be assigned to a variable. The assignment can be static text or might include the contents of other variables. In addition to the assignment, appending and prepending operations are also supported.

The following example shows some of the ways you can use variables in recipes:

```
S = "${WORKDIR}/postfix-${PV}"
CFLAGS += "-DNO_ASM"
SRC_URI_append = " file://fixup.patch"
```

• Functions: Functions provide a series of actions to be performed. You usually use functions to override the default implementation of a task function or to complement a default function (i.e. append or prepend to an existing function). Standard functions use sh shell syntax, although access to OpenEmbedded variables and internal methods are also available.

The following is an example function from the sed recipe:

```
do_install () {
    autotools_do_install
    install -d ${D}${base_bindir}
    mv ${D}${bindir}/sed ${D}${base_bindir}/sed
    rmdir ${D}${bindir}/
}
```

It is also possible to implement new functions that are called between existing tasks as long as the new functions are not replacing or complementing the default functions. You can implement functions in Python instead of shell. Both of these options are not seen in the majority of recipes.

• Keywords: BitBake recipes use only a few keywords. You use keywords to include common functions (inherit), load parts of a recipe from other files (include and require) and export variables to the environment (export).

The following example shows the use of some of these keywords:

```
export POSTCONF = "${STAGING_BINDIR}/postconf"
inherit autoconf
require otherfile.inc
```

• Comments: Any lines that begin with the hash character (#) are treated as comment lines and are ignored:

```
# This is a comment
```

This next list summarizes the most important and most commonly used parts of the recipe syntax. For more information on these parts of the syntax, you can reference the Syntax and Operators [http://www.yoctoproject.org/docs/1.7.2/bitbake-user-manual/bitbake-user-manual.html#bitbake-user-manual-metadata] chapter in the BitBake User Manual.

• Line Continuation: \ - Use the backward slash (\) character to split a statement over multiple lines. Place the slash character at the end of the line that is to be continued on the next line:

```
VAR = "A really long \
       line"
```

Note

You cannot have any characters including spaces or tabs after the slash character.

- Using Variables: ${...} - Use the ${varname} syntax to access the contents of a variable:

```
SRC_URI = "${SOURCEFORGE_MIRROR}/libpng/zlib-${PV}.tar.gz"
```

- Quote All Assignments: "value" - Use double quotes around the value in all variable assignments.

```
VAR1 = "${OTHERVAR}"
VAR2 = "The version is ${PV}"
```

- Conditional Assignment: ?= - Conditional assignment is used to assign a value to a variable, but only when the variable is currently unset. Use the question mark followed by the equal sign (?=) to make a "soft" assignment used for conditional assignment. Typically, "soft" assignments are used in the local.conf file for variables that are allowed to come through from the external environment.

Here is an example where VAR1 is set to "New value" if it is currently empty. However, if VAR1 has already been set, it remains unchanged:

```
VAR1 ?= "New value"
```

In this next example, VAR1 is left with the value "Original value":

```
VAR1 = "Original value"
VAR1 ?= "New value"
```

- Appending: += - Use the plus character followed by the equals sign (+=) to append values to existing variables.

Note

This operator adds a space between the existing content of the variable and the new content.

Here is an example:

```
SRC_URI += "file://fix-makefile.patch"
```

- Prepending: =+ - Use the equals sign followed by the plus character (=+) to prepend values to existing variables.

Note

This operator adds a space between the new content and the existing content of the variable.

Here is an example:

```
VAR =+ "Starts"
```

- Appending: _append - Use the _append operator to append values to existing variables. This operator does not add any additional space. Also, the operator is applied after all the +=, and =+ operators have been applied and after all = assignments have occurred.

  The following example shows the space being explicitly added to the start to ensure the appended value is not merged with the existing value:

  ```
  SRC_URI_append = " file://fix-makefile.patch"
  ```

  You can also use the _append operator with overrides, which results in the actions only being performed for the specified target or machine:

  ```
  SRC_URI_append_sh4 = " file://fix-makefile.patch"
  ```

- Prepending: _prepend - Use the _prepend operator to prepend values to existing variables. This operator does not add any additional space. Also, the operator is applied after all the +=, and =+ operators have been applied and after all = assignments have occurred.

  The following example shows the space being explicitly added to the end to ensure the prepended value is not merged with the existing value:

  ```
  CFLAGS_prepend = "-I${S}/myincludes "
  ```

  You can also use the _prepend operator with overrides, which results in the actions only being performed for the specified target or machine:

  ```
  CFLAGS_prepend_sh4 = "-I${S}/myincludes "
  ```

- Overrides: - You can use overrides to set a value conditionally, typically based on how the recipe is being built. For example, to set the KBRANCH [http://www.yoctoproject.org/docs/1.7.2/ref-manual/ref-manual.html#var-KBRANCH] variable's value to "standard/base" for any target MACHINE [http://www.yoctoproject.org/docs/1.7.2/ref-manual/ref-manual.html#var-MACHINE], except for qemuarm where it should be set to "standard/arm-versatile-926ejs", you would do the following:

  ```
  KBRANCH = "standard/base"
  KBRANCH_qemuarm = "standard/arm-versatile-926ejs"
  ```

  Overrides are also used to separate alternate values of a variable in other situations. For example, when setting variables such as FILES [http://www.yoctoproject.org/docs/1.7.2/ref-manual/ref-manual.html#var-FILES] and RDEPENDS [http://www.yoctoproject.org/docs/1.7.2/ref-manual/ref-manual.html#var-RDEPENDS] that are specific to individual packages produced by a recipe, you should always use an override that specifies the name of the package.

- Indentation: Use spaces for indentation rather than than tabs. For shell functions, both currently work. However, it is a policy decision of the Yocto Project to use tabs in shell functions. Realize that some layers have a policy to use spaces for all indentation.

- Using Python for Complex Operations: ${@python_code} - For more advanced processing, it is possible to use Python code during variable assignments (e.g. search and replacement on a variable).

  You indicate Python code using the ${@python_code} syntax for the variable assignment:

  ```
  SRC_URI = "ftp://ftp.info-zip.org/pub/infozip/src/zip${@d.getVar('PV',1).replace('.', '"
  ```

- Shell Function Syntax: Write shell functions as if you were writing a shell script when you describe a list of actions to take. You should ensure that your script works with a generic sh and that it does not require any bash or other shell-specific functionality. The same considerations apply to various system utilities (e.g. sed, grep, awk, and so forth) that you might wish to use. If in doubt, you should check with multiple implementations - including those from BusyBox.

5.3.5. Running a Build on the Recipe

Creating a new recipe is usually an iterative process that requires using BitBake to process the recipe multiple times in order to progressively discover and add information to the recipe file.

Assuming you have sourced a build environment setup script (i.e. oe-init-build-env [http://www.yoctoproject.org/docs/1.7.2/ref-manual/ref-manual.html#structure-core-script] or oe-init-build-env-memres [http://www.yoctoproject.org/docs/1.7.2/ref-manual/ref-manual.html#structure-memres-core-script]) and you are in the Build Directory [14], use BitBake to process your recipe. All you need to provide is the basename of the recipe as described in the previous section:

```
$ bitbake basename
```

During the build, the OpenEmbedded build system creates a temporary work directory for each recipe (${WORKDIR [http://www.yoctoproject.org/docs/1.7.2/ref-manual/ref-manual.html#var-WORKDIR]}) where it keeps extracted source files, log files, intermediate compilation and packaging files, and so forth.

The per-recipe temporary work directory is constructed as follows and depends on several factors:

```
BASE_WORKDIR ?= "${TMPDIR}/work"
WORKDIR = "${BASE_WORKDIR}/${MULTIMACH_TARGET_SYS}/${PN}/${EXTENDPE}${PV}-${PR}"
```

As an example, assume a Source Directory top-level folder named poky, a default Build Directory at poky/build, and a qemux86-poky-linux machine target system. Furthermore, suppose your recipe is named foo_1.3.0.bb. In this case, the work directory the build system uses to build the package would be as follows:

```
poky/build/tmp/work/qemux86-poky-linux/foo/1.3.0-r0
```

Inside this directory you can find sub-directories such as image, packages-split, and temp. After the build, you can examine these to determine how well the build went.

Note
You can find log files for each task in the recipe's temp directory (e.g. poky/build/tmp/work/qemux86-poky-linux/foo/1.3.0-r0/temp). Log files are named log.taskname (e.g. log.do_configure, log.do_fetch, and log.do_compile).

You can find more information about the build process in the "A Closer Look at the Yocto Project Development Environment [http://www.yoctoproject.org/docs/1.7.2/ref-manual/ref-manual.html#closer-look]" chapter of the Yocto Project Reference Manual.

You can also reference the following variables in the Yocto Project Reference Manual's glossary for more information:

- TMPDIR [http://www.yoctoproject.org/docs/1.7.2/ref-manual/ref-manual.html#var-TMPDIR]: The top-level build output directory

- MULTIMACH_TARGET_SYS [http://www.yoctoproject.org/docs/1.7.2/ref-manual/ref-manual.html#var-MULTIMACH_TARGET_SYS]: The target system identifier

- PN [http://www.yoctoproject.org/docs/1.7.2/ref-manual/ref-manual.html#var-PN]: The recipe name

- EXTENDPE   [http://www.yoctoproject.org/docs/1.7.2/ref-manual/ref-manual.html#var-EXTENDPE]: The epoch - (if PE [http://www.yoctoproject.org/docs/1.7.2/ref-manual/ref-manual.html#var-PE] is not specified, which is usually the case for most recipes, then EXTENDPE is blank)

- PV   [http://www.yoctoproject.org/docs/1.7.2/ref-manual/ref-manual.html#var-PV]:   The   recipe version

- PR   [http://www.yoctoproject.org/docs/1.7.2/ref-manual/ref-manual.html#var-PR]:   The   recipe revision

5.3.6. Fetching Code

The first thing your recipe must do is specify how to fetch the source files. Fetching is controlled mainly through the SRC_URI [http://www.yoctoproject.org/docs/1.7.2/ref-manual/ref-manual.html#var-SRC_URI] variable. Your recipe must have a SRC_URI variable that points to where the source is located. For a graphical representation of source locations, see the "Sources [http://www.yoctoproject.org/docs/1.7.2/ref-manual/ref-manual.html#sources-dev-environment]" section in the Yocto Project Reference Manual.

The do_fetch [http://www.yoctoproject.org/docs/1.7.2/ref-manual/ref-manual.html#ref-tasks-fetch] task uses the prefix of each entry in the SRC_URI variable value to determine which fetcher to use to get your source files. It is the SRC_URI variable that triggers the fetcher. The do_patch [http://www.yoctoproject.org/docs/1.7.2/ref-manual/ref-manual.html#ref-tasks-patch] task uses the variable after source is fetched to apply patches. The OpenEmbedded build system uses FILESOVERRIDES [http://www.yoctoproject.org/docs/1.7.2/ref-manual/ref-manual.html#var-FILESOVERRIDES] for scanning directory locations for local files in SRC_URI.

The SRC_URI variable in your recipe must define each unique location for your source files. It is good practice to not hard-code pathnames in an URL used in SRC_URI. Rather than hard-code these paths, use ${PV [http://www.yoctoproject.org/docs/1.7.2/ref-manual/ref-manual.html#var-PV]}, which causes the fetch process to use the version specified in the recipe filename. Specifying the version in this manner means that upgrading the recipe to a future version is as simple as renaming the recipe to match the new version.

Here   is   a   simple   example   from   the   meta/recipes-devtools/cdrtools/cdrtools-native_3.01a20.bb recipe where the source comes from a single tarball. Notice the use of the PV [http://www.yoctoproject.org/docs/1.7.2/ref-manual/ref-manual.html#var-PV] variable:

```
SRC_URI = "ftp://ftp.berlios.de/pub/cdrecord/alpha/cdrtools-${PV}.tar.bz2"
```

Files mentioned in SRC_URI whose names end in a typical archive extension (e.g. .tar, .tar.gz, .tar.bz2, .zip, and so forth), are automatically extracted during the do_unpack [http://www.yoctoproject.org/docs/1.7.2/ref-manual/ref-manual.html#ref-tasks-unpack] task. For another example that specifies these types of files, see the "Autotooled Package" section.

Another way of specifying source is from an SCM. For Git repositories, you must specify SRCREV [http://www.yoctoproject.org/docs/1.7.2/ref-manual/ref-manual.html#var-SRCREV] and you should specify PV [http://www.yoctoproject.org/docs/1.7.2/ref-manual/ref-manual.html#var-PV] to include the revision with SRCPV [http://www.yoctoproject.org/docs/1.7.2/ref-manual/ref-manual.html#var-SRCPV]. Here is an example from the recipe meta/recipes-kernel/blktrace/blktrace_git.bb:

```
SRCREV = "d6918c8832793b4205ed3bfede78c2f915c23385"

PR = "r6"
PV = "1.0.5+git${SRCPV}"

SRC_URI = "git://git.kernel.dk/blktrace.git \
           file://ldflags.patch"
```

If your SRC_URI statement includes URLs pointing to individual files fetched from a remote server other than a version control system, BitBake attempts to verify the files against checksums defined in your recipe to ensure they have not been tampered with or otherwise modified since the recipe was written. Two checksums are used: SRC_URI[md5sum] and SRC_URI[sha256sum].

If your SRC_URI variable points to more than a single URL (excluding SCM URLs), you need to provide the md5 and sha256 checksums for each URL. For these cases, you provide a name for each URL as part of the SRC_URI and then reference that name in the subsequent checksum statements. Here is an example:

```
SRC_URI = "${DEBIAN_MIRROR}/main/a/apmd/apmd_3.2.2.orig.tar.gz;name=tarball \
           ${DEBIAN_MIRROR}/main/a/apmd/apmd_${PV}.diff.gz;name=patch

SRC_URI[tarball.md5sum] = "b1e6309e8331e0f4e6efd311c2d97fa8"
SRC_URI[tarball.sha256sum] = "7f7d9f60b7766b852881d40b8ff91d8e39fccb0d1d913102a5c75a2dbb523:

SRC_URI[patch.md5sum] = "57e1b689264ea80f78353519eece0c92"
SRC_URI[patch.sha256sum] = "7905ff96be93d725544d0040e425c42f9c05580db3c272f11cff75b9aa89d43(
```

Proper values for md5 and sha256 checksums might be available with other signatures on the download page for the upstream source (e.g. md5, sha1, sha256, GPG, and so forth). Because the OpenEmbedded build system only deals with sha256sum and md5sum, you should verify all the signatures you find by hand.

If no SRC_URI checksums are specified when you attempt to build the recipe, the build will produce an error for each missing checksum. As part of the error message, the build system provides the checksum string corresponding to the fetched file. Once you have the correct checksums, you can copy and paste them into your recipe and then run the build again to continue.

Note

As mentioned, if the upstream source provides signatures for verifying the downloaded source code, you should verify those manually before setting the checksum values in the recipe and continuing with the build.

This final example is a bit more complicated and is from the meta/recipes-sato/rxvt-unicode/ rxvt-unicode_9.20.bb recipe. The example's SRC_URI statement identifies multiple files as the source files for the recipe: a tarball, a patch file, a desktop file, and an icon.

```
SRC_URI = "http://dist.schmorp.de/rxvt-unicode/Attic/rxvt-unicode-${PV}.tar.bz2 \
           file://xwc.patch \
           file://rxvt.desktop \
           file://rxvt.png"
```

When you specify local files using the file:// URI protocol, the build system fetches files from the local machine. The path is relative to the FILESPATH [http://www.yoctoproject.org/docs/1.7.2/ref-manual/ref-manual.html#var-FILESPATH] variable and searches specific directories in a certain order: ${BP [http://www.yoctoproject.org/docs/1.7.2/ref-manual/ref-manual.html#var-BP]}, ${BPN [http://www.yoctoproject.org/docs/1.7.2/ref-manual/ref-manual.html#var-BPN]}, and files. The directories are assumed to be subdirectories of the directory in which the recipe or append file resides. For another example that specifies these types of files, see the "Single .c File Package (Hello World!)" section.

The previous example also specifies a patch file. Patch files are files whose names end in .patch or .diff. The build system automatically applies patches as described in the "Patching Code" section.

5.3.7. Unpacking Code

During the build, the do_unpack [http://www.yoctoproject.org/docs/1.7.2/ref-manual/ref-manual.html#ref-tasks-unpack] task unpacks the source with ${S [http://www.yoctoproject.org/docs/1.7.2/ref-manual/ref-manual.html#var-S]} pointing to where it is unpacked.

If you are fetching your source files from an upstream source archived tarball and the tarball's internal structure matches the common convention of a top-level subdirectory named

${BPN [http://www.yoctoproject.org/docs/1.7.2/ref-manual/ref-manual.html#var-BPN]}-${PV [http://www.yoctoproject.org/docs/1.7.2/ref-manual/ref-manual.html#var-PV]}, then you do not need to set S. However, if SRC_URI specifies to fetch source from an archive that does not use this convention, or from an SCM like Git or Subversion, your recipe needs to define S.

If processing your recipe using BitBake successfully unpacks the source files, you need to be sure that the directory pointed to by ${S} matches the structure of the source.

5.3.8. Patching Code

Sometimes it is necessary to patch code after it has been fetched. Any files mentioned in SRC_URI whose names end in .patch or .diff are treated as patches. The do_patch [http://www.yoctoproject.org/docs/1.7.2/ref-manual/ref-manual.html#ref-tasks-patch] task automatically applies these patches.

The build system should be able to apply patches with the "-p1" option (i.e. one directory level in the path will be stripped off). If your patch needs to have more directory levels stripped off, specify the number of levels using the "striplevel" option in the SRC_URI entry for the patch. Alternatively, if your patch needs to be applied in a specific subdirectory that is not specified in the patch file, use the "patchdir" option in the entry.

As with all local files referenced in SRC_URI [http://www.yoctoproject.org/docs/1.7.2/ref-manual/ref-manual.html#var-SRC_URI] using file://, you should place patch files in a directory next to the recipe either named the same as the base name of the recipe (BPN [http://www.yoctoproject.org/docs/1.7.2/ref-manual/ref-manual.html#var-BPN]), or "files".

5.3.9. Licensing

Your recipe needs to have both the LICENSE [http://www.yoctoproject.org/docs/1.7.2/ref-manual/ref-manual.html#var-LICENSE] and LIC_FILES_CHKSUM [http://www.yoctoproject.org/docs/1.7.2/ref-manual/ref-manual.html#var-LIC_FILES_CHKSUM] variables:

- LICENSE: This variable specifies the license for the software. If you do not know the license under which the software you are building is distributed, you should go to the source code and look for that information. Typical files containing this information include COPYING, LICENSE, and README files. You could also find the information near the top of a source file. For example, given a piece of software licensed under the GNU General Public License version 2, you would set LICENSE as follows:

    ```
    LICENSE = "GPLv2"
    ```

    The licenses you specify within LICENSE can have any name as long as you do not use spaces, since spaces are used as separators between license names. For standard licenses, use the names of the files in meta/files/common-licenses/ or the SPDXLICENSEMAP flag names defined in meta/conf/licenses.conf.

- LIC_FILES_CHKSUM: The OpenEmbedded build system uses this variable to make sure the license text has not changed. If it has, the build produces an error and it affords you the chance to figure it out and correct the problem.

    You need to specify all applicable licensing files for the software. At the end of the configuration step, the build process will compare the checksums of the files to be sure the text has not changed. Any differences result in an error with the message containing the current checksum. For more explanation and examples of how to set the LIC_FILES_CHKSUM variable, see the "Tracking License Changes [http://www.yoctoproject.org/docs/1.7.2/ref-manual/ref-manual.html#usingpoky-configuring-LIC_FILES_CHKSUM]" section in the Yocto Project Reference Manual.

    To determine the correct checksum string, you can list the appropriate files in the LIC_FILES_CHKSUM variable with incorrect md5 strings, attempt to build the software, and then note the resulting error messages that will report the correct md5 strings. See the "Fetching Code" section for additional information.

    Here is an example that assumes the software has a COPYING file:

```
LIC_FILES_CHKSUM = "file://COPYING;md5=xxx"
```

When you try to build the software, the build system will produce an error and give you the correct string that you can substitute into the recipe file for a subsequent build.

5.3.10. Configuring the Recipe

Most software provides some means of setting build-time configuration options before compilation. Typically, setting these options is accomplished by running a configure script with some options, or by modifying a build configuration file.

A major part of build-time configuration is about checking for build-time dependencies and possibly enabling optional functionality as a result. You need to specify any build-time dependencies for the software you are building in your recipe's DEPENDS [http://www.yoctoproject.org/docs/1.7.2/ref-manual/ref-manual.html#var-DEPENDS] value, in terms of other recipes that satisfy those dependencies. You can often find build-time or runtime dependencies described in the software's documentation.

The following list provides configuration items of note based on how your software is built:

• Autotools: If your source files have a configure.ac file, then your software is built using Autotools. If this is the case, you just need to worry about modifying the configuration.

    When using Autotools, your recipe needs to inherit the autotools [http://www.yoctoproject.org/docs/1.7.2/ref-manual/ref-manual.html#ref-classes-autotools] class and your recipe does not have to contain a do_configure [http://www.yoctoproject.org/docs/1.7.2/ref-manual/ref-manual.html#ref-tasks-configure] task. However, you might still want to make some adjustments. For example, you can set EXTRA_OECONF [http://www.yoctoproject.org/docs/1.7.2/ref-manual/ref-manual.html#var-EXTRA_OECONF] to pass any needed configure options that are specific to the recipe.

• CMake: If your source files have a CMakeLists.txt file, then your software is built using CMake. If this is the case, you just need to worry about modifying the configuration.

    When you use CMake, your recipe needs to inherit the cmake [http://www.yoctoproject.org/docs/1.7.2/ref-manual/ref-manual.html#ref-classes-cmake] class and your recipe does not have to contain a do_configure [http://www.yoctoproject.org/docs/1.7.2/ref-manual/ref-manual.html#ref-tasks-configure] task. You can make some adjustments by setting EXTRA_OECMAKE [http://www.yoctoproject.org/docs/1.7.2/ref-manual/ref-manual.html#var-EXTRA_OECMAKE] to pass any needed configure options that are specific to the recipe.

• Other: If your source files do not have a configure.ac or CMakeLists.txt file, then your software is built using some method other than Autotools or CMake. If this is the case, you normally need to provide a do_configure [http://www.yoctoproject.org/docs/1.7.2/ref-manual/ref-manual.html#ref-tasks-configure] task in your recipe unless, of course, there is nothing to configure.

    Even if your software is not being built by Autotools or CMake, you still might not need to deal with any configuration issues. You need to determine if configuration is even a required step. You might need to modify a Makefile or some configuration file used for the build to specify necessary build options. Or, perhaps you might need to run a provided, custom configure script with the appropriate options.

    For the case involving a custom configure script, you would run ./configure ##help and look for the options you need to set.

Once configuration succeeds, it is always good practice to look at the log.do_configure file to ensure that the appropriate options have been enabled and no additional build-time dependencies need to be added to DEPENDS. For example, if the configure script reports that it found something not mentioned in DEPENDS, or that it did not find something that it needed for some desired optional functionality, then you would need to add those to DEPENDS. Looking at the log might also reveal items being checked for, enabled, or both that you do not want, or items not being found that are in DEPENDS, in which case you would need to look at passing extra options to the configure script as needed. For reference information on configure options specific to the software you are building, you can consult the output of the ./configure ##help command within ${S} or consult the software's upstream documentation.

5.3.11. Compilation

During a build, the do_compile task happens after source is fetched, unpacked, and configured. If the recipe passes through do_compile successfully, nothing needs to be done.

However, if the compile step fails, you need to diagnose the failure. Here are some common issues that cause failures:

- Parallel build failures: These failures manifest themselves as intermittent errors, or errors reporting that a file or directory that should be created by some other part of the build process could not be found. This type of failure can occur even if, upon inspection, the file or directory does exist after the build has failed, because that part of the build process happened in the wrong order.

  To fix the problem, you need to either satisfy the missing dependency in the Makefile or whatever script produced the Makefile, or (as a workaround) set PARALLEL_MAKE [http://www.yoctoproject.org/docs/1.7.2/ref-manual/ref-manual.html#var-PARALLEL_MAKE] to an empty string:

  ```
  PARALLEL_MAKE = ""
  ```

  For information on parallel Makefile issues, see the "Debugging Parallel Make Races" section.

- Improper host path usage: This failure applies to recipes building for the target or nativesdk only. The failure occurs when the compilation process uses improper headers, libraries, or other files from the host system when cross-compiling for the target.

  To fix the problem, examine the log.do_compile file to identify the host paths being used (e.g. /usr/include, /usr/lib, and so forth) and then either add configure options, apply a patch, or do both.

- Failure to find required libraries/headers: If a build-time dependency is missing because it has not been declared in DEPENDS [http://www.yoctoproject.org/docs/1.7.2/ref-manual/ref-manual.html#var-DEPENDS], or because the dependency exists but the path used by the build process to find the file is incorrect and the configure step did not detect it, the compilation process could fail. For either of these failures, the compilation process notes that files could not be found. In these cases, you need to go back and add additional options to the configure script as well as possibly add additional build-time dependencies to DEPENDS.

  Occasionally, it is necessary to apply a patch to the source to ensure the correct paths are used. If you need to specify paths to find files staged into the sysroot from other recipes, use the variables that the OpenEmbedded build system provides (e.g. STAGING_BINDIR, STAGING_INCDIR, STAGING_DATADIR, and so forth).

5.3.12. Installing

During do_install, the task copies the built files along with their hierarchy to locations that would mirror their locations on the target device. The installation process copies files from the ${S [http://www.yoctoproject.org/docs/1.7.2/ref-manual/ref-manual.html#var-S]}, ${B [http://www.yoctoproject.org/docs/1.7.2/ref-manual/ref-manual.html#var-B]}, and ${WORKDIR [http://www.yoctoproject.org/docs/1.7.2/ref-manual/ref-manual.html#var-WORKDIR]} directories to the ${D [http://www.yoctoproject.org/docs/1.7.2/ref-manual/ref-manual.html#var-D]} directory to create the structure as it should appear on the target system.

How your software is built affects what you must do to be sure your software is installed correctly. The following list describes what you must do for installation depending on the type of build system used by the software being built:

- Autotools and CMake: If the software your recipe is building uses Autotools or CMake, the OpenEmbedded build system understands how to install the software. Consequently, you do not have to have a do_install task as part of your recipe. You just need to make sure the install portion of the build completes with no issues. However, if you wish to install additional files not already being installed by make install, you should do this using a do_install_append function using the install command as described in the "Manual" bulleted item later in this list.

- Other (using make install): You need to define a do_install function in your recipe. The function should call oe_runmake install and will likely need to pass in the destination directory as well. How you pass that path is dependent on how the Makefile being run is written (e.g. DESTDIR= ${D}, PREFIX=${D}, INSTALLROOT=${D}, and so forth).

  For an example recipe using make install, see the "Makefile-Based Package" section.

- Manual: You need to define a do_install function in your recipe. The function must first use install -d to create the directories under ${D [http://www.yoctoproject.org/docs/1.7.2/ref-manual/ref-manual.html#var-D]}. Once the directories exist, your function can use install to manually install the built software into the directories.

  You can find more information on install at http://www.gnu.org/software/coreutils/manual/html_node/install-invocation.html.

For the scenarios that do not use Autotools or CMake, you need to track the installation and diagnose and fix any issues until everything installs correctly. You need to look in the default location of ${D}, which is ${WORKDIR}/image, to be sure your files have been installed correctly.

Notes

- During the installation process, you might need to modify some of the installed files to suit the target layout. For example, you might need to replace hard-coded paths in an initscript with values of variables provided by the build system, such as replacing /usr/bin/ with ${bindir}. If you do perform such modifications during do_install, be sure to modify the destination file after copying rather than before copying. Modifying after copying ensures that the build system can re-execute do_install if needed.

- oe_runmake install, which can be run directly or can be run indirectly by the autotools [http://www.yoctoproject.org/docs/1.7.2/ref-manual/ref-manual.html#ref-classes-autotools] and cmake [http://www.yoctoproject.org/docs/1.7.2/ref-manual/ref-manual.html#ref-classes-cmake] classes, runs make install in parallel. Sometimes, a Makefile can have missing dependencies between targets that can result in race conditions. If you experience intermittent failures during do_install, you might be able to work around them by disabling parallel Makefile installs by adding the following to the recipe:

  ```
  PARALLEL_MAKEINST = ""
  ```

  See PARALLEL_MAKEINST [http://www.yoctoproject.org/docs/1.7.2/ref-manual/ref-manual.html#var-PARALLEL_MAKEINST] for additional information.

5.3.13. Enabling System Services

If you want to install a service, which is a process that usually starts on boot and runs in the background, then you must include some additional definitions in your recipe.

If you are adding services and the service initialization script or the service file itself is not installed, you must provide for that installation in your recipe using a do_install_append function. If your recipe already has a do_install function, update the function near its end rather than adding an additional do_install_append function.

When you create the installation for your services, you need to accomplish what is normally done by make install. In other words, make sure your installation arranges the output similar to how it is arranged on the target system.

The OpenEmbedded build system provides support for starting services two different ways:

- SysVinit: SysVinit is a system and service manager that manages the init system used to control the very basic functions of your system. The init program is the first program started by the Linux kernel when the system boots. Init then controls the startup, running and shutdown of all other programs.

To enable a service using SysVinit, your recipe needs to inherit the update-rc.d [http://www.yoctoproject.org/docs/1.7.2/ref-manual/ref-manual.html#ref-classes-update-rc.d] class. The class helps facilitate safely installing the package on the target.

You will need to set the INITSCRIPT_PACKAGES [http://www.yoctoproject.org/docs/1.7.2/ref-manual/ref-manual.html#var-INITSCRIPT_PACKAGES], INITSCRIPT_NAME [http://www.yoctoproject.org/docs/1.7.2/ref-manual/ref-manual.html#var-INITSCRIPT_NAME], and INITSCRIPT_PARAMS [http://www.yoctoproject.org/docs/1.7.2/ref-manual/ref-manual.html#var-INITSCRIPT_PARAMS] variables within your recipe.

- systemd: System Management Daemon (systemd) was designed to replace SysVinit and to provide enhanced management of services. For more information on systemd, see the systemd homepage at http://freedesktop.org/wiki/Software/systemd/.

  To enable a service using systemd, your recipe needs to inherit the systemd [http://www.yoctoproject.org/docs/1.7.2/ref-manual/ref-manual.html#ref-classes-systemd] class. See the systemd.bbclass file located in your Source Directory [16]. section for more information.

5.3.14. Packaging

Successful packaging is a combination of automated processes performed by the OpenEmbedded build system and some specific steps you need to take. The following list describes the process:

- Splitting Files: The do_package task splits the files produced by the recipe into logical components. Even software that produces a single binary might still have debug symbols, documentation, and other logical components that should be split out. The do_package task ensures that files are split up and packaged correctly.

- Running QA Checks: The insane [http://www.yoctoproject.org/docs/1.7.2/ref-manual/ref-manual.html#ref-classes-insane] class adds a step to the package generation process so that output quality assurance checks are generated by the OpenEmbedded build system. This step performs a range of checks to be sure the build's output is free of common problems that show up during runtime. For information on these checks, see the insane [http://www.yoctoproject.org/docs/1.7.2/ref-manual/ref-manual.html#ref-classes-insane] class and the "QA Error and Warning Messages [http://www.yoctoproject.org/docs/1.7.2/ref-manual/ref-manual.html#ref-qa-checks]" chapter in the Yocto Project Reference Manual.

- Hand-Checking Your Packages: After you build your software, you need to be sure your packages are correct. Examine the ${WORKDIR [http://www.yoctoproject.org/docs/1.7.2/ref-manual/ref-manual.html#var-WORKDIR]}/packages-split directory and make sure files are where you expect them to be. If you discover problems, you can set PACKAGES [http://www.yoctoproject.org/docs/1.7.2/ref-manual/ref-manual.html#var-PACKAGES], FILES [http://www.yoctoproject.org/docs/1.7.2/ref-manual/ref-manual.html#var-FILES], do_install(_append), and so forth as needed.

- Splitting an Application into Multiple Packages: If you need to split an application into several packages, see the "Splitting an Application into Multiple Packages" section for an example.

- Installing a Post-Installation Script: For an example showing how to install a post-installation script, see the "Post-Installation Scripts" section.

- Marking Package Architecture: Depending on what your recipe is building and how it is configured, it might be important to mark the packages produced as being specific to a particular machine, or to mark them as not being specific to a particular machine or architecture at all. By default, packages produced for the target are marked as being specific to the architecture of the target machine because that is usually the desired result. However, if the recipe configures the software to be built specific to the target machine (e.g. the MACHINE [http://www.yoctoproject.org/docs/1.7.2/ref-manual/ref-manual.html#var-MACHINE] value is passed into the configure script or a patch is applied only for a particular machine), then you should mark the packages produced as being machine-specific by adding the following to the recipe:

      PACKAGE_ARCH = "${MACHINE_ARCH}"

  On the other hand, if the recipe produces packages that do not contain anything specific to the target machine or architecture at all (e.g. recipes that simply package script files or configuration files), you should use the `allarch` [http://www.yoctoproject.org/docs/1.7.2/ref-manual/ref-manual.html#ref-classes-allarch] class to do this for you by adding this to your recipe:

```
inherit allarch
```

Ensuring that the package architecture is correct is not critical while you are doing the first few builds of your recipe. However, it is important in order to ensure that your recipe rebuilds (or does not rebuild) appropriately in response to changes in configuration, and to ensure that you get the appropriate packages installed on the target machine, particularly if you run separate builds for more than one target machine.

5.3.15. Properly Versioning Pre-Release Recipes

Sometimes the name of a recipe can lead to versioning problems when the recipe is upgraded to a final release. For example, consider the `irssi_0.8.16-rc1.bb` recipe file in the list of example recipes in the "Storing and Naming the Recipe" section. This recipe is at a release candidate stage (i.e. "rc1"). When the recipe is released, the recipe filename becomes `irssi_0.8.16.bb`. The version change from `0.8.16-rc1` to `0.8.16` is seen as a decrease by the build system and package managers, so the resulting packages will not correctly trigger an upgrade.

In order to ensure the versions compare properly, the recommended convention is to set PV [http://www.yoctoproject.org/docs/1.7.2/ref-manual/ref-manual.html#var-PV] within the recipe to "previous_version+current_version". You can use an additional variable so that you can use the current version elsewhere. Here is an example:

```
REALPV = "0.8.16-rc1"
PV = "0.8.15+${REALPV}"
```

5.3.16. Post-Installation Scripts

Post-installation scripts run immediately after installing a package on the target or during image creation when a package is included in an image. To add a post-installation script to a package, add a pkg_postinst_PACKAGENAME() function to the recipe file (.bb) and replace PACKAGENAME with the name of the package you want to attach to the postinst script. To apply the post-installation script to the main package for the recipe, which is usually what is required, specify ${PN [http://www.yoctoproject.org/docs/1.7.2/ref-manual/ref-manual.html#var-PN]} in place of PACKAGENAME.

A post-installation function has the following structure:

```
pkg_postinst_PACKAGENAME() {
#!/bin/sh -e
# Commands to carry out
}
```

The script defined in the post-installation function is called when the root filesystem is created. If the script succeeds, the package is marked as installed. If the script fails, the package is marked as unpacked and the script is executed when the image boots again.

Sometimes it is necessary for the execution of a post-installation script to be delayed until the first boot. For example, the script might need to be executed on the device itself. To delay script execution until boot time, use the following structure in the post-installation script:

```
pkg_postinst_PACKAGENAME() {
#!/bin/sh -e
if [ x"$D" = "x" ]; then
    # Actions to carry out on the device go here
else
    exit 1
fi
```

```
    }
```

The previous example delays execution until the image boots again because the environment variable D points to the directory containing the image when the root filesystem is created at build time but is unset when executed on the first boot.

Note

Equivalent support for pre-install, pre-uninstall, and post-uninstall scripts exist by way of pkg_preinst, pkg_prerm, and pkg_postrm, respectively. These scrips work in exactly the same way as does pkg_postinst with the exception that they run at different times. Also, because of when they run, they are not applicable to being run at image creation time like pkg_postinst.

5.3.17. Testing

The final step for completing your recipe is to be sure that the software you built runs correctly. To accomplish runtime testing, add the build's output packages to your image and test them on the target.

For information on how to customize your image by adding specific packages, see the "Customizing Images" section.

5.3.18. Examples

To help summarize how to write a recipe, this section provides some examples given various scenarios:

• Recipes that use local files

• Using an Autotooled package

• Using a Makefile-based package

• Splitting an application into multiple packages

• Adding binaries to an image

5.3.18.1. Single .c File Package (Hello World!)

Building an application from a single file that is stored locally (e.g. under files) requires a recipe that has the file listed in the SRC_URI [http://www.yoctoproject.org/docs/1.7.2/ref-manual/ref-manual.html#var-SRC_URI] variable. Additionally, you need to manually write the do_compile and do_install tasks. The S [http://www.yoctoproject.org/docs/1.7.2/ref-manual/ref-manual.html#var-S] variable defines the directory containing the source code, which is set to WORKDIR [http://www.yoctoproject.org/docs/1.7.2/ref-manual/ref-manual.html#var-WORKDIR] in this case - the directory BitBake uses for the build.

```
SUMMARY = "Simple helloworld application"
SECTION = "examples"
LICENSE = "MIT"
LIC_FILES_CHKSUM = "file://${COMMON_LICENSE_DIR}/MIT;md5=0835ade698e0bcf8506ecda2f7b4f302"

SRC_URI = "file://helloworld.c"

S = "${WORKDIR}"

do_compile() {
 ${CC} helloworld.c -o helloworld
}

do_install() {
 install -d ${D}${bindir}
 install -m 0755 helloworld ${D}${bindir}
}
```

By default, the `helloworld`, `helloworld-dbg`, and `helloworld-dev` packages are built. For information on how to customize the packaging process, see the "Splitting an Application into Multiple Packages" section.

5.3.18.2. Autotooled Package

Applications that use Autotools such as autoconf and automake require a recipe that has a source archive listed in SRC_URI [http://www.yoctoproject.org/docs/1.7.2/ref-manual/ref-manual.html#var-SRC_URI] and also inherit the autotools [http://www.yoctoproject.org/docs/1.7.2/ref-manual/ref-manual.html#ref-classes-autotools] class, which contains the definitions of all the steps needed to build an Autotool-based application. The result of the build is automatically packaged. And, if the application uses NLS for localization, packages with local information are generated (one package per language). Following is one example: (hello_2.3.bb)

```
SUMMARY = "GNU Helloworld application"
SECTION = "examples"
LICENSE = "GPLv2+"
LIC_FILES_CHKSUM = "file://COPYING;md5=751419260aa954499f7abaabaa882bbe"

SRC_URI = "${GNU_MIRROR}/hello/hello-${PV}.tar.gz"

inherit autotools gettext
```

The variable LIC_FILES_CHKSUM [http://www.yoctoproject.org/docs/1.7.2/ref-manual/ref-manual.html#var-LIC_FILES_CHKSUM] is used to track source license changes as described in the "Tracking License Changes [http://www.yoctoproject.org/docs/1.7.2/ref-manual/ref-manual.html#usingpoky-configuring-LIC_FILES_CHKSUM]" section. You can quickly create Autotool-based recipes in a manner similar to the previous example.

5.3.18.3. Makefile-Based Package

Applications that use GNU make also require a recipe that has the source archive listed in SRC_URI [http://www.yoctoproject.org/docs/1.7.2/ref-manual/ref-manual.html#var-SRC_URI]. You do not need to add a do_compile step since by default BitBake starts the make command to compile the application. If you need additional make options, you should store them in the EXTRA_OEMAKE [http://www.yoctoproject.org/docs/1.7.2/ref-manual/ref-manual.html#var-EXTRA_OEMAKE] variable. BitBake passes these options into the GNU make invocation. Note that a do_install task is still required. Otherwise, BitBake runs an empty do_install task by default.

Some applications might require extra parameters to be passed to the compiler. For example, the application might need an additional header path. You can accomplish this by adding to the CFLAGS [http://www.yoctoproject.org/docs/1.7.2/ref-manual/ref-manual.html#var-CFLAGS] variable. The following example shows this:

```
CFLAGS_prepend = "-I ${S}/include "
```

In the following example, `mtd-utils` is a makefile-based package:

```
SUMMARY = "Tools for managing memory technology devices"
SECTION = "base"
DEPENDS = "zlib lzo e2fsprogs util-linux"
HOMEPAGE = "http://www.linux-mtd.infradead.org/"
LICENSE = "GPLv2+"
LIC_FILES_CHKSUM = "file://COPYING;md5=0636e73ff0215e8d672dc4c32c317bb3 \
                    file://include/common.h;beginline=1;endline=17;md5=ba05b07912a44ea2bf81c

# Use the latest version at 26 Oct, 2013
SRCREV = "9f107132a6a073cce37434ca9cda6917dd8d866b"
```

```
SRC_URI = "git://git.infradead.org/mtd-utils.git \
               file://add-exclusion-to-mkfs-jffs2-git-2.patch \
          "

PV = "1.5.1+git${SRCPV}"

S = "${WORKDIR}/git/"

EXTRA_OEMAKE = "'CC=${CC}' 'RANLIB=${RANLIB}' 'AR=${AR}' 'CFLAGS=${CFLAGS} -I${S}/include

do_install () {
          oe_runmake install DESTDIR=${D} SBINDIR=${sbindir} MANDIR=${mandir} INCLUDEDIR=${
}

PACKAGES =+ "mtd-utils-jffs2 mtd-utils-ubifs mtd-utils-misc"

FILES_mtd-utils-jffs2 = "${sbindir}/mkfs.jffs2 ${sbindir}/jffs2dump ${sbindir}/jffs2reade
FILES_mtd-utils-ubifs = "${sbindir}/mkfs.ubifs ${sbindir}/ubi*"
FILES_mtd-utils-misc = "${sbindir}/nftl* ${sbindir}/ftl* ${sbindir}/rfd* ${sbindir}/doc*

PARALLEL_MAKE = ""

BBCLASSEXTEND = "native"
```

5.3.18.4. Splitting an Application into Multiple Packages

You can use the variables PACKAGES [http://www.yoctoproject.org/docs/1.7.2/ref-manual/
ref-manual.html#var-PACKAGES] and FILES [http://www.yoctoproject.org/docs/1.7.2/ref-
manual/ref-manual.html#var-FILES] to split an application into multiple packages.

Following is an example that uses the libxpm recipe. By default, this recipe generates a single
package that contains the library along with a few binaries. You can modify the recipe to split the
binaries into separate packages:

```
require xorg-lib-common.inc

SUMMARY = "X11 Pixmap library"
LICENSE = "X-BSD"
LIC_FILES_CHKSUM = "file://COPYING;md5=3e07763d16963c3af12db271a31abaa5"
DEPENDS += "libxext libsm libxt"
PR = "r3"
PE = "1"

XORG_PN = "libXpm"

PACKAGES =+ "sxpm cxpm"
FILES_cxpm = "${bindir}/cxpm"
FILES_sxpm = "${bindir}/sxpm"
```

In the previous example, we want to ship the sxpm and cxpm binaries in separate packages.
Since bindir would be packaged into the main PN [http://www.yoctoproject.org/docs/1.7.2/
ref-manual/ref-manual.html#var-PN] package by default, we prepend the PACKAGES variable so
additional package names are added to the start of list. This results in the extra FILES_* variables
then containing information that define which files and directories go into which packages. Files
included by earlier packages are skipped by latter packages. Thus, the main PN package does not
include the above listed files.

5.3.18.5. Packaging Externally Produced Binaries

Sometimes, you need to add pre-compiled binaries to an image. For example, suppose that binaries
for proprietary code exist, which are created by a particular division of a company. Your part
of the company needs to use those binaries as part of an image that you are building using

the OpenEmbedded build system. Since you only have the binaries and not the source code, you cannot use a typical recipe that expects to fetch the source specified in SRC_URI [http://www.yoctoproject.org/docs/1.7.2/ref-manual/ref-manual.html#var-SRC_URI] and then compile it.

One method is to package the binaries and then install them as part of the image. Generally, it is not a good idea to package binaries since, among other things, it can hinder the ability to reproduce builds and could lead to compatibility problems with ABI in the future. However, sometimes you have no choice.

The easiest solution is to create a recipe that uses the bin_package [http://www.yoctoproject.org/docs/1.7.2/ref-manual/ref-manual.html#ref-classes-bin-package] class and to be sure that you are using default locations for build artifacts. In most cases, the bin_package class handles "skipping" the configure and compile steps as well as sets things up to grab packages from the appropriate area. In particular, this class sets noexec on both the do_configure [http://www.yoctoproject.org/docs/1.7.2/ref-manual/ref-manual.html#ref-tasks-configure] and do_compile [http://www.yoctoproject.org/docs/1.7.2/ref-manual/ref-manual.html#ref-tasks-compile] tasks, sets FILES_${PN} to "/" so that it picks up all files, and sets up a do_install [http://www.yoctoproject.org/docs/1.7.2/ref-manual/ref-manual.html#ref-tasks-install] task, which effectively copies all files from ${S} to ${D}. The bin_package class works well when the files extracted into ${S} are already laid out in the way they should be laid out on the target. For more information on these variables, see the FILES [http://www.yoctoproject.org/docs/1.7.2/ref-manual/ref-manual.html#var-FILES], PN [http://www.yoctoproject.org/docs/1.7.2/ref-manual/ref-manual.html#var-PN], S [http://www.yoctoproject.org/docs/1.7.2/ref-manual/ref-manual.html#var-S], and D [http://www.yoctoproject.org/docs/1.7.2/ref-manual/ref-manual.html#var-D] variables in the Yocto Project Reference Manual's variable glossary.

If you can't use the bin_package class, you need to be sure you are doing the following:

- Create a recipe where the do_configure and do_compile tasks do nothing:

```
do_configure[noexec] = "1"
do_compile[noexec] = "1"
```

Alternatively, you can make these tasks an empty function.

- Make sure your do_install task installs the binaries appropriately.

- Ensure that you set up FILES (usually FILES_${PN}) to point to the files you have installed, which of course depends on where you have installed them and whether those files are in different locations than the defaults.

5.4. Adding a New Machine

Adding a new machine to the Yocto Project is a straightforward process. This section describes how to add machines that are similar to those that the Yocto Project already supports.

Note

Although well within the capabilities of the Yocto Project, adding a totally new architecture might require changes to gcc/glibc and to the site information, which is beyond the scope of this manual.

For a complete example that shows how to add a new machine, see the "Creating a New BSP Layer Using the yocto-bsp Script [http://www.yoctoproject.org/docs/1.7.2/bsp-guide/bsp-guide.html#creating-a-new-bsp-layer-using-the-yocto-bsp-script]" section in the Yocto Project Board Support Package (BSP) Developer's Guide.

5.4.1. Adding the Machine Configuration File

To add a new machine, you need to add a new machine configuration file to the layer's conf/machine directory. This configuration file provides details about the device you are adding.

The OpenEmbedded build system uses the root name of the machine configuration file to reference the new machine. For example, given a machine configuration file named crownbay.conf, the build system recognizes the machine as "crownbay".

The most important variables you must set in your machine configuration file or include from a lower-level configuration file are as follows:

- TARGET_ARCH   [http://www.yoctoproject.org/docs/1.7.2/ref-manual/ref-manual.html#var-TARGET_ARCH] (e.g. "arm")

- PREFERRED_PROVIDER   [http://www.yoctoproject.org/docs/1.7.2/ref-manual/ref-manual.html#var-PREFERRED_PROVIDER]_virtual/kernel

- MACHINE_FEATURES   [http://www.yoctoproject.org/docs/1.7.2/ref-manual/ref-manual.html#var-MACHINE_FEATURES] (e.g. "apm screen wifi")

You might also need these variables:

- SERIAL_CONSOLES   [http://www.yoctoproject.org/docs/1.7.2/ref-manual/ref-manual.html#var-SERIAL_CONSOLES] (e.g. "115200;ttyS0 115200;ttyS1")

- KERNEL_IMAGETYPE   [http://www.yoctoproject.org/docs/1.7.2/ref-manual/ref-manual.html#var-KERNEL_IMAGETYPE] (e.g. "zImage")

- IMAGE_FSTYPES   [http://www.yoctoproject.org/docs/1.7.2/ref-manual/ref-manual.html#var-IMAGE_FSTYPES] (e.g. "tar.gz jffs2")

You can find full details on these variables in the reference section. You can leverage existing machine .conf files from meta-yocto-bsp/conf/machine/.

5.4.2. Adding a Kernel for the Machine

The OpenEmbedded build system needs to be able to build a kernel for the machine. You need to either create a new kernel recipe for this machine, or extend an existing kernel recipe. You can find several kernel recipe examples in the Source Directory at meta/recipes-kernel/linux that you can use as references.

If you are creating a new kernel recipe, normal recipe-writing rules apply for setting up a SRC_URI   [http://www.yoctoproject.org/docs/1.7.2/ref-manual/ref-manual.html#var-SRC_URI]. Thus, you need to specify any necessary patches and set S   [http://www.yoctoproject.org/docs/1.7.2/ref-manual/ref-manual.html#var-S] to point at the source code. You need to create a do_configure task that configures the unpacked kernel with a defconfig file. You can do this by using a make defconfig command or, more commonly, by copying in a suitable defconfig file and then running make oldconfig. By making use of inherit kernel and potentially some of the linux-*.inc files, most other functionality is centralized and the defaults of the class normally work well.

If you are extending an existing kernel recipe, it is usually a matter of adding a suitable defconfig file. The file needs to be added into a location similar to defconfig files used for other machines in a given kernel recipe. A possible way to do this is by listing the file in the SRC_URI and adding the machine to the expression in COMPATIBLE_MACHINE [http://www.yoctoproject.org/docs/1.7.2/ref-manual/ref-manual.html#var-COMPATIBLE_MACHINE]:

```
COMPATIBLE_MACHINE = '(qemux86|qemumips)'
```

5.4.3. Adding a Formfactor Configuration File

A formfactor configuration file provides information about the target hardware for which the image is being built and information that the build system cannot obtain from other sources such as the kernel. Some examples of information contained in a formfactor configuration file include framebuffer orientation, whether or not the system has a keyboard, the positioning of the keyboard in relation to the screen, and the screen resolution.

The build system uses reasonable defaults in most cases. However, if customization is necessary, you need to create a machconfig file in the meta/recipes-bsp/formfactor/files directory. This directory contains directories for specific machines such as qemuarm and qemux86. For information about the settings available and the defaults, see the meta/recipes-bsp/formfactor/files/config file found in the same area.

Following is an example for "qemuarm" machine:

```
HAVE_TOUCHSCREEN=1
HAVE_KEYBOARD=1

DISPLAY_CAN_ROTATE=0
DISPLAY_ORIENTATION=0
#DISPLAY_WIDTH_PIXELS=640
#DISPLAY_HEIGHT_PIXELS=480
#DISPLAY_BPP=16
DISPLAY_DPI=150
DISPLAY_SUBPIXEL_ORDER=vrgb
```

5.5. Working With Libraries

Libraries are an integral part of your system. This section describes some common practices you might find helpful when working with libraries to build your system:

• How to include static library files

• How to use the Multilib feature to combine multiple versions of library files into a single image

• How to install multiple versions of the same library in parallel on the same system

5.5.1. Including Static Library Files

If you are building a library and the library offers static linking, you can control which static library files (*.a files) get included in the built library.

The PACKAGES [http://www.yoctoproject.org/docs/1.7.2/ref-manual/ref-manual.html#var-PACKAGES] and FILES_* [http://www.yoctoproject.org/docs/1.7.2/ref-manual/ref-manual.html#var-FILES] variables in the meta/conf/bitbake.conf configuration file define how files installed by the do_install task are packaged. By default, the PACKAGES variable includes ${PN}-staticdev, which represents all static library files.

Note
Some previously released versions of the Yocto Project defined the static library files through ${PN}-dev.

Following is part of the BitBake configuration file, where you can see how the static library files are defined:

```
PACKAGE_BEFORE_PN ?= ""
PACKAGES = "${PN}-dbg ${PN}-staticdev ${PN}-dev ${PN}-doc ${PN}-locale ${PACKAGE_BEFORE_PN}
PACKAGES_DYNAMIC = "^${PN}-locale-.*"
FILES = ""

FILES_${PN} = "${bindir}/* ${sbindir}/* ${libexecdir}/* ${libdir}/lib*${SOLIBS} \
            ${sysconfdir} ${sharedstatedir} ${localstatedir} \
            ${base_bindir}/* ${base_sbindir}/* \
            ${base_libdir}/*${SOLIBS} \
            ${base_prefix}/lib/udev/rules.d ${prefix}/lib/udev/rules.d \
            ${datadir}/${BPN} ${libdir}/${BPN}/* \
            ${datadir}/pixmaps ${datadir}/applications \
            ${datadir}/idl ${datadir}/omf ${datadir}/sounds \
            ${libdir}/bonobo/servers"

FILES_${PN}-bin = "${bindir}/* ${sbindir}/*"

FILES_${PN}-doc = "${docdir} ${mandir} ${infodir} ${datadir}/gtk-doc \
            ${datadir}/gnome/help"
SECTION_${PN}-doc = "doc"
```

```
FILES_SOLIBSDEV ?= "${base_libdir}/lib*${SOLIBSDEV} ${libdir}/lib*${SOLIBSDEV}"
FILES_${PN}-dev = "${includedir} ${FILES_SOLIBSDEV} ${libdir}/*.la \
                ${libdir}/*.o ${libdir}/pkgconfig ${datadir}/pkgconfig \
                ${datadir}/aclocal ${base_libdir}/*.o \
                ${libdir}/${BPN}/*.la ${base_libdir}/*.la"
SECTION_${PN}-dev = "devel"
ALLOW_EMPTY_${PN}-dev = "1"
RDEPENDS_${PN}-dev = "${PN} (= ${EXTENDPKGV})"

FILES_${PN}-staticdev = "${libdir}/*.a ${base_libdir}/*.a ${libdir}/${BPN}/*.a"
SECTION_${PN}-staticdev = "devel"
RDEPENDS_${PN}-staticdev = "${PN}-dev (= ${EXTENDPKGV})"
```

5.5.2. Combining Multiple Versions of Library Files into One Image

The build system offers the ability to build libraries with different target optimizations or architecture formats and combine these together into one system image. You can link different binaries in the image against the different libraries as needed for specific use cases. This feature is called "Multilib."

An example would be where you have most of a system compiled in 32-bit mode using 32-bit libraries, but you have something large, like a database engine, that needs to be a 64-bit application and uses 64-bit libraries. Multilib allows you to get the best of both 32-bit and 64-bit libraries.

While the Multilib feature is most commonly used for 32 and 64-bit differences, the approach the build system uses facilitates different target optimizations. You could compile some binaries to use one set of libraries and other binaries to use a different set of libraries. The libraries could differ in architecture, compiler options, or other optimizations.

This section overviews the Multilib process only. For more details on how to implement Multilib, see the Multilib [https://wiki.yoctoproject.org/wiki/Multilib] wiki page.

Aside from this wiki page, several examples exist in the `meta-skeleton` layer found in the Source Directory [16]:

- `conf/multilib-example.conf` configuration file

- `conf/multilib-example2.conf` configuration file

- `recipes-multilib/images/core-image-multilib-example.bb` recipe

5.5.2.1. Preparing to Use Multilib

User-specific requirements drive the Multilib feature. Consequently, there is no one "out-of-the-box" configuration that likely exists to meet your needs.

In order to enable Multilib, you first need to ensure your recipe is extended to support multiple libraries. Many standard recipes are already extended and support multiple libraries. You can check in the `meta/conf/multilib.conf` configuration file in the Source Directory [16] to see how this is done using the BBCLASSEXTEND [http://www.yoctoproject.org/docs/1.7.2/ref-manual/ref-manual.html#var-BBCLASSEXTEND] variable. Eventually, all recipes will be covered and this list will not be needed.

For the most part, the Multilib class extension works automatically to extend the package name from ${PN} to ${MLPREFIX}${PN}, where MLPREFIX is the particular multilib (e.g. "lib32-" or "lib64-"). Standard variables such as DEPENDS [http://www.yoctoproject.org/docs/1.7.2/ref-manual/ref-manual.html#var-DEPENDS], RDEPENDS [http://www.yoctoproject.org/docs/1.7.2/ref-manual/ref-manual.html#var-RDEPENDS], RPROVIDES [http://www.yoctoproject.org/docs/1.7.2/ref-manual/ref-manual.html#var-RPROVIDES], RRECOMMENDS [http://www.yoctoproject.org/docs/1.7.2/ref-manual/ref-manual.html#var-RRECOMMENDS], PACKAGES [http://www.yoctoproject.org/docs/1.7.2/ref-manual/ref-manual.html#var-PACKAGES], and PACKAGES_DYNAMIC [http://www.yoctoproject.org/docs/1.7.2/ref-manual/ref-manual.html#var-PACKAGES_DYNAMIC] are automatically extended by the system. If you are extending any manual code in the recipe, you can use the ${MLPREFIX} variable to ensure those names are extended correctly. This automatic extension code resides in `multilib.bbclass`.

5.5.2.2. Using Multilib

After you have set up the recipes, you need to define the actual combination of multiple libraries you want to build. You accomplish this through your local.conf configuration file in the Build Directory [14]. An example configuration would be as follows:

```
MACHINE = "qemux86-64"
require conf/multilib.conf
MULTILIBS = "multilib:lib32"
DEFAULTTUNE_virtclass-multilib-lib32 = "x86"
IMAGE_INSTALL = "lib32-connman"
```

This example enables an additional library named lib32 alongside the normal target packages. When combining these "lib32" alternatives, the example uses "x86" for tuning. For information on this particular tuning, see meta/conf/machine/include/ia32/arch-ia32.inc.

The example then includes lib32-connman in all the images, which illustrates one method of including a multiple library dependency. You can use a normal image build to include this dependency, for example:

```
$ bitbake core-image-sato
```

You can also build Multilib packages specifically with a command like this:

```
$ bitbake lib32-connman
```

5.5.2.3. Additional Implementation Details

Different packaging systems have different levels of native Multilib support. For the RPM Package Management System, the following implementation details exist:

- A unique architecture is defined for the Multilib packages, along with creating a unique deploy folder under tmp/deploy/rpm in the Build Directory [14]. For example, consider lib32 in a qemux86-64 image. The possible architectures in the system are "all", "qemux86_64", "lib32_qemux86_64", and "lib32_x86".

- The ${MLPREFIX} variable is stripped from ${PN} during RPM packaging. The naming for a normal RPM package and a Multilib RPM package in a qemux86-64 system resolves to something similar to bash-4.1-r2.x86_64.rpm and bash-4.1.r2.lib32_x86.rpm, respectively.

- When installing a Multilib image, the RPM backend first installs the base image and then installs the Multilib libraries.

- The build system relies on RPM to resolve the identical files in the two (or more) Multilib packages.

For the IPK Package Management System, the following implementation details exist:

- The ${MLPREFIX} is not stripped from ${PN} during IPK packaging. The naming for a normal RPM package and a Multilib IPK package in a qemux86-64 system resolves to something like bash_4.1-r2.x86_64.ipk and lib32-bash_4.1-rw_x86.ipk, respectively.

- The IPK deploy folder is not modified with ${MLPREFIX} because packages with and without the Multilib feature can exist in the same folder due to the ${PN} differences.

- IPK defines a sanity check for Multilib installation using certain rules for file comparison, overridden, etc.

5.5.3. Installing Multiple Versions of the Same Library

Situations can exist where you need to install and use multiple versions of the same library on the same system at the same time. These situations almost always exist when a library API changes and you have multiple pieces of software that depend on the separate versions of the library. To accommodate these situations, you can install multiple versions of the same library in parallel on the same system.

The process is straightforward as long as the libraries use proper versioning. With properly versioned libraries, all you need to do to individually specify the libraries is create separate, appropriately named recipes where the PN [http://www.yoctoproject.org/docs/1.7.2/ref-manual/ref-manual.html#var-PN] part of the name includes a portion that differentiates each library version (e.g.the major part of the version number). Thus, instead of having a single recipe that loads one version of a library (e.g. clutter), you provide multiple recipes that result in different versions of the libraries you want. As an example, the following two recipes would allow the two separate versions of the clutter library to co-exist on the same system:

```
clutter-1.6_1.6.20.bb
clutter-1.8_1.8.4.bb
```

Additionally, if you have other recipes that depend on a given library, you need to use the DEPENDS [http://www.yoctoproject.org/docs/1.7.2/ref-manual/ref-manual.html#var-DEPENDS] variable to create the dependency. Continuing with the same example, if you want to have a recipe depend on the 1.8 version of the clutter library, use the following in your recipe:

```
DEPENDS = "clutter-1.8"
```

5.6. Creating Partitioned Images

Creating an image for a particular hardware target using the OpenEmbedded build system does not necessarily mean you can boot that image as is on your device. Physical devices accept and boot images in various ways depending on the specifics of the device. Usually, information about the hardware can tell you what image format the device requires. Should your device require multiple partitions on an SD card, flash, or an HDD, you can use the OpenEmbedded Image Creator, wic, to create the properly partitioned image.

The wic command generates partitioned images from existing OpenEmbedded build artifacts. Image generation is driven by partitioning commands contained in an Openembedded kickstart file (.wks) specified either directly on the command line or as one of a selection of canned .wks files as shown with the wic list images command in the "Using an Existing Kickstart File" section. When applied to a given set of build artifacts, the result is an image or set of images that can be directly written onto media and used on a particular system.

The wic command and the infrastructure it is based on is by definition incomplete. Its purpose is to allow the generation of customized images, and as such was designed to be completely extensible through a plugin interface. See the "Plugins" section for information on these plugins.

This section provides some background information on wic, describes what you need to have in place to run the tool, provides instruction on how to use wic, and provides several examples.

5.6.1. Background

This section provides some background on the wic utility. While none of this information is required to use wic, you might find it interesting.

- The name "wic" is derived from OpenEmbedded Image Creator (oeic). The "oe" diphthong in "oeic" was promoted to the letter "w", because "oeic" is both difficult to remember and pronounce.

- wic is loosely based on the Meego Image Creator (mic) framework. The wic implementation has been heavily modified to make direct use of OpenEmbedded build artifacts instead of package installation and configuration, which are already incorporated within the OpenEmbedded artifacts.

- wic is a completely independent standalone utility that initially provides easier-to-use and more flexible replacements for a couple bits of existing functionality in OE Core's boot-directdisk.bbclass and mkefidisk.sh scripts. The difference between wic and those examples is that with wic the functionality of those scripts is implemented by a general-purpose partitioning language, which is based on Redhat kickstart syntax.

5.6.2. Requirements

In order to use the `wic` utility with the OpenEmbedded Build system, your system needs to meet the following requirements:

• The Linux distribution on your development host must support the Yocto Project. See the "Supported Linux Distributions [http://www.yoctoproject.org/docs/1.7.2/ref-manual/ref-manual.html#detailed-supported-distros]" section in the Yocto Project Reference Manual for this list of distributions.

• The standard system utilities, such as `cp`, must be installed on your development host system.

• The GNU Parted [http://www.gnu.org/software/parted/] package must be installed on your development host system.

• You need to have the build artifacts already available, which typically means that you must have already created an image using the Openembedded build system (e.g. `core-image-minimal`). While it might seem redundant to generate an image in order to create an image using `wic`, the current version of `wic` requires the artifacts in the form generated by the build system.

• You must have sourced one of the build environment setup scripts (i.e. `oe-init-build-env` [http://www.yoctoproject.org/docs/1.7.2/ref-manual/ref-manual.html#structure-core-script] or `oe-init-build-env-memres` [http://www.yoctoproject.org/docs/1.7.2/ref-manual/ref-manual.html#structure-memres-core-script]) found in the Build Directory [14].

5.6.3. Getting Help

You can get general help for the `wic` by entering the `wic` command by itself or by entering the command with a help argument as follows:

```
$ wic -h
$ wic ##help
```

Currently, `wic` supports two commands: `create` and `list`. You can get help for these commands as follows:

```
$ wic help command
```

You can also get detailed help on a number of topics from the help system. The output of `wic ##help` displays a list of available help topics under a "Help topics" heading. You can have the help system display the help text for a given topic by prefacing the topic with `wic help`:

```
$ wic help help_topic
```

You can find out more about the images `wic` creates using the existing kickstart files with the following form of the command:

```
$ wic list image help
```

where image is either `directdisk` or `mkefidisk`.

5.6.4. Operational Modes

You can use `wic` in two different modes, depending on how much control you need for specifying the Openembedded build artifacts that are used for creating the image: Raw and Cooked:

• Raw Mode: You explicitly specify build artifacts through command-line arguments.

• Cooked Mode: The current `MACHINE` [http://www.yoctoproject.org/docs/1.7.2/ref-manual/ref-manual.html#var-MACHINE] setting and image name are used to automatically locate and provide the build artifacts.

Regardless of the mode you use, you need to have the build artifacts ready and available. Additionally, the environment must be set up using the oe-init-build-env [http://www.yoctoproject.org/docs/1.7.2/ref-manual/ref-manual.html#structure-core-script] or oe-init-build-env-memres [http://www.yoctoproject.org/docs/1.7.2/ref-manual/ref-manual.html#structure-memres-core-script] script found in the Build Directory [14].

5.6.4.1. Raw Mode

The general form of the 'wic' command in raw mode is:

```
$ wic create image_name.wks [options] [...]

    Where:

        image_name.wks
                        An OpenEmbedded kickstart file.  You can provide
                        your own custom file or use a file from a set of
                        existing files as described by further options.

        -o OUTDIR, ##outdir=OUTDIR
                        The name of a directory in which to create image.

        -i PROPERTIES_FILE, ##infile=PROPERTIES_FILE
                        The name of a file containing the values for image
                        properties as a JSON file.

        -e IMAGE_NAME, ##image-name=IMAGE_NAME
                        The name of the image from which to use the artifacts
                        (e.g. core-image-sato).

        -r ROOTFS_DIR, ##rootfs-dir=ROOTFS_DIR
                        The path to the /rootfs directory to use as the
                        .wks rootfs source.

        -b BOOTIMG_DIR, ##bootimg-dir=BOOTIMG_DIR
                        The path to the directory containing the boot artifacts
                        (e.g. /EFI or /syslinux) to use as the .wks bootimg
                        source.

        -k KERNEL_DIR, ##kernel-dir=KERNEL_DIR
                        The path to the directory containing the kernel to use
                        in the .wks boot image.

        -n NATIVE_SYSROOT, ##native-sysroot=NATIVE_SYSROOT
                        The path to the native sysroot containing the tools to use
                        to build the image.

        -s, ##skip-build-check
                        Skips the build check.

        -D, ##debug
                        Output debug information.
```

Note

You do not need root privileges to run wic. In fact, you should not run as root when using the utility.

5.6.4.2. Cooked Mode

The general form of the wic command using Cooked Mode is:

```
$ wic create kickstart_file -e image_name
```

Where:

kickstart_file

An OpenEmbedded kickstart file. You can provide your own custom file or supplied file.

image_name

Specifies the image built using the OpenEmbedded build system.

This form is the simplest and most user-friendly, as it does not require specifying all individual parameters. All you need to provide is your own .wks file or one provided with the release.

5.6.5. Using an Existing Kickstart File

If you do not want to create your own .wks file, you can use an existing file provided by the wic installation. Use the following command to list the available files:

```
$ wic list images
directdisk Create a 'pcbios' direct disk image
mkefidisk Create an EFI disk image
```

When you use an existing file, you do not have to use the .wks extension. Here is an example in Raw Mode that uses the directdisk file:

```
$ wic create directdisk -r rootfs_dir -b bootimg_dir \
    -k kernel_dir -n native_sysroot
```

Here are the actual partition language commands used in the mkefidisk.wks file to generate an image:

```
# short-description: Create an EFI disk image
# long-description: Creates a partitioned EFI disk image that the user
# can directly dd to boot media.

part /boot --source bootimg-efi --ondisk sda --label msdos --active --align 1024

part / --source rootfs --ondisk sda --fstype=ext3 --label platform --align 1024

part swap --ondisk sda --size 44 --label swap1 --fstype=swap

bootloader  --timeout=10  --append="rootwait rootfstype=ext3 console=ttyPCH0,115200 console=
```

5.6.6. Examples

This section provides several examples that show how to use the wic utility. All the examples assume the list of requirements in the "Requirements" section have been met. The examples assume the previously generated image is core-image-minimal.

5.6.6.1. Generate an Image using an Existing Kickstart File

This example runs in Cooked Mode and uses the mkefidisk kickstart file:

```
$ wic create mkefidisk -e core-image-minimal
Checking basic build environment...
```

```
Done.

Creating image(s)...

Info: The new image(s) can be found here:
 /var/tmp/wic/build/mkefidisk-201310230946-sda.direct

The following build artifacts were used to create the image(s):
 ROOTFS_DIR: /home/trz/yocto/yocto-image/build/tmp/work/minnow-poky-linux/core-image-minim
 BOOTIMG_DIR: /home/trz/yocto/yocto-image/build/tmp/work/minnow-poky-linux/core-image-mini
 KERNEL_DIR: /home/trz/yocto/yocto-image/build/tmp/sysroots/minnow/usr/src/kernel
 NATIVE_SYSROOT: /home/trz/yocto/yocto-image/build/tmp/sysroots/x86_64-linux


The image(s) were created using OE kickstart file:
 /home/trz/yocto/yocto-image/scripts/lib/image/canned-wks/mkefidisk.wks
```

This example shows the easiest way to create an image by running in Cooked Mode and using the -e option with an existing kickstart file. All that is necessary is to specify the image used to generate the artifacts. Your local.conf needs to have the MACHINE [http://www.yoctoproject.org/docs/1.7.2/ref-manual/ref-manual.html#var-MACHINE] variable set to the machine you are using, which is "minnow" in this example.

The output specifies the exact created as well as where it was created. The output also names the artifacts used and the exact .wks script that was used to generate the image.

Note
You should always verify the details provided in the output to make sure that the image was indeed created exactly as expected.

Continuing with the example, you can now directly dd the image to a USB stick, or whatever media for which you built your image, and boot the resulting media:

```
$ sudo dd if=/var/tmp/wic/build/mkefidisk-201310230946-sda.direct of=/dev/sdb
[sudo] password for trz:
182274+0 records in
182274+0 records out
93324288 bytes (93 MB) copied, 14.4777 s, 6.4 MB/s
[trz@empanada ~]$ sudo eject /dev/sdb
```

5.6.6.2. Using a Modified Kickstart File

Because wic image creation is driven by the kickstart file, it is easy to affect image creation by changing the parameters in the file. This next example demonstrates that through modification of the directdisk kickstart file.

As mentioned earlier, you can use the command wic list images to show the list of existing kickstart files. The directory in which these files reside is scripts/lib/image/canned-wks/ located in the Source Directory [16]. Because the available files reside in this directory, you can create and add your own custom files to the directory. Subsequent use of the wic list images command would then include your kickstart files.

In this example, the existing directdisk file already does most of what is needed. However, for the hardware in this example, the image will need to boot from sdb instead of sda, which is what the directdisk kickstart file uses.

The example begins by making a copy of the directdisk.wks file in the scripts/lib/image/canned-wks directory and then changing the lines that specify the target disk from which to boot.

```
$ cp /home/trz/yocto/yocto-image/scripts/lib/image/canned-wks/directdisk.wks \
     /home/trz/yocto/yocto-image/scripts/lib/image/canned-wks/directdisksdb.wks
```

Next, the example modifies the `directdisksdb.wks` file and changes all instances of "##ondisk sda" to "##ondisk sdb". The example changes the following two lines and leaves the remaining lines untouched:

```
part /boot ##source bootimg-pcbios ##ondisk sdb ##label boot ##active ##align 1024
part / ##source rootfs ##ondisk sdb ##fstype=ext3 ##label platform ##align 1024
```

Once the lines are changed, the example generates the `directdisksdb` image. The command points the process at the `core-image-minimal` artifacts for the Next Unit of Computing (nuc) MACHINE [http://www.yoctoproject.org/docs/1.7.2/ref-manual/ref-manual.html#var-MACHINE] the `local.conf`.

```
$ wic create directdisksdb -e core-image-minimal
Checking basic build environment...
Done.

Creating image(s)...

Info: The new image(s) can be found here:
 /var/tmp/wic/build/directdisksdb-201310231131-sdb.direct

The following build artifacts were used to create the image(s):
 ROOTFS_DIR: /home/trz/yocto/yocto-image/build/tmp/work/nuc-poky-linux/core-image-minimal/1.
 BOOTIMG_DIR: /home/trz/yocto/yocto-image/build/tmp/sysroots/nuc/usr/share
 KERNEL_DIR: /home/trz/yocto/yocto-image/build/tmp/sysroots/nuc/usr/src/kernel
 NATIVE_SYSROOT: /home/trz/yocto/yocto-image/build/tmp/sysroots/x86_64-linux


The image(s) were created using OE kickstart file:
 /home/trz/yocto/yocto-image/scripts/lib/image/canned-wks/directdisksdb.wks
```

Continuing with the example, you can now directly dd the image to a USB stick, or whatever media for which you built your image, and boot the resulting media:

```
$ sudo dd if=/var/tmp/wic/build/directdisksdb-201310231131-sdb.direct of=/dev/sdb
86018+0 records in
86018+0 records out
44041216 bytes (44 MB) copied, 13.0734 s, 3.4 MB/s
[trz@empanada tmp]$ sudo eject /dev/sdb
```

5.6.6.3. Creating an Image Based on **core-image-minimal** and **crownbay-noemgd**

This example creates an image based on core-image-minimal and a crownbay-noemgd MACHINE [http://www.yoctoproject.org/docs/1.7.2/ref-manual/ref-manual.html#var-MACHINE] that works right out of the box.

```
$ wic create directdisk -e core-image-minimal

Checking basic build environment...
Done.

Creating image(s)...

Info: The new image(s) can be found here:
 /var/tmp/wic/build/directdisk-201309252350-sda.direct

The following build artifacts were used to create the image(s):
```

```
ROOTFS_DIR: /home/trz/yocto/yocto-image/build/tmp/work/crownbay_noemgd-poky-linux/core-ima
BOOTIMG_DIR: /home/trz/yocto/yocto-image/build/tmp/sysroots/crownbay-noemgd/usr/share
KERNEL_DIR: /home/trz/yocto/yocto-image/build/tmp/sysroots/crownbay-noemgd/usr/src/kernel
NATIVE_SYSROOT: /home/trz/yocto/yocto-image/build/tmp/sysroots/crownbay-noemgd/usr/src/ker

The image(s) were created using OE kickstart file:
 /home/trz/yocto/yocto-image/scripts/lib/image/canned-wks/directdisk.wks
```

5.6.6.4. Using a Modified Kickstart File and Running in Raw Mode

This next example manually specifies each build artifact (runs in Raw Mode) and uses a modified kickstart file. The example also uses the -o option to cause wic to create the output somewhere other than the default /var/tmp/wic directory:

```
$ wic create ~/test.wks -o /home/trz/testwic ##rootfs-dir \
    /home/trz/yocto/yocto-image/build/tmp/work/crownbay_noemgd-poky-linux/core-image-mini
    ##bootimg-dir /home/trz/yocto/yocto-image/build/tmp/sysroots/crownbay-noemgd/usr/shar
    ##kernel-dir /home/trz/yocto/yocto-image/build/tmp/sysroots/crownbay-noemgd/usr/src/k
    ##native-sysroot /home/trz/yocto/yocto-image/build/tmp/sysroots/x86_64-linux

Creating image(s)...

Info: The new image(s) can be found here:
 /home/trz/testwic/build/test-201309260032-sda.direct

The following build artifacts were used to create the image(s):

ROOTFS_DIR: /home/trz/yocto/yocto-image/build/tmp/work/crownbay_noemgd-poky-linux/core-ima
BOOTIMG_DIR: /home/trz/yocto/yocto-image/build/tmp/sysroots/crownbay-noemgd/usr/share
KERNEL_DIR: /home/trz/yocto/yocto-image/build/tmp/sysroots/crownbay-noemgd/usr/src/kernel
NATIVE_SYSROOT: /home/trz/yocto/yocto-image/build/tmp/sysroots/crownbay-noemgd/usr/src/ke

The image(s) were created using OE kickstart file:
 /home/trz/test.wks
```

For this example, MACHINE [http://www.yoctoproject.org/docs/1.7.2/ref-manual/ref-manual.html#var-MACHINE] did not have to be specified in the local.conf file since the artifact is manually specified.

5.6.7. Plugins

Plugins allow wic functionality to be extended and specialized by users. This section documents the plugin interface, which is currently restricted to source plugins.

Source plugins provide a mechanism to customize various aspects of the image generation process in wic, mainly the contents of partitions. The plugins provide a mechanism for mapping values specified in .wks files using the ##source keyword to a particular plugin implementation that populates a corresponding partition.

A source plugin is created as a subclass of SourcePlugin. The plugin file containing it is added to scripts/lib/mic/plugins/source/ to make the plugin implementation available to the wic implementation. For more information, see scripts/lib/mic/pluginbase.py.

Source plugins can also be implemented and added by external layers. As such, any plugins found in a scripts/lib/mic/plugins/source/ directory in an external layer are also made available.

When the wic implementation needs to invoke a partition-specific implementation, it looks for the plugin that has the same name as the ##source parameter given to that partition. For example, if the partition is set up as follows:

```
part /boot ##source bootimg-pcbios   ...
```

The methods defined as class members of the plugin having the matching bootimg-pcbios.name class member are used.

To be more concrete, here is the plugin definition that matches a ##source bootimg-pcbios usage, along with an example method called by the wic implementation when it needs to invoke an implementation-specific partition-preparation function:

```
class BootimgPcbiosPlugin(SourcePlugin):
    name = 'bootimg-pcbios'

@classmethod
    def do_prepare_partition(self, part, ...)
```

If the subclass itself does not implement a function, a default version in a superclass is located and used, which is why all plugins must be derived from SourcePlugin.

The SourcePlugin class defines the following methods, which is the current set of methods that can be implemented or overridden by ##source plugins. Any methods not implemented by a SourcePlugin subclass inherit the implementations present in the SourcePlugin class. For more information, see the SourcePlugin source for details:

- do_prepare_partition(): Called to do the actual content population for a partition. In other words, the method prepares the final partition image that is incorporated into the disk image.

- do_configure_partition(): Called before do_prepare_partition(). This method is typically used to create custom configuration files for a partition (e.g. syslinux or grub configuration files).

- do_install_disk(): Called after all partitions have been prepared and assembled into a disk image. This method provides a hook to allow finalization of a disk image, (e.g. writing an MBR).

- do_stage_partition(): Special content-staging hook called before do_prepare_partition(). This method is normally empty.

  Typically, a partition just uses the passed-in parameters (e.g. the unmodified value of bootimg_dir). However, in some cases things might need to be more tailored. As an example, certain files might additionally need to be taken from bootimg_dir + /boot. This hook allows those files to be staged in a customized fashion.

Note
get_bitbake_var() allows you to access non-standard variables that you might want to use for this.

This scheme is extensible. Adding more hooks is a simple matter of adding more plugin methods to SourcePlugin and derived classes. The code that then needs to call the plugin methods uses plugin.get_source_plugin_methods() to find the method or methods needed by the call. Retrieval of those methods is accomplished by filling up a dict with keys containing the method names of interest. On success, these will be filled in with the actual methods. Please see the wic implementation for examples and details.

5.6.8. OpenEmbedded Kickstart (.wks) Reference

The current wic implementation supports only the basic kickstart partitioning commands: partition (or part for short) and bootloader.

Note
Future updates will implement more commands and options. If you use anything that is not specifically supported, results can be unpredictable.

The following is a list of the commands, their syntax, and meanings. The commands are based on the Fedora kickstart versions but with modifications to reflect wic capabilities. You can see the original documentation for those commands at the following links:

- http://fedoraproject.org/wiki/Anaconda/Kickstart#part_or_partition

• http://fedoraproject.org/wiki/Anaconda/Kickstart#bootloader

5.6.8.1. Command: part or partition

This command creates a partition on the system and uses the following syntax:

```
part mntpoint
```

The `mntpoint` is where the partition will be mounted and must be of one of the following forms:

• /path: For example, /, /usr, and /home

• swap: The partition will be used as swap space.

Following are the supported options:

• ##size: The minimum partition size in MBytes. Specify an integer value such as 500. Do not append the number with "MB". You do not need this option if you use ##source.

• ##source: This option is a `wic`-specific option that names the source of the data that populates the partition. The most common value for this option is "rootfs", but you can use any value that maps to a valid source plugin. For information on the source plugins, see the "Plugins" section.

   If you use ##source rootfs, `wic` creates a partition as large as needed and to fill it with the contents of the root filesystem pointed to by the -r command-line option or the equivalent rootfs derived from the -e command-line option. The filesystem type used to create the partition is driven by the value of the ##fstype option specified for the partition. See the entry on ##fstype that follows for more information.

   If you use ##source plugin-name, `wic` creates a partition as large as needed and fills it with the contents of the partition that is generated by the specified plugin name using the data pointed to by the -r command-line option or the equivalent rootfs derived from the -e command-line option. Exactly what those contents and filesystem type end up being are dependent on the given plugin implementation.

• ##ondisk or ##ondrive: Forces the partition to be created on a particular disk.

• ##fstype: Sets the file system type for the partition. Valid values are:

   • ext4

   • ext3

   • ext2

   • btrfs

   • squashfs

   • swap

• ##fsoptions: Specifies a free-form string of options to be used when mounting the filesystem. This string will be copied into the /etc/fstab file of the installed system and should be enclosed in quotes. If not specified, the default string is "defaults".

• ##label label: Specifies the label to give to the filesystem to be made on the partition. If the given label is already in use by another filesystem, a new label is created for the partition.

• ##active: Marks the partition as active.

• ##align (in KBytes): This option is a `wic`-specific option that says to start a partition on an x KBytes boundary.

5.6.8.2. Command: bootloader

This command specifies how the boot loader should be configured and supports the following options:

Note

Bootloader functionality and boot partitions are implemented by the various ##source plugins that implement bootloader functionality. The bootloader command essentially provides a means of modifying bootloader configuration.

- ##timeout: Specifies the number of seconds before the bootloader times out and boots the default option.

- ##append: Specifies kernel parameters. These parameters will be added to the syslinux APPEND or grub kernel command line.

5.7. Configuring the Kernel

Configuring the Yocto Project kernel consists of making sure the .config file has all the right information in it for the image you are building. You can use the menuconfig tool and configuration fragments to make sure your .config file is just how you need it. This section describes how to use menuconfig, create and use configuration fragments, and how to interactively modify your .config file to create the leanest kernel configuration file possible.

For more information on kernel configuration, see the "Changing the Configuration [http:// www.yoctoproject.org/docs/1.7.2/kernel-dev/kernel-dev.html#changing-the-configuration]" section in the Yocto Project Linux Kernel Development Manual.

5.7.1. Using **menuconfig**

The easiest way to define kernel configurations is to set them through the menuconfig tool. This tool provides an interactive method with which to set kernel configurations. For general information on menuconfig, see http://en.wikipedia.org/wiki/Menuconfig.

To use the menuconfig tool in the Yocto Project development environment, you must launch it using BitBake. Thus, the environment must be set up using the oe-init-build-env [http:// www.yoctoproject.org/docs/1.7.2/ref-manual/ref-manual.html#structure-core-script] or oe-init-build-env-memres [http://www.yoctoproject.org/docs/1.7.2/ref-manual/ref-manual.html#structure-memres-core-script] script found in the Build Directory [14]. The following commands run menuconfig assuming the Source Directory [16] top-level folder is ~/poky:

```
$ cd poky
$ source oe-init-build-env
$ bitbake linux-yocto -c menuconfig
```

Once menuconfig comes up, its standard interface allows you to interactively examine and configure all the kernel configuration parameters. After making your changes, simply exit the tool and save your changes to create an updated version of the .config configuration file.

Consider an example that configures the linux-yocto-3.14 kernel. The OpenEmbedded build system recognizes this kernel as linux-yocto. Thus, the following commands from the shell in which you previously sourced the environment initialization script cleans the shared state cache and the WORKDIR [http://www.yoctoproject.org/docs/1.7.2/ref-manual/ref-manual.html#var-WORKDIR] directory and then runs menuconfig:

```
$ bitbake linux-yocto -c menuconfig
```

Once menuconfig launches, use the interface to navigate through the selections to find the configuration settings in which you are interested. For example, consider the CONFIG_SMP configuration setting. You can find it at Processor Type and Features under the configuration selection Symmetric Multi-processing Support. After highlighting the selection, use the arrow keys to select or deselect the setting. When you are finished with all your selections, exit out and save them.

Saving the selections updates the .config configuration file. This is the file that the OpenEmbedded build system uses to configure the kernel during the build. You can find and examine this file in the

Build Directory in tmp/work/. The actual .config is located in the area where the specific kernel is built. For example, if you were building a Linux Yocto kernel based on the Linux 3.14 kernel and you were building a QEMU image targeted for x86 architecture, the .config file would be located here:

```
poky/build/tmp/work/qemux86-poky-linux/linux-yocto-3.14.11+git1+84f...
    ...656ed30-r1/linux-qemux86-standard-build
```

Note

The previous example directory is artificially split and many of the characters in the actual filename are omitted in order to make it more readable. Also, depending on the kernel you are using, the exact pathname for linux-yocto-3.14... might differ.

Within the .config file, you can see the kernel settings. For example, the following entry shows that symmetric multi-processor support is not set:

```
# CONFIG_SMP is not set
```

A good method to isolate changed configurations is to use a combination of the menuconfig tool and simple shell commands. Before changing configurations with menuconfig, copy the existing .config and rename it to something else, use menuconfig to make as many changes as you want and save them, then compare the renamed configuration file against the newly created file. You can use the resulting differences as your base to create configuration fragments to permanently save in your kernel layer.

Note

Be sure to make a copy of the .config and don't just rename it. The build system needs an existing .config from which to work.

5.7.2. Creating Configuration Fragments

Configuration fragments are simply kernel options that appear in a file placed where the OpenEmbedded build system can find and apply them. Syntactically, the configuration statement is identical to what would appear in the .config file, which is in the Build Directory [14] in tmp/work/ <arch>-poky-linux/linux-yocto-<release-specific-string>/linux-<arch>-<build-type>.

It is simple to create a configuration fragment. For example, issuing the following from the shell creates a configuration fragment file named my_smp.cfg that enables multi-processor support within the kernel:

```
$ echo "CONFIG_SMP=y" >> my_smp.cfg
```

Note

All configuration files must use the .cfg extension in order for the OpenEmbedded build system to recognize them as a configuration fragment.

Where do you put your configuration files? You can place these configuration files in the same area pointed to by SRC_URI [http://www.yoctoproject.org/docs/1.7.2/ref-manual/ref-manual.html#var-SRC_URI]. The OpenEmbedded build system will pick up the configuration and add it to the kernel's configuration. For example, suppose you had a set of configuration options in a file called myconfig.cfg. If you put that file inside a directory named linux-yocto that resides in the same directory as the kernel's append file and then add a SRC_URI statement such as the following to the kernel's append file, those configuration options will be picked up and applied when the kernel is built.

```
SRC_URI += "file://myconfig.cfg"
```

As mentioned earlier, you can group related configurations into multiple files and name them all in the SRC_URI statement as well. For example, you could group separate configurations specifically for Ethernet and graphics into their own files and add those by using a SRC_URI statement like the following in your append file:

```
SRC_URI += "file://myconfig.cfg \
        file://eth.cfg \
        file://gfx.cfg"
```

5.7.3. Fine-Tuning the Kernel Configuration File

You can make sure the .config file is as lean or efficient as possible by reading the output of the kernel configuration fragment audit, noting any issues, making changes to correct the issues, and then repeating.

As part of the kernel build process, the do_kernel_configcheck task runs. This task validates the kernel configuration by checking the final .config file against the input files. During the check, the task produces warning messages for the following issues:

• Requested options that did not make the final .config file.

• Configuration items that appear twice in the same configuration fragment.

• Configuration items tagged as "required" that were overridden.

• A board overrides a non-board specific option.

• Listed options not valid for the kernel being processed. In other words, the option does not appear anywhere.

Note
The do_kernel_configcheck task can also optionally report if an option is overridden during processing.

For each output warning, a message points to the file that contains a list of the options and a pointer to the config fragment that defines them. Collectively, the files are the key to streamlining the configuration.

To streamline the configuration, do the following:

1. Start with a full configuration that you know works - it builds and boots successfully. This configuration file will be your baseline.

2. Separately run the do_configme and do_kernel_configcheck tasks.

3. Take the resulting list of files from the do_kernel_configcheck task warnings and do the following:

   • Drop values that are redefined in the fragment but do not change the final .config file.

   • Analyze and potentially drop values from the .config file that override required configurations.

   • Analyze and potentially remove non-board specific options.

   • Remove repeated and invalid options.

4. After you have worked through the output of the kernel configuration audit, you can re-run the do_configme and do_kernel_configcheck tasks to see the results of your changes. If you have more issues, you can deal with them as described in the previous step.

Iteratively working through steps two through four eventually yields a minimal, streamlined configuration file. Once you have the best .config, you can build the Linux Yocto kernel.

5.8. Patching the Kernel

Patching the kernel involves changing or adding configurations to an existing kernel, changing or adding recipes to the kernel that are needed to support specific hardware features, or even altering the source code itself.

Note

You can use the yocto-kernel script found in the Source Directory [16] under scripts to manage kernel patches and configuration. See the "Managing kernel Patches and Config Items with yocto-kernel [http://www.yoctoproject.org/docs/1.7.2/bsp-guide/bsp-guide.html#managing-kernel-patches-and-config-items-with-yocto-kernel]" section in the Yocto Project Board Support Packages (BSP) Developer's Guide for more information.

This example creates a simple patch by adding some QEMU emulator console output at boot time through printk statements in the kernel's calibrate.c source code file. Applying the patch and booting the modified image causes the added messages to appear on the emulator's console.

The example assumes a clean build exists for the qemux86 machine in a Source Directory [16] named poky. Furthermore, the Build Directory [14] is build and is located in poky and the kernel is based on the Linux 3.4 kernel. For general information on how to configure the most efficient build, see the "Building an Image [http://www.yoctoproject.org/docs/1.7.2/yocto-project-qs/yocto-project-qs.html#building-image]" section in the Yocto Project Quick Start.

Also, for more information on patching the kernel, see the "Applying Patches [http://www.yoctoproject.org/docs/1.7.2/kernel-dev/kernel-dev.html#applying-patches]" section in the Yocto Project Linux Kernel Development Manual.

5.8.1. Create a Layer for your Changes

The first step is to create a layer so you can isolate your changes. Rather than use the yocto-layer script to create the layer, this example steps through the process by hand. If you want information on the script that creates a general layer, see the "Creating a General Layer Using the yocto-layer Script" section.

These two commands create a directory you can use for your layer:

```
$ cd ~/poky
$ mkdir meta-mylayer
```

Creating a directory that follows the Yocto Project layer naming conventions sets up the layer for your changes. The layer is where you place your configuration files, append files, and patch files. To learn more about creating a layer and filling it with the files you need, see the "Understanding and Creating Layers" section.

5.8.2. Finding the Kernel Source Code

Each time you build a kernel image, the kernel source code is fetched and unpacked into the following directory:

```
${S}/linux
```

See the "Finding the Temporary Source Code" section and the S [http://www.yoctoproject.org/docs/1.7.2/ref-manual/ref-manual.html#var-S] variable for more information about where source is kept during a build.

For this example, we are going to patch the init/calibrate.c file by adding some simple console printk statements that we can see when we boot the image using QEMU.

5.8.3. Creating the Patch

Two methods exist by which you can create the patch: Git workflow and Quilt workflow. For kernel patches, the Git workflow is more appropriate. This section assumes the Git workflow and shows the steps specific to this example.

1. Change the working directory: Change to where the kernel source code is before making your edits to the calibrate.c file:

```
$ cd ~/poky/build/tmp/work/qemux86-poky-linux/linux-yocto-${PV}-${PR}/linux
```

Because you are working in an established Git repository, you must be in this directory in order to commit your changes and create the patch file.

Note

The PV [http://www.yoctoproject.org/docs/1.7.2/ref-manual/ref-manual.html#var-PV] and PR [http://www.yoctoproject.org/docs/1.7.2/ref-manual/ref-manual.html#var-PR] variables represent the version and revision for the linux-yocto recipe. The PV variable includes the Git meta and machine hashes, which make the directory name longer than you might expect.

2. Edit the source file: Edit the init/calibrate.c file to have the following changes:

```
void calibrate_delay(void)
{
    unsigned long lpj;
    static bool printed;
    int this_cpu = smp_processor_id();

    printk("***********************************\n");
    printk("*                                 *\n");
    printk("*        HELLO YOCTO KERNEL        *\n");
    printk("*                                 *\n");
    printk("***********************************\n");

 if (per_cpu(cpu_loops_per_jiffy, this_cpu)) {
             .
             .
             .
```

3. Stage and commit your changes: These Git commands display the modified file, stage it, and then commit the file:

```
$ git status
$ git add init/calibrate.c
$ git commit -m "calibrate: Add printk example"
```

4. Generate the patch file: This Git command creates the a patch file named 0001-calibrate-Add-printk-example.patch in the current directory.

```
$ git format-patch -1
```

5.8.4. Set Up Your Layer for the Build

These steps get your layer set up for the build:

1. Create additional structure: Create the additional layer structure:

```
$ cd ~/poky/meta-mylayer
$ mkdir conf
$ mkdir recipes-kernel
$ mkdir recipes-kernel/linux
$ mkdir recipes-kernel/linux/linux-yocto
```

The conf directory holds your configuration files, while the recipes-kernel directory holds your append file and your patch file.

2. Create the layer configuration file: Move to the meta-mylayer/conf directory and create the layer.conf file as follows:

```
# We have a conf and classes directory, add to BBPATH
BBPATH .= ":${LAYERDIR}"

# We have recipes-* directories, add to BBFILES
BBFILES += "${LAYERDIR}/recipes-*/*/*.bb \
            ${LAYERDIR}/recipes-*/*/*.bbappend"

BBFILE_COLLECTIONS += "mylayer"
BBFILE_PATTERN_mylayer = "^${LAYERDIR}/"
BBFILE_PRIORITY_mylayer = "5"
```

Notice mylayer as part of the last three statements.

3. Create the kernel recipe append file: Move to the meta-mylayer/recipes-kernel/linux directory and create the linux-yocto_3.4.bbappend file as follows:

```
FILESEXTRAPATHS_prepend := "${THISDIR}/${PN}:"

SRC_URI += "file://0001-calibrate-Add-printk-example.patch"
```

The FILESEXTRAPATHS [http://www.yoctoproject.org/docs/1.7.2/ref-manual/ref-manual.html#var-FILESEXTRAPATHS] and SRC_URI [http://www.yoctoproject.org/docs/1.7.2/ref-manual.html#var-SRC_URI] statements enable the OpenEmbedded build system to find the patch file. For more information on using append files, see the "Using .bbappend Files" section.

4. Put the patch file in your layer: Move the 0001-calibrate-Add-printk-example.patch file to the meta-mylayer/recipes-kernel/linux/linux-yocto directory.

5.8.5. Set Up for the Build

Do the following to make sure the build parameters are set up for the example. Once you set up these build parameters, they do not have to change unless you change the target architecture of the machine you are building:

• Build for the correct target architecture: Your selected MACHINE [http://www.yoctoproject.org/docs/1.7.2/ref-manual/ref-manual.html#var-MACHINE] definition within the local.conf file in the Build Directory [14] specifies the target architecture used when building the Linux kernel. By default, MACHINE is set to qemux86, which specifies a 32-bit Intel® Architecture target machine suitable for the QEMU emulator.

• Identify your meta-mylayer layer: The BBLAYERS [http://www.yoctoproject.org/docs/1.7.2/ref-manual/ref-manual.html#var-BBLAYERS] variable in the bblayers.conf file found in the poky/build/conf directory needs to have the path to your local meta-mylayer layer. By default, the BBLAYERS variable contains paths to meta, meta-yocto, and meta-yocto-bsp in the poky Git repository. Add the path to your meta-mylayer location:

```
BBLAYERS ?= " \
  $HOME/poky/meta \
  $HOME/poky/meta-yocto \
  $HOME/poky/meta-yocto-bsp \
  $HOME/poky/meta-mylayer \
  "

BBLAYERS_NON_REMOVABLE ?= " \
  $HOME/poky/meta \
  $HOME/poky/meta-yocto \
  "
```

5.8.6. Build the Modified QEMU Kernel Image

The following steps build your modified kernel image:

1. Be sure your build environment is initialized: Your environment should be set up since you previously sourced the oe-init-build-env [http://www.yoctoproject.org/docs/1.7.2/ref-manual/ref-manual.html#structure-core-script] script. If it is not, source the script again from poky.

```
$ cd ~/poky
$ source oe-init-build-env
```

2. Clean up: Be sure to clean the shared state out by using BitBake to run from within the Build Directory the do_cleansstate [http://www.yoctoproject.org/docs/1.7.2/ref-manual/ref-manual.html#ref-tasks-cleansstate] task as follows:

```
$ bitbake -c cleansstate linux-yocto
```

Note

Never remove any files by hand from the tmp/deploy directory inside the Build Directory [14]. Always use the various BitBake clean tasks to clear out previous build artifacts. For information on the clean tasks, see the "do_clean [http://www.yoctoproject.org/docs/1.7.2/ref-manual/ref-manual.html#ref-tasks-clean]", "do_cleanall [http://www.yoctoproject.org/docs/1.7.2/ref-manual/ref-manual.html#ref-tasks-cleanall]", and "do_cleansstate [http://www.yoctoproject.org/docs/1.7.2/ref-manual/ref-manual.html#ref-tasks-cleansstate]" sections all in the Yocto Project Reference Manual.

3. Build the image: Next, build the kernel image using this command:

```
$ bitbake -k linux-yocto
```

5.8.7. Boot the Image and Verify Your Changes

These steps boot the image and allow you to see the changes

1. Boot the image: Boot the modified image in the QEMU emulator using this command:

```
$ runqemu qemux86
```

2. Verify the changes: Log into the machine using root with no password and then use the following shell command to scroll through the console's boot output.

```
# dmesg | less
```

You should see the results of your printk statements as part of the output.

5.9. Making Images More Secure

Security is of increasing concern for embedded devices. Consider the issues and problems discussed in just this sampling of work found across the Internet:

- "Security Risks of Embedded Systems [https://www.schneier.com/blog/archives/2014/01/security_risks_9.html]" by Bruce Schneier

- "Internet Census 2012 [http://internetcensus2012.bitbucket.org/paper.html]" by Carna Botnet

- "Security Issues for Embedded Devices [http://elinux.org/images/6/6f/Security-issues.pdf]" by Jake Edge

- "They ought to know better: Exploiting Security Gateways via their Web Interfaces [https://www.nccgroup.com/media/18475/exploiting_security_gateways_via_their_web_interfaces.pdf]" by Ben Williams

When securing your image is of concern, there are steps, tools, and variables that you can consider to help you reach the security goals you need for your particular device. Not all situations are identical when it comes to making an image secure. Consequently, this section provides some guidance and suggestions for consideration when you want to make your image more secure.

Note
Because the security requirements and risks are different for every type of device, this section cannot provide a complete reference on securing your custom OS. It is strongly recommended that you also consult other sources of information on embedded Linux system hardening and on security.

5.9.1. General Considerations

General considerations exist that help you create more secure images. You should consider the following suggestions to help make your device more secure:

- Scan additional code you are adding to the system (e.g. application code) by using static analysis tools. Look for buffer overflows and other potential security problems.

- Pay particular attention to the security for any web-based administration interface.

  Web interfaces typically need to perform administrative functions and tend to need to run with elevated privileges. Thus, the consequences resulting from the interface's security becoming compromised can be serious. Look for common web vulnerabilities such as cross-site-scripting (XSS), unvalidated inputs, and so forth.

  As with system passwords, the default credentials for accessing a web-based interface should not be the same across all devices. This is particularly true if the interface is enabled by default as it can be assumed that many end-users will not change the credentials.

- Ensure you can update the software on the device to mitigate vulnerabilities discovered in the future. This consideration especially applies when your device is network-enabled.

- Ensure you remove or disable debugging functionality before producing the final image. For information on how to do this, see the "Considerations Specific to the OpenEmbedded Build System" section.

- Ensure you have no network services listening that are not needed.

- Remove any software from the image that is not needed.

- Enable hardware support for secure boot functionality when your device supports this functionality.

5.9.2. Security Flags

The Yocto Project has security flags that you can enable that help make your build output more secure. The security flags are in the meta/conf/distro/include/security_flags.inc file in your Source Directory [16] (e.g. poky).

Note
Depending on the recipe, certain security flags are enabled and disabled by default.

Use the following line in your local.conf file or in your custom distribution configuration file to enable the security compiler and linker flags for your build:

```
require conf/distro/include/security_flags.inc
```

5.9.3. Considerations Specific to the OpenEmbedded Build System

You can take some steps that are specific to the OpenEmbedded build system to make your images more secure:

- Ensure "debug-tweaks" is not one of your selected IMAGE_FEATURES [http://www.yoctoproject.org/docs/1.7.2/ref-manual/ref-manual.html#var-IMAGE_FEATURES]. When creating a new project, the default is to provide you with an initial local.conf file that enables this feature using the EXTRA_IMAGE_FEATURES [http://www.yoctoproject.org/docs/1.7.2/ref-manual/ref-manual.html#var-EXTRA_IMAGE_FEATURES] variable with the line:

      EXTRA_IMAGE_FEATURES = "debug-tweaks"

  To disable that feature, simply comment out that line in your local.conf file, or make sure IMAGE_FEATURES does not contain "debug-tweaks" before producing your final image. Among other things, leaving this in place sets the root password as blank, which makes logging in for debugging or inspection easy during development but also means anyone can easily log in during production.

- It is possible to set a root password for the image and also to set passwords for any extra users you might add (e.g. administrative or service type users). When you set up passwords for multiple images or users, you should not duplicate passwords.

  To set up passwords, use the extrausers [http://www.yoctoproject.org/docs/1.7.2/ref-manual/ref-manual.html#ref-classes-extrausers] class, which is the preferred method. For an example on how to set up both root and user passwords, see the "extrausers.bbclass [http://www.yoctoproject.org/docs/1.7.2/ref-manual/ref-manual.html#ref-classes-extrausers]" section.

  ### Note
  When adding extra user accounts or setting a root password, be cautious about setting the same password on every device. If you do this, and the password you have set is exposed, then every device is now potentially compromised. If you need this access but want to ensure security, consider setting a different, random password for each device. Typically, you do this as a separate step after you deploy the image onto the device.

- Consider enabling a Mandatory Access Control (MAC) framework such as SMACK or SELinux and tuning it appropriately for your device's usage. You can find more information in the meta-selinux [http://git.yoctoproject.org/cgit/cgit.cgi/meta-selinux/] layer.

5.9.4. Tools for Hardening Your Image

The Yocto Project provides tools for making your image more secure. You can find these tools in the meta-security layer of the Yocto Project Source Repositories [http://git.yoctoproject.org/cgit/cgit.cgi].

5.10. Creating Your Own Distribution

When you build an image using the Yocto Project and do not alter any distribution Metadata [16], you are creating a Poky distribution. If you wish to gain more control over package alternative selections, compile-time options, and other low-level configurations, you can create your own distribution.

To create your own distribution, the basic steps consist of creating your own distribution layer, creating your own distribution configuration file, and then adding any needed code and Metadata to the layer. The following steps provide some more detail:

- Create a layer for your new distro: Create your distribution layer so that you can keep your Metadata and code for the distribution separate. It is strongly recommended that you create and use your own layer for configuration and code. Using your own layer as compared to just placing configurations in a local.conf configuration file makes it easier to reproduce the same build configuration when using multiple build machines. See the "Creating a General Layer Using the yocto-layer Script" section for information on how to quickly set up a layer.

- Create the distribution configuration file: The distribution configuration file needs to be created in the conf/distro directory of your layer. You need to name it using your distribution name (e.g. mydistro.conf).

Note
The DISTRO [http://www.yoctoproject.org/docs/1.7.2/ref-manual/ref-manual.html#var-DISTRO] variable in your local.conf file determines the name of your distribution.

You can split out parts of your configuration file into include files and then "require" them from within your distribution configuration file. Be sure to place the include files in the conf/distro/include directory of your layer. A common example usage of include files would be to separate out the selection of desired version and revisions for individual recipes.

Your configuration file needs to set the following required variables:

    DISTRO_NAME [http://www.yoctoproject.org/docs/1.7.2/ref-manual/ref-manual.html#var-DISTF
    DISTRO_VERSION [http://www.yoctoproject.org/docs/1.7.2/ref-manual/ref-manual.html#var-D}

These following variables are optional and you typically set them from the distribution configuration file:

    DISTRO_FEATURES [http://www.yoctoproject.org/docs/1.7.2/ref-manual/ref-manual.html#var-[
    DISTRO_EXTRA_RDEPENDS [http://www.yoctoproject.org/docs/1.7.2/ref-manual/ref-manual.htm}
    DISTRO_EXTRA_RRECOMMENDS [http://www.yoctoproject.org/docs/1.7.2/ref-manual/ref-manual.}
    TCLIBC [http://www.yoctoproject.org/docs/1.7.2/ref-manual/ref-manual.html#var-TCLIBC]

Tip
If you want to base your distribution configuration file on the very basic configuration from OE-Core, you can use conf/distro/defaultsetup.conf as a reference and just include variables that differ as compared to defaultsetup.conf. Alternatively, you can create a distribution configuration file from scratch using the defaultsetup.conf file or configuration files from other distributions such as Poky or Angstrom as references.

- Provide miscellaneous variables: Be sure to define any other variables for which you want to create a default or enforce as part of the distribution configuration. You can include nearly any variable from the local.conf file. The variables you use are not limited to the list in the previous bulleted item.

- Point to Your distribution configuration file: In your local.conf file in the Build Directory [14], set your DISTRO [http://www.yoctoproject.org/docs/1.7.2/ref-manual/ref-manual.html#var-DISTRO] variable to point to your distribution's configuration file. For example, if your distribution's configuration file is named mydistro.conf, then you point to it as follows:

    DISTRO = "mydistro"

- Add more to the layer if necessary: Use your layer to hold other information needed for the distribution:

  - Add recipes for installing distro-specific configuration files that are not already installed by another recipe. If you have distro-specific configuration files that are included by an existing recipe, you should add an append file (.bbappend) for those. For general information and recommendations on how to add recipes to your layer, see the "Creating Your Own Layer" and "Best Practices to Follow When Creating Layers" sections.

  - Add any image recipes that are specific to your distribution.

  - Add a psplash append file for a branded splash screen. For information on append files, see the "Using .bbappend Files" section.

  - Add any other append files to make custom changes that are specific to individual recipes.

5.11. Creating a Custom Template Configuration Directory

If you are producing your own customized version of the build system for use by other users, you might want to customize the message shown by the setup script or you might want to change the template configuration files (i.e. local.conf and bblayers.conf) that are created in a new build directory.

The OpenEmbedded build system uses the environment variable TEMPLATECONF to locate the directory from which it gathers configuration information that ultimately ends up in the Build Directory's [14] conf directory. By default, TEMPLATECONF is set as follows in the poky repository:

```
TEMPLATECONF=${TEMPLATECONF:-meta-yocto/conf}
```

This is the directory used by the build system to find templates from which to build some key configuration files. If you look at this directory, you will see the bblayers.conf.sample, local.conf.sample, and conf-notes.txt files. The build system uses these files to form the respective bblayers.conf file, local.conf file, and display the list of BitBake targets when running the setup script.

To override these default configuration files with configurations you want used within every new Build Directory, simply set the TEMPLATECONF variable to your directory. The TEMPLATECONF variable is set in the .templateconf file, which is in the top-level Source Directory [16] folder (e.g. poky). Edit the .templateconf so that it can locate your directory.

Best practices dictate that you should keep your template configuration directory in your custom distribution layer. For example, suppose you have a layer named meta-mylayer located in your home directory and you want your template configuration directory named myconf. Changing the .templateconf as follows causes the OpenEmbedded build system to look in your directory and base its configuration files on the *.sample configuration files it finds. The final configuration files (i.e. local.conf and bblayers.conf ultimately still end up in your Build Directory, but they are based on your *.sample files.

```
TEMPLATECONF=${TEMPLATECONF:-meta-mylayer/myconf}
```

Aside from the *.sample configuration files, the conf-notes.txt also resides in the default meta-yocto/conf directory. The scripts that set up the build environment (i.e. oe-init-build-env [http://www.yoctoproject.org/docs/1.7.2/ref-manual/ref-manual.html#structure-core-script] and oe-init-build-env-memres [http://www.yoctoproject.org/docs/1.7.2/ref-manual/ref-manual.html#structure-memres-core-script]) use this file to display BitBake targets as part of the script output. Customizing this conf-notes.txt file is a good way to make sure your list of custom targets appears as part of the script's output.

Here is the default list of targets displayed as a result of running either of the setup scripts:

```
You can now run 'bitbake <target>'

Common targets are:
    core-image-minimal
    core-image-sato
    meta-toolchain
    adt-installer
    meta-ide-support
```

Changing the listed common targets is as easy as editing your version of conf-notes.txt in your custom template configuration directory and making sure you have TEMPLATECONF set to your directory.

5.12. Building a Tiny System

Very small distributions have some significant advantages such as requiring less on-die or in-package memory (cheaper), better performance through efficient cache usage, lower power requirements due to less memory, faster boot times, and reduced development overhead. Some real-world examples where a very small distribution gives you distinct advantages are digital cameras, medical devices, and small headless systems.

This section presents information that shows you how you can trim your distribution to even smaller sizes than the poky-tiny distribution, which is around 5 Mbytes, that can be built out-of-the-box using the Yocto Project.

5.12.1. Overview

The following list presents the overall steps you need to consider and perform to create distributions with smaller root filesystems, achieve faster boot times, maintain your critical functionality, and avoid initial RAM disks:

* Determine your goals and guiding principles.

* Understand what contributes to your image size.

* Reduce the size of the root filesystem.

* Reduce the size of the kernel.

* Eliminate packaging requirements.

* Look for other ways to minimize size.

* Iterate on the process.

5.12.2. Goals and Guiding Principles

Before you can reach your destination, you need to know where you are going. Here is an example list that you can use as a guide when creating very small distributions:

* Determine how much space you need (e.g. a kernel that is 1 Mbyte or less and a root filesystem that is 3 Mbytes or less).

* Find the areas that are currently taking 90% of the space and concentrate on reducing those areas.

* Do not create any difficult "hacks" to achieve your goals.

* Leverage the device-specific options.

* Work in a separate layer so that you keep changes isolated. For information on how to create layers, see the "Understanding and Creating Layers" section.

5.12.3. Understand What Contributes to Your Image Size

It is easiest to have something to start with when creating your own distribution. You can use the Yocto Project out-of-the-box to create the poky-tiny distribution. Ultimately, you will want to make changes in your own distribution that are likely modeled after poky-tiny.

Note

To use poky-tiny in your build, set the DISTRO [http://www.yoctoproject.org/docs/1.7.2/ref-manual/ref-manual.html#var-DISTRO] variable in your local.conf file to "poky-tiny" as described in the "Creating Your Own Distribution" section.

Understanding some memory concepts will help you reduce the system size. Memory consists of static, dynamic, and temporary memory. Static memory is the TEXT (code), DATA (initialized data in the code), and BSS (uninitialized data) sections. Dynamic memory represents memory that is allocated at runtime: stacks, hash tables, and so forth. Temporary memory is recovered after the boot process. This memory consists of memory used for decompressing the kernel and for the __init__ functions.

To help you see where you currently are with kernel and root filesystem sizes, you can use two tools found in the Source Directory [16] in the `scripts/tiny/` directory:

- `ksize.py`: Reports component sizes for the kernel build objects.

- `dirsize.py`: Reports component sizes for the root filesystem.

This next tool and command help you organize configuration fragments and view file dependencies in a human-readable form:

- `merge_config.sh`: Helps you manage configuration files and fragments within the kernel. With this tool, you can merge individual configuration fragments together. The tool allows you to make overrides and warns you of any missing configuration options. The tool is ideal for allowing you to iterate on configurations, create minimal configurations, and create configuration files for different machines without having to duplicate your process.

  The `merge_config.sh` script is part of the Linux Yocto kernel Git repositories (i.e. linux-yocto-3.14, linux-yocto-3.10, linux-yocto-3.8, and so forth) in the `scripts/kconfig` directory.

  For more information on configuration fragments, see the "Generating Configuration Files [http://www.yoctoproject.org/docs/1.7.2/kernel-dev/kernel-dev.html#generating-configuration-files]" section of the Yocto Project Linux Kernel Development Manual and the "Creating Configuration Fragments" section, which is in this manual.

- `bitbake -u depexp -g bitbake_target`: Using the BitBake command with these options brings up a Dependency Explorer from which you can view file dependencies. Understanding these dependencies allows you to make informed decisions when cutting out various pieces of the kernel and root filesystem.

5.12.4. Trim the Root Filesystem

The root filesystem is made up of packages for booting, libraries, and applications. To change things, you can configure how the packaging happens, which changes the way you build them. You can also modify the filesystem itself or select a different filesystem.

First, find out what is hogging your root filesystem by running the `dirsize.py` script from your root directory:

```
$ cd root-directory-of-image
$ dirsize.py 100000 > dirsize-100k.log
$ cat dirsize-100k.log
```

You can apply a filter to the script to ignore files under a certain size. The previous example filters out any files below 100 Kbytes. The sizes reported by the tool are uncompressed, and thus will be smaller by a relatively constant factor in a compressed root filesystem. When you examine your log file, you can focus on areas of the root filesystem that take up large amounts of memory.

You need to be sure that what you eliminate does not cripple the functionality you need. One way to see how packages relate to each other is by using the Dependency Explorer UI with the BitBake command:

```
$ cd image-directory
$ bitbake -u depexp -g image
```

Use the interface to select potential packages you wish to eliminate and see their dependency relationships.

When deciding how to reduce the size, get rid of packages that result in minimal impact on the feature set. For example, you might not need a VGA display. Or, you might be able to get by with `devtmpfs` and mdev instead of udev.

Use your `local.conf` file to make changes. For example, to eliminate udev and `glib`, set the following in the local configuration file:

```
VIRTUAL-RUNTIME_dev_manager = ""
```

Finally, you should consider exactly the type of root filesystem you need to meet your needs while also reducing its size. For example, consider `cramfs`, `squashfs`, `ubifs`, ext2, or an `initramfs` using `initramfs`. Be aware that ext3 requires a 1 Mbyte journal. If you are okay with running read-only, you do not need this journal.

Note

After each round of elimination, you need to rebuild your system and then use the tools to see the effects of your reductions.

5.12.5. Trim the Kernel

The kernel is built by including policies for hardware-independent aspects. What subsystems do you enable? For what architecture are you building? Which drivers do you build by default?

Note

You can modify the kernel source if you want to help with boot time.

Run the `ksize.py` script from the top-level Linux build directory to get an idea of what is making up the kernel:

```
$ cd top-level-linux-build-directory
$ ksize.py > ksize.log
$ cat ksize.log
```

When you examine the log, you will see how much space is taken up with the built-in .o files for drivers, networking, core kernel files, filesystem, sound, and so forth. The sizes reported by the tool are uncompressed, and thus will be smaller by a relatively constant factor in a compressed kernel image. Look to reduce the areas that are large and taking up around the "90% rule."

To examine, or drill down, into any particular area, use the -d option with the script:

```
$ ksize.py -d > ksize.log
```

Using this option breaks out the individual file information for each area of the kernel (e.g. drivers, networking, and so forth).

Use your log file to see what you can eliminate from the kernel based on features you can let go. For example, if you are not going to need sound, you do not need any drivers that support sound.

After figuring out what to eliminate, you need to reconfigure the kernel to reflect those changes during the next build. You could run `menuconfig` and make all your changes at once. However, that makes it difficult to see the effects of your individual eliminations and also makes it difficult to replicate the changes for perhaps another target device. A better method is to start with no configurations using `allnoconfig`, create configuration fragments for individual changes, and then manage the fragments into a single configuration file using `merge_config.sh`. The tool makes it easy for you to iterate using the configuration change and build cycle.

Each time you make configuration changes, you need to rebuild the kernel and check to see what impact your changes had on the overall size.

5.12.6. Remove Package Management Requirements

Packaging requirements add size to the image. One way to reduce the size of the image is to remove all the packaging requirements from the image. This reduction includes both removing the package manager and its unique dependencies as well as removing the package management data itself.

To eliminate all the packaging requirements for an image, be sure that "package-management" is not part of your IMAGE_FEATURES [http://www.yoctoproject.org/docs/1.7.2/ref-manual/ref-manual.html#var-IMAGE_FEATURES] statement for the image. When you remove this feature, you are removing the package manager as well as its dependencies from the root filesystem.

5.12.7. Look for Other Ways to Minimize Size

Depending on your particular circumstances, other areas that you can trim likely exist. The key to finding these areas is through tools and methods described here combined with experimentation and iteration. Here are a couple of areas to experiment with:

- glibc: In general, follow this process:

  1. Remove glibc features from DISTRO_FEATURES [http://www.yoctoproject.org/docs/1.7.2/ref-manual/ref-manual.html#var-DISTRO_FEATURES] that you think you do not need.

  2. Build your distribution.

  3. If the build fails due to missing symbols in a package, determine if you can reconfigure the package to not need those features. For example, change the configuration to not support wide character support as is done for ncurses. Or, if support for those characters is needed, determine what glibc features provide the support and restore the configuration.

  4. Rebuild and repeat the process.

- busybox: For BusyBox, use a process similar as described for glibc. A difference is you will need to boot the resulting system to see if you are able to do everything you expect from the running system. You need to be sure to integrate configuration fragments into Busybox because BusyBox handles its own core features and then allows you to add configuration fragments on top.

5.12.8. Iterate on the Process

If you have not reached your goals on system size, you need to iterate on the process. The process is the same. Use the tools and see just what is taking up 90% of the root filesystem and the kernel. Decide what you can eliminate without limiting your device beyond what you need.

Depending on your system, a good place to look might be Busybox, which provides a stripped down version of Unix tools in a single, executable file. You might be able to drop virtual terminal services or perhaps ipv6.

5.13. Working with Packages

This section describes a few tasks that involve packages:

- Excluding packages from an image

- Incrementing a package revision number

- Handling a package name alias

- Handling optional module packaging

- Using Runtime Package Management

- Setting up and running package test (ptest)

5.13.1. Excluding Packages from an Image

You might find it necessary to prevent specific packages from being installed into an image. If so, you can use several variables to direct the build system to essentially ignore installing recommended packages or to not install a package at all.

The following list introduces variables you can use to prevent packages from being installed into your image. Each of these variables only works with IPK and RPM package types. Support for Debian packages does not exist. Also, you can use these variables from your local.conf file or attach them to a specific image recipe by using a recipe name override. For more detail on the variables, see the descriptions in the Yocto Project Reference Manual's glossary chapter.

- BAD_RECOMMENDATIONS [http://www.yoctoproject.org/docs/1.7.2/ref-manual/ref-manual.html#var-BAD_RECOMMENDATIONS]: Use this variable to specify "recommended-only" packages that you do not want installed.

- NO_RECOMMENDATIONS [http://www.yoctoproject.org/docs/1.7.2/ref-manual/ref-manual.html#var-NO_RECOMMENDATIONS]: Use this variable to prevent all "recommended-only" packages from being installed.

- PACKAGE_EXCLUDE [http://www.yoctoproject.org/docs/1.7.2/ref-manual/ref-manual.html#var-PACKAGE_EXCLUDE]: Use this variable to prevent specific packages from being installed regardless of whether they are "recommended-only" or not. You need to realize that the build process could fail with an error when you prevent the installation of a package whose presence is required by an installed package.

5.13.2. Incrementing a Package Revision Number

If a committed change results in changing the package output, then the value of the PR [http://www.yoctoproject.org/docs/1.7.2/ref-manual/ref-manual.html#var-PR] variable needs to be increased (or "bumped"). Increasing PR occurs one of two ways:

- Automatically using a Package Revision Service (PR Service).

- Manually incrementing the PR variable.

Given that one of the challenges any build system and its users face is how to maintain a package feed that is compatible with existing package manager applications such as RPM, APT, and OPKG, using an automated system is much preferred over a manual system. In either system, the main requirement is that version numbering increases in a linear fashion and that a number of version components exist that support that linear progression.

The following two sections provide information on the PR Service and on manual PR bumping.

5.13.2.1. Working With a PR Service

As mentioned, attempting to maintain revision numbers in the Metadata [http://www.yoctoproject.org/docs/1.7.2/dev-manual/dev-manual.html#metadata] is error prone, inaccurate, and causes problems for people submitting recipes. Conversely, the PR Service automatically generates increasing numbers, particularly the revision field, which removes the human element.

Note

For additional information on using a PR Service, you can see the PR Service [https://wiki.yoctoproject.org/wiki/PR_Service] wiki page.

The Yocto Project uses variables in order of decreasing priority to facilitate revision numbering (i.e. PE [http://www.yoctoproject.org/docs/1.7.2/ref-manual/ref-manual.html#var-PE], PV [http://www.yoctoproject.org/docs/1.7.2/ref-manual/ref-manual.html#var-PV], and PR [http://www.yoctoproject.org/docs/1.7.2/ref-manual/ref-manual.html#var-PR] for epoch, version, and revision, respectively). The values are highly dependent on the policies and procedures of a given distribution and package feed.

Because the OpenEmbedded build system uses "signatures [http://www.yoctoproject.org/docs/1.7.2/ref-manual/ref-manual.html#checksums]", which are unique to a given build, the build system knows when to rebuild packages. All the inputs into a given task are represented by a signature, which can trigger a rebuild when different. Thus, the build system itself does not rely on the PR numbers to trigger a rebuild. The signatures, however, can be used to generate PR values.

The PR Service works with both OEBasic and OEBasicHash generators. The value of PR bumps when the checksum changes and the different generator mechanisms change signatures under different circumstances.

As implemented, the build system includes values from the PR Service into the PR field as an addition using the form ".x" so r0 becomes r0.1, r0.2 and so forth. This scheme allows existing PR values to be used for whatever reasons, which include manual PR bumps, should it be necessary.

By default, the PR Service is not enabled or running. Thus, the packages generated are just "self consistent". The build system adds and removes packages and there are no guarantees about upgrade paths but images will be consistent and correct with the latest changes.

The simplest form for a PR Service is for it to exist for a single host development system that builds the package feed (building system). For this scenario, you can enable a local PR Service by setting PRSERV_HOST [http://www.yoctoproject.org/docs/1.7.2/ref-manual/ref-manual.html#var-PRSERV_HOST] in your local.conf file in the Build Directory [http://www.yoctoproject.org/docs/1.7.2/dev-manual/dev-manual.html#build-directory]:

```
PRSERV_HOST = "localhost:0"
```

Once the service is started, packages will automatically get increasing PR values and BitBake will take care of starting and stopping the server.

If you have a more complex setup where multiple host development systems work against a common, shared package feed, you have a single PR Service running and it is connected to each building system. For this scenario, you need to start the PR Service using the bitbake-prserv command:

```
bitbake-prserv ##host ip ##port port ##start
```

In addition to hand-starting the service, you need to update the local.conf file of each building system as described earlier so each system points to the server and port.

It is also recommended you use build history, which adds some sanity checks to package versions, in conjunction with the server that is running the PR Service. To enable build history, add the following to each building system's local.conf file:

```
# It is recommended to activate "buildhistory" for testing the PR service
INHERIT += "buildhistory"
BUILDHISTORY_COMMIT = "1"
```

For information on build history, see the "Maintaining Build Output Quality [http://www.yoctoproject.org/docs/1.7.2/ref-manual/ref-manual.html#maintaining-build-output-quality]" section in the Yocto Project Reference Manual.

Note

The OpenEmbedded build system does not maintain PR information as part of the shared state (sstate) packages. If you maintain an sstate feed, its expected that either all your building systems that contribute to the sstate feed use a shared PR Service, or you do not run a PR Service on any of your building systems. Having some systems use a PR Service while others do not leads to obvious problems.

For more information on shared state, see the "Shared State Cache [http://www.yoctoproject.org/docs/1.7.2/ref-manual/ref-manual.html#shared-state-cache]" section in the Yocto Project Reference Manual.

5.13.2.2. Manually Bumping PR

The alternative to setting up a PR Service is to manually bump the PR [http://www.yoctoproject.org/docs/1.7.2/ref-manual/ref-manual.html#var-PR] variable.

If a committed change results in changing the package output, then the value of the PR variable needs to be increased (or "bumped") as part of that commit. For new recipes you should add the PR variable and set its initial value equal to "r0", which is the default. Even though the default value is "r0", the practice of adding it to a new recipe makes it harder to forget to bump the variable when you make changes to the recipe in future.

If you are sharing a common .inc file with multiple recipes, you can also use the INC_PR [http://www.yoctoproject.org/docs/1.7.2/ref-manual/ref-manual.html#var-

INC_PR] variable to ensure that the recipes sharing the .inc file are rebuilt when the .inc file itself is changed. The .inc file must set INC_PR (initially to "r0"), and all recipes referring to it should set PR to "$(INC_PR).0" initially, incrementing the last number when the recipe is changed. If the .inc file is changed then its INC_PR should be incremented.

When upgrading the version of a package, assuming the PV [http://www.yoctoproject.org/docs/1.7.2/ref-manual/ref-manual.html#var-PV] changes, the PR variable should be reset to "r0" (or "$(INC_PR).0" if you are using INC_PR).

Usually, version increases occur only to packages. However, if for some reason PV changes but does not increase, you can increase the PE [http://www.yoctoproject.org/docs/1.7.2/ref-manual/ref-manual.html#var-PE] variable (Package Epoch). The PE variable defaults to "0".

Version numbering strives to follow the Debian Version Field Policy Guidelines [http://www.debian.org/doc/debian-policy/ch-controlfields.html]. These guidelines define how versions are compared and what "increasing" a version means.

5.13.3. Handling a Package Name Alias

Sometimes a package name you are using might exist under an alias or as a similarly named package in a different distribution. The OpenEmbedded build system implements a do_distro_check task that automatically connects to major distributions and checks for these situations. If the package exists under a different name in a different distribution, you get a distro_check mismatch. You can resolve this problem by defining a per-distro recipe name alias using the DISTRO_PN_ALIAS [http://www.yoctoproject.org/docs/1.7.2/ref-manual/ref-manual.html#var-DISTRO_PN_ALIAS] variable.

Following is an example that shows how you specify the DISTRO_PN_ALIAS variable:

```
DISTRO_PN_ALIAS_pn-PACKAGENAME = "distro1=package_name_alias1 \
                                  distro2=package_name_alias2 \
                                  distro3=package_name_alias3 \
                                  ..."
```

If you have more than one distribution alias, separate them with a space. Note that the build system currently automatically checks the Fedora, OpenSUSE, Debian, Ubuntu, and Mandriva distributions for source package recipes without having to specify them using the DISTRO_PN_ALIAS variable. For example, the following command generates a report that lists the Linux distributions that include the sources for each of the recipes.

```
$ bitbake world -f -c distro_check
```

The results are stored in the build/tmp/log/distro_check-${DATETIME}.results file found in the Source Directory [16].

5.13.4. Handling Optional Module Packaging

Many pieces of software split functionality into optional modules (or plug-ins) and the plug-ins that are built might depend on configuration options. To avoid having to duplicate the logic that determines what modules are available in your recipe or to avoid having to package each module by hand, the OpenEmbedded build system provides functionality to handle module packaging dynamically.

To handle optional module packaging, you need to do two things:

• Ensure the module packaging is actually done.

• Ensure that any dependencies on optional modules from other recipes are satisfied by your recipe.

5.13.4.1. Making Sure the Packaging is Done

To ensure the module packaging actually gets done, you use the do_split_packages function within the populate_packages Python function in your recipe. The do_split_packages function searches for a pattern of files or directories under a specified path and creates a package for each one it finds by appending to the PACKAGES [http://www.yoctoproject.org/docs/1.7.2/ref-manual/ref-manual.html#var-PACKAGES] variable and setting the appropriate values for FILES_packagename, RDEPENDS_packagename, DESCRIPTION_packagename, and so forth. Here is an example from the lighttpd recipe:

```
python populate_packages_prepend () {
    lighttpd_libdir = d.expand('${libdir}')
    do_split_packages(d, lighttpd_libdir, '^mod_(.*)\.so$',
                      'lighttpd-module-%s', 'Lighttpd module for %s',
                      extra_depends='')
}
```

The previous example specifies a number of things in the call to do_split_packages.

• A directory within the files installed by your recipe through do_install in which to search.

• A regular expression used to match module files in that directory. In the example, note the parentheses () that mark the part of the expression from which the module name should be derived.

• A pattern to use for the package names.

• A description for each package.

• An empty string for extra_depends, which disables the default dependency on the main lighttpd package. Thus, if a file in ${libdir} called mod_alias.so is found, a package called lighttpd-module-alias is created for it and the DESCRIPTION [http://www.yoctoproject.org/docs/1.7.2/ref-manual/ref-manual.html#var-DESCRIPTION] is set to "Lighttpd module for alias".

Often, packaging modules is as simple as the previous example. However, more advanced options exist that you can use within do_split_packages to modify its behavior. And, if you need to, you can add more logic by specifying a hook function that is called for each package. It is also perfectly acceptable to call do_split_packages multiple times if you have more than one set of modules to package.

For more examples that show how to use do_split_packages, see the connman.inc file in the meta/recipes-connectivity/connman/ directory of the poky source repository. You can also find examples in meta/classes/kernel.bbclass.

Following is a reference that shows do_split_packages mandatory and optional arguments:

```
Mandatory arguments

root
    The path in which to search
file_regex
    Regular expression to match searched files.
    Use parentheses () to mark the part of this
    expression that should be used to derive the
    module name (to be substituted where %s is
    used in other function arguments as noted below)
output_pattern
    Pattern to use for the package names. Must
    include %s.
description
    Description to set for each package. Must
    include %s.

Optional arguments

postinst
    Postinstall script to use for all packages
    (as a string)
recursive
    True to perform a recursive search - default
```

```
            False
hook
      A hook function to be called for every match.
      The function will be called with the following
      arguments (in the order listed):

      f
            Full path to the file/directory match
      pkg
            The package name
      file_regex
            As above
      output_pattern
            As above
      modulename
            The module name derived using file_regex

extra_depends
      Extra runtime dependencies (RDEPENDS) to be
      set for all packages. The default value of None
      causes a dependency on the main package
      (${PN}) - if you do not want this, pass empty
      string '' for this parameter.
aux_files_pattern
      Extra item(s) to be added to FILES for each
      package. Can be a single string item or a list
      of strings for multiple items. Must include %s.
postrm
      postrm script to use for all packages (as a
      string)
allow_dirs
      True to allow directories to be matched -
      default False
prepend
      If True, prepend created packages to PACKAGES
      instead of the default False which appends them
match_path
      match file_regex on the whole relative path to
      the root rather than just the file name
aux_files_pattern_verbatim
      Extra item(s) to be added to FILES for each
      package, using the actual derived module name
      rather than converting it to something legal
      for a package name. Can be a single string item
      or a list of strings for multiple items. Must
      include %s.
allow_links
      True to allow symlinks to be matched - default
      False
summary
      Summary to set for each package. Must include %s;
      defaults to description if not set.
```

5.13.4.2. Satisfying Dependencies

The second part for handling optional module packaging is to ensure that any dependencies on optional modules from other recipes are satisfied by your recipe. You can be sure these dependencies are satisfied by using the PACKAGES_DYNAMIC [http://www.yoctoproject.org/docs/1.7.2/ref-manual/ref-manual.html#var-PACKAGES_DYNAMIC] variable. Here is an example that continues with the lighttpd recipe shown earlier:

```
PACKAGES_DYNAMIC = "lighttpd-module-.*"
```

The name specified in the regular expression can of course be anything. In this example, it is lighttpd-module- and is specified as the prefix to ensure that any RDEPENDS [http://www.yoctoproject.org/docs/1.7.2/ref-manual/ref-manual.html#var-RDEPENDS] and RRECOMMENDS [http://www.yoctoproject.org/docs/1.7.2/ref-manual/ref-manual.html#var-RRECOMMENDS] on a package name starting with the prefix are satisfied during build time. If you are using do_split_packages as described in the previous section, the value you put in PACKAGES_DYNAMIC should correspond to the name pattern specified in the call to do_split_packages.

5.13.5. Using Runtime Package Management

During a build, BitBake always transforms a recipe into one or more packages. For example, BitBake takes the bash recipe and currently produces the bash-dbg, bash-staticdev, bash-dev, bash-doc, bash-locale, and bash packages. Not all generated packages are included in an image.

In several situations, you might need to update, add, remove, or query the packages on a target device at runtime (i.e. without having to generate a new image). Examples of such situations include:

• You want to provide in-the-field updates to deployed devices (e.g. security updates).

• You want to have a fast turn-around development cycle for one or more applications that run on your device.

• You want to temporarily install the "debug" packages of various applications on your device so that debugging can be greatly improved by allowing access to symbols and source debugging.

• You want to deploy a more minimal package selection of your device but allow in-the-field updates to add a larger selection for customization.

In all these situations, you have something similar to a more traditional Linux distribution in that in-field devices are able to receive pre-compiled packages from a server for installation or update. Being able to install these packages on a running, in-field device is what is termed "runtime package management".

In order to use runtime package management, you need a host/server machine that serves up the pre-compiled packages plus the required metadata. You also need package manipulation tools on the target. The build machine is a likely candidate to act as the server. However, that machine does not necessarily have to be the package server. The build machine could push its artifacts to another machine that acts as the server (e.g. Internet-facing).

A simple build that targets just one device produces more than one package database. In other words, the packages produced by a build are separated out into a couple of different package groupings based on criteria such as the target's CPU architecture, the target board, or the C library used on the target. For example, a build targeting the qemuarm device produces the following three package databases: all, armv5te, and qemuarm. If you wanted your qemuarm device to be aware of all the packages that were available to it, you would need to point it to each of these databases individually. In a similar way, a traditional Linux distribution usually is configured to be aware of a number of software repositories from which it retrieves packages.

Using runtime package management is completely optional and not required for a successful build or deployment in any way. But if you want to make use of runtime package management, you need to do a couple things above and beyond the basics. The remainder of this section describes what you need to do.

5.13.5.1. Build Considerations

This section describes build considerations that you need to be aware of in order to provide support for runtime package management.

When BitBake generates packages it needs to know what format or formats to use. In your configuration, you use the PACKAGE_CLASSES [http://www.yoctoproject.org/docs/1.7.2/ref-manual/ref-manual.html#var-PACKAGE_CLASSES] variable to specify the format.

Note
You can choose to have more than one format but you must provide at least one.

If you would like your image to start off with a basic package database of the packages in your current build as well as have the relevant tools available on the target for runtime package management, you can include "package-management" in the IMAGE_FEATURES [http://www.yoctoproject.org/docs/1.7.2/ref-manual/ref-manual.html#var-IMAGE_FEATURES] variable. Including "package-management" in this configuration variable ensures that when the image is assembled for your target, the image includes the currently-known package databases as well as the target-specific tools required for runtime package management to be performed on the target. However, this is not strictly necessary. You could start your image off without any databases but only include the required on-target package tool(s). As an example, you could include "opkg" in your IMAGE_INSTALL [http://www.yoctoproject.org/docs/1.7.2/ref-manual/ref-manual.html#var-IMAGE_INSTALL] variable if you are using the IPK package format. You can then initialize your target's package database(s) later once your image is up and running.

Whenever you perform any sort of build step that can potentially generate a package or modify an existing package, it is always a good idea to re-generate the package index with:

```
$ bitbake package-index
```

Realize that it is not sufficient to simply do the following:

```
$ bitbake some-package package-index
```

This is because BitBake does not properly schedule the package-index target fully after any other target has completed. Thus, be sure to run the package update step separately.

As described below in the "Using IPK" section, if you are using IPK as your package format, you can make use of the distro-feed-configs recipe provided by meta-oe in order to configure your target to use your IPK databases.

When your build is complete, your packages reside in the ${TMPDIR}/deploy/package-format directory. For example, if ${TMPDIR} is tmp and your selected package type is IPK, then your IPK packages are available in tmp/deploy/ipk.

5.13.5.2. Host or Server Machine Setup

Typically, packages are served from a server using HTTP. However, other protocols are possible. If you want to use HTTP, then setup and configure a web server, such as Apache 2 or lighttpd, on the machine serving the packages.

As previously mentioned, the build machine can act as the package server. In the following sections that describe server machine setups, the build machine is assumed to also be the server.

5.13.5.2.1. Serving Packages via Apache 2

This example assumes you are using the Apache 2 server:

1. Add the directory to your Apache configuration, which you can find at /etc/httpd/conf/httpd.conf. Use commands similar to these on the development system. These example commands assume a top-level Source Directory [16] named poky in your home directory. The example also assumes an RPM package type. If you are using a different package type, such as IPK, use "ipk" in the pathnames:

```
<VirtualHost *:80>
    ....
    Alias /rpm ~/poky/build/tmp/deploy/rpm
    <Directory "~/poky/build/tmp/deploy/rpm">
      Options +Indexes
    </Directory>
</VirtualHost>
```

2. Reload the Apache configuration as described in this step. For all commands, be sure you have root privileges.

If your development system is using Fedora or CentOS, use the following:

```
# service httpd reload
```

For Ubuntu and Debian, use the following:

```
# /etc/init.d/apache2 reload
```

For OpenSUSE, use the following:

```
# /etc/init.d/apache2 reload
```

3. If you are using Security-Enhanced Linux (SELinux), you need to label the files as being accessible through Apache. Use the following command from the development host. This example assumes RPM package types:

```
# chcon -R -h -t httpd_sys_content_t tmp/deploy/rpm
```

5.13.5.2.2. Serving Packages via lighttpd

If you are using lighttpd, all you need to do is to provide a link from your ${TMPDIR}/deploy/package-format directory to lighttpd's document-root. You can determine the specifics of your lighttpd installation by looking through its configuration file, which is usually found at: /etc/lighttpd/lighttpd.conf.

For example, if you are using IPK, lighttpd's document-root is set to /var/www/lighttpd, and you had packages for a target named "BOARD", then you might create a link from your build location to lighttpd's document-root as follows:

```
# ln -s $(PWD)/tmp/deploy/ipk /var/www/lighttpd/BOARD-dir
```

At this point, you need to start the lighttpd server. The method used to start the server varies by distribution. However, one basic method that starts it by hand is:

```
# lighttpd -f /etc/lighttpd/lighttpd.conf
```

5.13.5.3. Target Setup

Setting up the target differs depending on the package management system. This section provides information for RPM and IPK.

5.13.5.3.1. Using RPM

The application for performing runtime package management of RPM packages on the target is called smart.

On the target machine, you need to inform smart of every package database you want to use. As an example, suppose your target device can use the following three package databases from a server named server.name: all, i586, and qemux86. Given this example, issue the following commands on the target:

```
# smart channel ##add all type=rpm-md baseurl=http://server.name/rpm/all
# smart channel ##add i585 type=rpm-md baseurl=http://server.name/rpm/i586
# smart channel ##add qemux86 type=rpm-md baseurl=http://server.name/rpm/qemux86
```

Also from the target machine, fetch the repository information using this command:

```
# smart update
```

You can now use the `smart query` and `smart install` commands to find and install packages from the repositories.

5.13.5.3.2. Using IPK

The application for performing runtime package management of IPK packages on the target is called opkg.

In order to inform opkg of the package databases you want to use, simply create one or more `*.conf` files in the `/etc/opkg` directory on the target. The opkg application uses them to find its available package databases. As an example, suppose you configured your HTTP server on your machine named `www.mysite.com` to serve files from a `BOARD-dir` directory under its document-root. In this case, you might create a configuration file on the target called `/etc/opkg/base-feeds.conf` that contains:

```
src/gz all http://www.mysite.com/BOARD-dir/all
src/gz armv7a http://www.mysite.com/BOARD-dir/armv7a
src/gz beaglebone http://www.mysite.com/BOARD-dir/beaglebone
```

As a way of making it easier to generate and make these IPK configuration files available on your target, simply define FEED_DEPLOYDIR_BASE_URI [http://www.yoctoproject.org/docs/1.7.2/ref-manual/ref-manual.html#var-FEED_DEPLOYDIR_BASE_URI] to point to your server and the location within the document-root which contains the databases. For example: if you are serving your packages over HTTP, your server's IP address is 192.168.7.1, and your databases are located in a directory called BOARD-dir underneath your HTTP server's document-root, you need to set FEED_DEPLOYDIR_BASE_URI to `http://192.168.7.1/BOARD-dir` and a set of configuration files will be generated for you in your target to work with this feed.

On the target machine, fetch (or refresh) the repository information using this command:

```
# opkg update
```

You can now use the `opkg list` and `opkg install` commands to find and install packages from the repositories.

5.13.6. Testing Packages With ptest

A Package Test (ptest) runs tests against packages built by the OpenEmbedded build system on the target machine. A ptest contains at least two items: the actual test, and a shell script (run-ptest) that starts the test. The shell script that starts the test must not contain the actual test - the script only starts the test. On the other hand, the test can be anything from a simple shell script that runs a binary and checks the output to an elaborate system of test binaries and data files.

The test generates output in the format used by Automake:

```
result: testname
```

where the result can be PASS, FAIL, or SKIP, and the testname can be any identifying string.

For a list of Yocto Project recipes that are already enabled with ptest, see the Ptest [https://wiki.yoctoproject.org/wiki/Ptest] wiki page.

Note
A recipe is "ptest-enabled" if it inherits the ptest [http://www.yoctoproject.org/docs/1.7.2/ref-manual/ref-manual.html#ref-classes-ptest] class.

5.13.6.1. Adding ptest to Your Build

To add package testing to your build, add the DISTRO_FEATURES [http://www.yoctoproject.org/docs/1.7.2/ref-manual/ref-manual.html#var-DISTRO_FEATURES] and EXTRA_IMAGE_FEATURES [http://www.yoctoproject.org/docs/1.7.2/ref-manual/ref-manual.html#var-EXTRA_IMAGE_FEATURES] variables to your local.conf file, which is found in the Build Directory [14]:

```
DISTRO_FEATURES_append = " ptest"
EXTRA_IMAGE_FEATURES += "ptest-pkgs"
```

Once your build is complete, the ptest files are installed into the /usr/lib/package/ptest directory within the image, where package is the name of the package.

5.13.6.2. Running ptest

The ptest-runner package installs a shell script that loops through all installed ptest test suites and runs them in sequence. Consequently, you might want to add this package to your image.

5.13.6.3. Getting Your Package Ready

In order to enable a recipe to run installed ptests on target hardware, you need to prepare the recipes that build the packages you want to test. Here is what you have to do for each recipe:

- Be sure the recipe inherits the ptest [http://www.yoctoproject.org/docs/1.7.2/ref-manual/ref-manual.html#ref-classes-ptest] class: Include the following line in each recipe:

```
inherit ptest
```

- Create run-ptest: This script starts your test. Locate the script where you will refer to it using SRC_URI [http://www.yoctoproject.org/docs/1.7.2/ref-manual/ref-manual.html#var-SRC_URI]. Here is an example that starts a test for dbus:

```
#!/bin/sh
cd test
make -k runtest-TESTS
```

- Ensure dependencies are met: If the test adds build or runtime dependencies that normally do not exist for the package (such as requiring "make" to run the test suite), use the DEPENDS [http://www.yoctoproject.org/docs/1.7.2/ref-manual/ref-manual.html#var-DEPENDS] and RDEPENDS [http://www.yoctoproject.org/docs/1.7.2/ref-manual/ref-manual.html#var-RDEPENDS] variables in your recipe in order for the package to meet the dependencies. Here is an example where the package has a runtime dependency on "make":

```
RDEPENDS_${PN}-ptest += "make"
```

- Add a function to build the test suite: Not many packages support cross-compilation of their test suites. Consequently, you usually need to add a cross-compilation function to the package.

  Many packages based on Automake compile and run the test suite by using a single command such as make check. However, the native make check builds and runs on the same computer, while cross-compiling requires that the package is built on the host but executed on the target. The built version of Automake that ships with the Yocto Project includes a patch that separates building and execution. Consequently, packages that use the unaltered, patched version of make check automatically cross-compiles.

  Regardless, you still must add a do_compile_ptest function to build the test suite. Add a function similar to the following to your recipe:

```
do_compile_ptest() {
    oe_runmake buildtest-TESTS
}
```

- Ensure special configurations are set: If the package requires special configurations prior to compiling the test code, you must insert a do_configure_ptest function into the recipe.

- Install the test suite: The ptest class automatically copies the file run-ptest to the target and then runs make install-ptest to run the tests. If this is not enough, you need to create a do_install_ptest function and make sure it gets called after the "make install-ptest" completes.

5.14. Working with Source Files

The OpenEmbedded build system works with source files located through the SRC_URI [http://www.yoctoproject.org/docs/1.7.2/ref-manual/ref-manual.html#var-SRC_URI] variable. When you build something using BitBake, a big part of the operation is locating and downloading all the source tarballs. For images, downloading all the source for various packages can take a significant amount of time.

This section presents information for working with source files that can lead to more efficient use of resources and time.

5.14.1. Setting up Effective Mirrors

As mentioned, a good deal that goes into a Yocto Project build is simply downloading all of the source tarballs. Maybe you have been working with another build system (OpenEmbedded or Angstrom) for which you have built up a sizable directory of source tarballs. Or, perhaps someone else has such a directory for which you have read access. If so, you can save time by adding statements to your configuration file so that the build process checks local directories first for existing tarballs before checking the Internet.

Here is an efficient way to set it up in your local.conf file:

```
SOURCE_MIRROR_URL ?= "file:///home/you/your-download-dir/"
INHERIT += "own-mirrors"
BB_GENERATE_MIRROR_TARBALLS = "1"
# BB_NO_NETWORK = "1"
```

In the previous example, the BB_GENERATE_MIRROR_TARBALLS [http://www.yoctoproject.org/docs/1.7.2/ref-manual/ref-manual.html#var-BB_GENERATE_MIRROR_TARBALLS] variable causes the OpenEmbedded build system to generate tarballs of the Git repositories and store them in the DL_DIR [http://www.yoctoproject.org/docs/1.7.2/ref-manual/ref-manual.html#var-DL_DIR] directory. Due to performance reasons, generating and storing these tarballs is not the build system's default behavior.

You can also use the PREMIRRORS [http://www.yoctoproject.org/docs/1.7.2/ref-manual/ref-manual.html#var-PREMIRRORS] variable. For an example, see the variable's glossary entry in the Yocto Project Reference Manual.

5.14.2. Getting Source Files and Suppressing the Build

Another technique you can use to ready yourself for a successive string of build operations, is to pre-fetch all the source files without actually starting a build. This technique lets you work through any download issues and ultimately gathers all the source files into your download directory build/downloads [http://www.yoctoproject.org/docs/1.7.2/ref-manual/ref-manual.html#structure-build-downloads], which is located with DL_DIR [http://www.yoctoproject.org/docs/1.7.2/ref-manual/ref-manual.html#var-DL_DIR].

Use the following BitBake command form to fetch all the necessary sources without starting the build:

```
$ bitbake -c fetchall target
```

This variation of the BitBake command guarantees that you have all the sources for that BitBake target should you disconnect from the Internet and want to do the build later offline.

5.15. Building Software from an External Source

By default, the OpenEmbedded build system uses the Build Directory [14] when building source code. The build process involves fetching the source files, unpacking them, and then patching them if necessary before the build takes place.

Situations exist where you might want to build software from source files that are external to and thus outside of the OpenEmbedded build system. For example, suppose you have a project that includes a new BSP with a heavily customized kernel. And, you want to minimize exposing the build system to the development team so that they can focus on their project and maintain everyone's workflow as much as possible. In this case, you want a kernel source directory on the development machine where the development occurs. You want the recipe's SRC_URI [http://www.yoctoproject.org/docs/1.7.2/ref-manual/ref-manual.html#var-SRC_URI] variable to point to the external directory and use it as is, not copy it.

To build from software that comes from an external source, all you need to do is inherit the externalsrc [http://www.yoctoproject.org/docs/1.7.2/ref-manual/ref-manual.html#ref-classes-externalsrc] class and then set the EXTERNALSRC [http://www.yoctoproject.org/docs/1.7.2/ref-manual/ref-manual.html#var-EXTERNALSRC] variable to point to your external source code. Here are the statements to put in your local.conf file:

```
INHERIT += "externalsrc"
EXTERNALSRC_pn-myrecipe = "path-to-your-source-tree"
```

This next example shows how to accomplish the same thing by setting EXTERNALSRC in the recipe itself or in the recipe's append file:

```
EXTERNALSRC = "path"
EXTERNALSRC_BUILD = "path"
```

Note

In order for these settings to take effect, you must globally or locally inherit the externalsrc [http://www.yoctoproject.org/docs/1.7.2/ref-manual/ref-manual.html#ref-classes-externalsrc] class.

By default, externalsrc.bbclass builds the source code in a directory separate from the external source directory as specified by EXTERNALSRC [http://www.yoctoproject.org/docs/1.7.2/ref-manual/ref-manual.html#var-EXTERNALSRC]. If you need to have the source built in the same directory in which it resides, or some other nominated directory, you can set EXTERNALSRC_BUILD [http://www.yoctoproject.org/docs/1.7.2/ref-manual/ref-manual.html#var-EXTERNALSRC_BUILD] to point to that directory:

```
EXTERNALSRC_BUILD_pn-myrecipe = "path-to-your-source-tree"
```

5.16. Selecting an Initialization Manager

By default, the Yocto Project uses SysVinit as the initialization manager. However, support also exists for systemd, which is a full replacement for init with parallel starting of services, reduced shell overhead and other features that are used by many distributions.

If you want to use SysVinit, you do not have to do anything. But, if you want to use systemd, you must take some steps as described in the following sections.

5.16.1. Using systemd Exclusively

Set the these variables in your distribution configuration file as follows:

```
DISTRO_FEATURES_append = " systemd"
VIRTUAL-RUNTIME_init_manager = "systemd"
```

You can also prevent the SysVinit distribution feature from being automatically enabled as follows:

```
DISTRO_FEATURES_BACKFILL_CONSIDERED = "sysvinit"
```

Doing so removes any redundant SysVinit scripts.

To remove initscripts from your image altogether, set this variable also:

```
VIRTUAL-RUNTIME_initscripts = ""
```

For information on the backfill variable, see DISTRO_FEATURES_BACKFILL_CONSIDERED [http://www.yoctoproject.org/docs/1.7.2/ref-manual/ref-manual.html#var-DISTRO_FEATURES_BACKFILL_CONSIDERED].

5.16.2. Using systemd for the Main Image and Using SysVinit for the Rescue Image

Set these variables in your distribution configuration file as follows:

```
DISTRO_FEATURES_append = " systemd"
VIRTUAL-RUNTIME_init_manager = "systemd"
```

Doing so causes your main image to use the packagegroup-core-boot.bb recipe and systemd. The rescue/minimal image cannot use this package group. However, it can install SysVinit and the appropriate packages will have support for both systemd and SysVinit.

5.17. Using an External SCM

If you're working on a recipe that pulls from an external Source Code Manager (SCM), it is possible to have the OpenEmbedded build system notice new recipe changes added to the SCM and then build the resulting packages that depend on the new recipes by using the latest versions. This only works for SCMs from which it is possible to get a sensible revision number for changes. Currently, you can do this with Apache Subversion (SVN), Git, and Bazaar (BZR) repositories.

To enable this behavior, the PV [http://www.yoctoproject.org/docs/1.7.2/ref-manual/ref-manual.html#var-PV] of the recipe needs to reference SRCPV [http://www.yoctoproject.org/docs/1.7.2/ref-manual/ref-manual.html#var-SRCPV]. Here is an example:

```
PV = "1.2.3+git${SRCPV}
```

Then, you can add the following to your local.conf:

```
SRCREV_pn-PN = "${AUTOREV}"
```

PN [http://www.yoctoproject.org/docs/1.7.2/ref-manual/ref-manual.html#var-PN] is the name of the recipe for which you want to enable automatic source revision updating.

If you do not want to update your local configuration file, you can add the following directly to the recipe to finish enabling the feature:

```
SRCREV = "${AUTOREV}"
```

The Yocto Project provides a distribution named poky-bleeding, whose configuration file contains the line:

```
require conf/distro/include/poky-floating-revisions.inc
```

This line pulls in the listed include file that contains numerous lines of exactly that form:

```
SRCREV_pn-gconf-dbus ?= "${AUTOREV}"
SRCREV_pn-matchbox-common ?= "${AUTOREV}"
SRCREV_pn-matchbox-config-gtk ?= "${AUTOREV}"
SRCREV_pn-matchbox-desktop ?= "${AUTOREV}"
SRCREV_pn-matchbox-keyboard ?= "${AUTOREV}"
SRCREV_pn-matchbox-panel ?= "${AUTOREV}"
SRCREV_pn-matchbox-panel-2 ?= "${AUTOREV}"
SRCREV_pn-matchbox-themes-extra ?= "${AUTOREV}"
SRCREV_pn-matchbox-terminal ?= "${AUTOREV}"
SRCREV_pn-matchbox-wm ?= "${AUTOREV}"
SRCREV_pn-matchbox-wm-2 ?= "${AUTOREV}"
SRCREV_pn-settings-daemon ?= "${AUTOREV}"
SRCREV_pn-screenshot ?= "${AUTOREV}"
SRCREV_pn-libfakekey ?= "${AUTOREV}"
SRCREV_pn-oprofileui ?= "${AUTOREV}"
            .
            .
            .
```

These lines allow you to experiment with building a distribution that tracks the latest development source for numerous packages.

Caution

The poky-bleeding distribution is not tested on a regular basis. Keep this in mind if you use it.

5.18. Creating a Read-Only Root Filesystem

Suppose, for security reasons, you need to disable your target device's root filesystem's write permissions (i.e. you need a read-only root filesystem). Or, perhaps you are running the device's operating system from a read-only storage device. For either case, you can customize your image for that behavior.

Note

Supporting a read-only root filesystem requires that the system and applications do not try to write to the root filesystem. You must configure all parts of the target system to write elsewhere, or to gracefully fail in the event of attempting to write to the root filesystem.

5.18.1. Creating the Root Filesystem

To create the read-only root filesystem, simply add the "read-only-rootfs" feature to your image. Using either of the following statements in your image recipe or from within the local.conf file found in the Build Directory [14] causes the build system to create a read-only root filesystem:

```
IMAGE_FEATURES = "read-only-rootfs"
```

or

```
EXTRA_IMAGE_FEATURES += "read-only-rootfs"
```

For more information on how to use these variables, see the "Customizing Images Using Custom IMAGE_FEATURES and EXTRA_IMAGE_FEATURES" section. For information on the variables, see IMAGE_FEATURES [http://www.yoctoproject.org/docs/1.7.2/ref-manual/ref-manual.html#var-IMAGE_FEATURES] and EXTRA_IMAGE_FEATURES [http://www.yoctoproject.org/docs/1.7.2/ref-manual/ref-manual.html#var-EXTRA_IMAGE_FEATURES].

5.18.2. Post-Installation Scripts

It is very important that you make sure all post-Installation (pkg_postinst) scripts for packages that are installed into the image can be run at the time when the root filesystem is created during the build on the host system. These scripts cannot attempt to run during first-boot on the target device. With the "read-only-rootfs" feature enabled, the build system checks during root filesystem creation to make sure all post-installation scripts succeed. If any of these scripts still need to be run after the root filesystem is created, the build immediately fails. These build-time checks ensure that the build fails rather than the target device fails later during its initial boot operation.

Most of the common post-installation scripts generated by the build system for the out-of-the-box Yocto Project are engineered so that they can run during root filesystem creation (e.g. post-installation scripts for caching fonts). However, if you create and add custom scripts, you need to be sure they can be run during this file system creation.

Here are some common problems that prevent post-installation scripts from running during root filesystem creation:

- Not using $D in front of absolute paths: The build system defines $D [http://www.yoctoproject.org/docs/1.7.2/ref-manual/ref-manual.html#var-D] when the root filesystem is created. Furthermore, $D is blank when the script is run on the target device. This implies two purposes for $D: ensuring paths are valid in both the host and target environments, and checking to determine which environment is being used as a method for taking appropriate actions.

- Attempting to run processes that are specific to or dependent on the target architecture: You can work around these attempts by using native tools to accomplish the same tasks, or by alternatively running the processes under QEMU, which has the qemu_run_binary function. For more information, see the qemu [http://www.yoctoproject.org/docs/1.7.2/ref-manual/ref-manual.html#ref-classes-qemu] class.

5.18.3. Areas With Write Access

With the "read-only-rootfs" feature enabled, any attempt by the target to write to the root filesystem at runtime fails. Consequently, you must make sure that you configure processes and applications that attempt these types of writes do so to directories with write access (e.g. /tmp or /var/run).

5.19. Performing Automated Runtime Testing

The OpenEmbedded build system makes available a series of automated tests for images to verify runtime functionality. You can run these tests on either QEMU or actual target hardware. Tests are written in Python making use of the unittest module, and the majority of them run commands on the target system over SSH. This section describes how you set up the environment to use these tests, run available tests, and write and add your own tests.

5.19.1. Enabling Tests

Depending on whether you are planning to run tests using QEMU or on the hardware, you have to take different steps to enable the tests. See the following subsections for information on how to enable both types of tests.

5.19.1.1. Enabling Runtime Tests on QEMU

In order to run tests, you need to do the following:

- Set up to avoid interaction with sudo for networking: To accomplish this, you must do one of the following:

- Add NOPASSWD for your user in /etc/sudoers either for all commands or just for runqemu-ifup. You must provide the full path as that can change if you are using multiple clones of the source repository.

   ## Note

   On some distributions, you also need to comment out "Defaults requiretty" in /etc/ sudoers.

- Manually configure a tap interface for your system.

- Run as root the script in scripts/runqemu-gen-tapdevs, which should generate a list of tap devices. This is the option typically chosen for Autobuilder-type environments.

- Set the DISPLAY variable: You need to set this variable so that you have an X server available (e.g. start vncserver for a headless machine).

- Be sure your host's firewall accepts incoming connections from 192.168.7.0/24: Some of the tests (in particular smart tests) start an HTTP server on a random high number port, which is used to serve files to the target. The smart module serves ${DEPLOY_DIR}/rpm so it can run smart channel commands. That means your host's firewall must accept incoming connections from 192.168.7.0/24, which is the default IP range used for tap devices by runqemu.

Once you start running the tests, the following happens:

1. A copy of the root filesystem is written to ${WORKDIR}/testimage.

2. The image is booted under QEMU using the standard runqemu script.

3. A default timeout of 500 seconds occurs to allow for the boot process to reach the login prompt. You can change the timeout period by setting TEST_QEMUBOOT_TIMEOUT [http://www.yoctoproject.org/ docs/1.7.2/ref-manual/ref-manual.html#var-TEST_QEMUBOOT_TIMEOUT] in the local.conf file.

4. Once the boot process is reached and the login prompt appears, the tests run. The full boot log is written to ${WORKDIR}/testimage/qemu_boot_log.

5. Each test module loads in the order found in TEST_SUITES. You can find the full output of the commands run over SSH in ${WORKDIR}/testimgage/ssh_target_log.

6. If no failures occur, the task running the tests ends successfully. You can find the output from the unittest in the task log at ${WORKDIR}/temp/log.do_testimage.

5.19.1.2. Enabling Runtime Tests on Hardware

The OpenEmbedded build system can run tests on real hardware, and for certain devices it can also deploy the image to be tested onto the device beforehand.

For automated deployment, a "master image" is installed onto the hardware once as part of setup. Then, each time tests are to be run, the following occurs:

1. The master image is booted into and used to write the image to be tested to a second partition.

2. The device is then rebooted using an external script that you need to provide.

3. The device boots into the image to be tested.

When running tests (independent of whether the image has been deployed automatically or not), the device is expected to be connected to a network on a pre-determined IP address. You can either use static IP addresses written into the image, or set the image to use DHCP and have your DHCP server on the test network assign a known IP address based on the MAC address of the device.

In order to run tests on hardware, you need to set TEST_TARGET to an appropriate value. For QEMU, you do not have to change anything, the default value is "QemuTarget". For running tests on hardware, the following options exist:

- "SimpleRemoteTarget": Choose "SimpleRemoteTarget" if you are going to run tests on a target system that is already running the image to be tested and is available on the network. You can use "SimpleRemoteTarget" in conjunction with either real hardware or an image running within a separately started QEMU or any other virtual machine manager.

- "GummibootTarget": Choose "GummibootTarget" if your hardware is an EFI-based machine with gummiboot as bootloader and `core-image-testmaster` (or something similar) is installed. Also, your hardware under test must be in a DHCP-enabled network that gives it the same IP address for each reboot.

  If you choose "GummibootTarget", there are additional requirements and considerations. See the "Selecting GummibootTarget" section, which follows, for more information.

- "BeagleBoneTarget": Choose "BeagleBoneTarget" if you are deploying images and running tests on the BeagleBone "Black" or original "White" hardware. For information on how to use these tests, see the comments at the top of the BeagleBoneTarget `meta-yocto-bsp/lib/oeqa/controllers/ beaglebonetarget.py` file.

- "EdgeRouterTarget": Choose "EdgeRouterTarget" is you are deploying images and running tests on the Ubiquiti Networks EdgeRouter Lite. For information on how to use these tests, see the comments at the top of the EdgeRouterTarget `meta-yocto-bsp/lib/oeqa/controllers/ edgeroutertarget.py` file.

- "GrubTarget": Choose the "supports deploying images and running tests on any generic PC that boots using GRUB. For information on how to use these tests, see the comments at the top of the GrubTarget `meta-yocto-bsp/lib/oeqa/controllers/grubtarget.py` file.

- "your-target": Create your own custom target if you want to run tests when you are deploying images and running tests on a custom machine within your BSP layer. To do this, you need to add a Python unit that defines the target class under `lib/oeqa/controllers/` within your layer. You must also provide an empty `__init__.py`. For examples, see files in `meta-yocto-bsp/lib/oeqa/ controllers/`.

5.19.1.3. Selecting GummibootTarget

If you did not set TEST_TARGET to "GummibootTarget", then you do not need any information in this section. You can skip down to the "Running Tests" section.

If you did set TEST_TARGET to "GummibootTarget", you also need to perform a one-time setup of your master image by doing the following:

1. Set EFI_PROVIDER: Be sure that EFI_PROVIDER is as follows:

   ```
   EFI_PROVIDER = "gummiboot"
   ```

2. Build the master image: Build the `core-image-testmaster` image. The `core-image-testmaster` recipe is provided as an example for a "master" image and you can customize the image recipe as you would any other recipe.

   Here are the image recipe requirements:

   - Inherits `core-image` so that kernel modules are installed.

   - Installs normal linux utilities not busybox ones (e.g. `bash`, `coreutils`, `tar`, `gzip`, and `kmod`).

   - Uses a custom Initial RAM Disk (initramfs) image with a custom installer. A normal image that you can install usually creates a single rootfs partition. This image uses another installer that creates a specific partition layout. Not all Board Support Packages (BSPs) can use an installer. For such cases, you need to manually create the following partition layout on the target:

     - First partition mounted under /boot, labeled "boot".

     - The main rootfs partition where this image gets installed, which is mounted under /.

     - Another partition labeled "testrootfs" where test images get deployed.

3. Install image: Install the image that you just built on the target system.

The final thing you need to do when setting TEST_TARGET to "GummibootTarget" is to set up the test image:

1. Set up your local.conf file: Make sure you have the following statements in your local.conf file:

```
IMAGE_FSTYPES += "tar.gz"
INHERIT += "testimage"
TEST_TARGET = "GummibootTarget"
TEST_TARGET_IP = "192.168.2.3"
```

2. Build your test image: Use BitBake to build the image:

```
$ bitbake core-image-sato
```

5.19.1.4. Power Control

For most hardware targets other than SimpleRemoteTarget, you can control power:

• You can use TEST_POWERCONTROL_CMD together with TEST_POWERCONTROL_EXTRA_ARGS as a command that runs on the host and does power cycling. The test code passes one argument to that command: off, on or cycle (off then on). Here is an example that could appear in your local.conf file:

```
TEST_POWERCONTROL_CMD = "powercontrol.exp test 10.11.12.1 nuc1"
```

In this example, the expect script does the following:

```
ssh test@10.11.12.1 "pyctl nuc1 arg"
```

It then runs a Python script that controls power for a label called nuc1.

Note
You need to customize TEST_POWERCONTROL_CMD and TEST_POWERCONTROL_EXTRA_ARGS for your own setup. The one requirement is that it accepts "on", "off", and "cycle" as the last argument.

• When no command is defined, it connects to the device over SSH and uses the classic reboot command to reboot the device. Classic reboot is fine as long as the machine actually reboots (i.e. the SSH test has not failed). It is useful for scenarios where you have a simple setup, typically with a single board, and where some manual interaction is okay from time to time.

If you have no hardware to automatically perform power control but still wish to experiment with automated hardware testing, you can use the dialog-power-control script that shows a dialog prompting you to perform the required power action. This script requires either KDialog or Zenity to be installed. To use this script, set the TEST_POWERCONTROL_CMD [http://www.yoctoproject.org/docs/1.7.2/ref-manual/ref-manual.html#var-TEST_POWERCONTROL_CMD] variable as follows:

```
TEST_POWERCONTROL_CMD = "${COREBASE}/scripts/contrib/dialog-power-control"
```

5.19.1.5. Serial Console Connection

For test target classes requiring a serial console to interact with the bootloader (e.g. BeagleBoneTarget, EdgeRouterTarget, and GrubTarget), you need to specify a command to use to connect to the serial console of the target machine by using the TEST_POWERCONTROL_CMD [http://www.yoctoproject.org/docs/1.7.2/ref-manual/ref-manual.html#var-TEST_POWERCONTROL_CMD] variable and optionally the TEST_SERIALCONTROL_EXTRA_ARGS [http://www.yoctoproject.org/docs/1.7.2/ref-manual/ref-manual.html#var-TEST_SERIALCONTROL_EXTRA_ARGS] variable.

These cases could be a serial terminal program if the machine is connected to a local serial port, or a telnet or ssh command connecting to a remote console server. Regardless of the case, the command simply needs to connect to the serial console and forward that connection to standard input and output as any normal terminal program does. For example, to use the picocom terminal program on serial device /dev/ttyUSB0 at 115200bps, you would set the variable as follows:

```
TEST_SERIALCONTROL_CMD = "picocom /dev/ttyUSB0 -b 115200"
```

For local devices where the serial port device disappears when the device reboots, an additional "serdevtry" wrapper script is provided. To use this wrapper, simply prefix the terminal command with ${COREBASE}/scripts/contrib/serdevtry:

```
TEST_SERIALCONTROL_CMD = "${COREBASE}/scripts/contrib/serdevtry picocom -b
115200 /dev/ttyUSB0"
```

5.19.2. Running Tests

You can start the tests automatically or manually:

- Automatically running tests: To run the tests automatically after the OpenEmbedded build system successfully creates an image, first set the TEST_IMAGE [http://www.yoctoproject.org/docs/1.7.2/ref-manual/ref-manual.html#var-TEST_IMAGE] variable to "1" in your local.conf file in the Build Directory [http://www.yoctoproject.org/docs/1.7.2/dev-manual/dev-manual.html#build-directory]:

```
TEST_IMAGE = "1"
```

Next, build your image. If the image successfully builds, the tests will be run:

```
bitbake core-image-sato
```

- Manually running tests: To manually run the tests, first globally inherit the testimage [http://www.yoctoproject.org/docs/1.7.2/ref-manual/ref-manual.html#ref-classes-testimage] class by editing your local.conf file:

```
INHERIT += "testimage"
```

Next, use BitBake to run the tests:

```
bitbake -c testimage image
```

All test files reside in meta/lib/oeqa/runtime in the Source Directory [16]. A test name maps directly to a Python module. Each test module may contain a number of individual tests. Tests are usually grouped together by the area tested (e.g tests for systemd reside in meta/lib/oeqa/runtime/systemd.py).

You can add tests to any layer provided you place them in the proper area and you extend BBPATH [http://www.yoctoproject.org/docs/1.7.2/ref-manual/ref-manual.html#var-BBPATH] in the local.conf file as normal. Be sure that tests reside in layer/lib/oeqa/runtime.

Note
Be sure that module names do not collide with module names used in the default set of test modules in meta/lib/oeqa/runtime.

You can change the set of tests run by appending or overriding TEST_SUITES [http://www.yoctoproject.org/docs/1.7.2/ref-manual/ref-manual.html#var-TEST_SUITES] variable in local.conf. Each name in TEST_SUITES represents a required test for the image. Test modules named within TEST_SUITES cannot be skipped even if a test is not suitable for an image (e.g. running the RPM tests on an image without rpm). Appending "auto" to TEST_SUITES causes the build system to try to run all tests that are suitable for the image (i.e. each test module may elect to skip itself).

The order you list tests in TEST_SUITES is important and influences test dependencies. Consequently, tests that depend on other tests should be added after the test on which they depend. For example, since the ssh test depends on the ping test, "ssh" needs to come after "ping" in the list. The test class provides no re-ordering or dependency handling.

Note
Each module can have multiple classes with multiple test methods. And, Python unittest rules apply.

Here are some things to keep in mind when running tests:

- The default tests for the image are defined as:

      DEFAULT_TEST_SUITES_pn-image = "ping ssh df connman syslog xorg scp vnc date rpm smart dme

- Add your own test to the list of the by using the following:

      TEST_SUITES_append = " mytest"

- Run a specific list of tests as follows:

      TEST_SUITES = "test1 test2 test3"

Remember, order is important. Be sure to place a test that is dependent on another test later in the order.

5.19.3. Exporting Tests

You can export tests so that they can run independently of the build system. Exporting tests is required if you want to be able to hand the test execution off to a scheduler. You can only export tests that are defined in TEST_SUITES [http://www.yoctoproject.org/docs/1.7.2/ref-manual/ref-manual.html#var-TEST_SUITES].

If your image is already built, make sure the following are set in your local.conf file. Be sure to provide the IP address you need:

      TEST_EXPORT_ONLY = "1"
      TEST_TARGET = "simpleremote"
      TEST_TARGET_IP = "192.168.7.2"
      TEST_SERVER_IP = "192.168.7.1"

You can then export the tests with the following:

      $ bitbake core-image-sato -c testimage

Exporting the tests places them in the Build Directory [14] in tmp/testimage/core-image-sato, which is controlled by the TEST_EXPORT_DIR variable.

You can now run the tests outside of the build environment:

```
$ cd tmp/testimage/core-image-sato
$ ./runexported.py testdata.json
```

Note

This "export" feature does not deploy or boot the target image. Your target (be it a Qemu or hardware one) has to already be up and running when you call runexported.py

The exported data (i.e. testdata.json) contains paths to the Build Directory. Thus, the contents of the directory can be moved to another machine as long as you update some paths in the JSON. Usually, you only care about the ${DEPLOY_DIR}/rpm directory (assuming the RPM and Smart tests are enabled). Consequently, running the tests on other machine means that you have to move the contents and call runexported.py with "##deploy-dir path" as follows:

```
./runexported.py ##deploy-dir /new/path/on/this/machine testdata.json
```

runexported.py accepts other arguments as well as described using ##help.

5.19.4. Writing New Tests

As mentioned previously, all new test files need to be in the proper place for the build system to find them. New tests for additional functionality outside of the core should be added to the layer that adds the functionality, in layer/lib/oeqa/runtime (as long as BBPATH [http://www.yoctoproject.org/docs/1.7.2/ref-manual/ref-manual.html#var-BBPATH] is extended in the layer's layer.conf file as normal). Just remember that filenames need to map directly to test (module) names and that you do not use module names that collide with existing core tests.

To create a new test, start by copying an existing module (e.g. syslog.py or gcc.py are good ones to use). Test modules can use code from meta/lib/oeqa/utils, which are helper classes.

Note

Structure shell commands such that you rely on them and they return a single code for success. Be aware that sometimes you will need to parse the output. See the df.py and date.py modules for examples.

You will notice that all test classes inherit oeRuntimeTest, which is found in meta/lib/oetest.py. This base class offers some helper attributes, which are described in the following sections:

5.19.4.1. Class Methods

Class methods are as follows:

- hasPackage(pkg): Returns "True" if pkg is in the installed package list of the image, which is based on the manifest file that is generated during the do_rootfs task.

- hasFeature(feature): Returns "True" if the feature is in IMAGE_FEATURES [http://www.yoctoproject.org/docs/1.7.2/ref-manual/ref-manual.html#var-IMAGE_FEATURES] or DISTRO_FEATURES [http://www.yoctoproject.org/docs/1.7.2/ref-manual/ref-manual.html#var-DISTRO_FEATURES].

5.19.4.2. Class Attributes

Class attributes are as follows:

- pscmd: Equals "ps -ef" if procps is installed in the image. Otherwise, pscmd equals "ps" (busybox).

- tc: The called text context, which gives access to the following attributes:

  - d: The BitBake datastore, which allows you to use stuff such as oeRuntimeTest.tc.d.getVar("VIRTUAL-RUNTIME_init_manager").

  - testslist and testsrequired: Used internally. The tests do not need these.

- filesdir: The absolute path to meta/lib/oeqa/runtime/files, which contains helper files for tests meant for copying on the target such as small files written in C for compilation.

- target: The target controller object used to deploy and start an image on a particular target (e.g. QemuTarget, SimpleRemote, and GummibootTarget). Tests usually use the following:

  - ip: The target's IP address.

  - server_ip: The host's IP address, which is usually used by the "smart" test suite.

  - run(cmd, timeout=None): The single, most used method. This command is a wrapper for: ssh root@host "cmd". The command returns a tuple: (status, output), which are what their names imply - the return code of "cmd" and whatever output it produces. The optional timeout argument represents the number of seconds the test should wait for "cmd" to return. If the argument is "None", the test uses the default instance's timeout period, which is 300 seconds. If the argument is "0", the test runs until the command returns.

  - copy_to(localpath, remotepath): scp localpath root@ip:remotepath.

  - copy_from(remotepath, localpath): scp root@host:remotepath localpath.

5.19.4.3. Instance Attributes

A single instance attribute exists, which is target. The target instance attribute is identical to the class attribute of the same name, which is described in the previous section. This attribute exists as both an instance and class attribute so tests can use self.target.run(cmd) in instance methods instead of oeRuntimeTest.tc.target.run(cmd).

5.20. Debugging With the GNU Project Debugger (GDB) Remotely

GDB allows you to examine running programs, which in turn helps you to understand and fix problems. It also allows you to perform post-mortem style analysis of program crashes. GDB is available as a package within the Yocto Project and is installed in SDK images by default. See the "Images [http://www.yoctoproject.org/docs/1.7.2/ref-manual/ref-manual.html#ref-images]" chapter in the Yocto Project Reference Manual for a description of these images. You can find information on GDB at http://sourceware.org/gdb/.

Tip
For best results, install debug (-dbg) packages for the applications you are going to debug. Doing so makes extra debug symbols available that give you more meaningful output.

Sometimes, due to memory or disk space constraints, it is not possible to use GDB directly on the remote target to debug applications. These constraints arise because GDB needs to load the debugging information and the binaries of the process being debugged. Additionally, GDB needs to perform many computations to locate information such as function names, variable names and values, stack traces and so forth - even before starting the debugging process. These extra computations place more load on the target system and can alter the characteristics of the program being debugged.

To help get past the previously mentioned constraints, you can use Gdbserver. Gdbserver runs on the remote target and does not load any debugging information from the debugged process. Instead, a GDB instance processes the debugging information that is run on a remote computer - the host GDB. The host GDB then sends control commands to Gdbserver to make it stop or start the debugged program, as well as read or write memory regions of that debugged program. All the debugging information loaded and processed as well as all the heavy debugging is done by the host GDB. Offloading these processes gives the Gdbserver running on the target a chance to remain small and fast.

Note
By default, source files are part of the *-dbg packages in order to enable GDB to show source lines in its output. You can save further space on the target by setting

the PACKAGE_DEBUG_SPLIT_STYLE [http://www.yoctoproject.org/docs/1.7.2/ref-manual/ref-manual.html#var-PACKAGE_DEBUG_SPLIT_STYLE] variable to "debug-without-src" so that these packages do not include the source files.

Because the host GDB is responsible for loading the debugging information and for doing the necessary processing to make actual debugging happen, you have to make sure the host can access the unstripped binaries complete with their debugging information and also be sure the target is compiled with no optimizations. The host GDB must also have local access to all the libraries used by the debugged program. Because Gdbserver does not need any local debugging information, the binaries on the remote target can remain stripped. However, the binaries must also be compiled without optimization so they match the host's binaries.

To remain consistent with GDB documentation and terminology, the binary being debugged on the remote target machine is referred to as the "inferior" binary. For documentation on GDB see the GDB site [http://sourceware.org/gdb/documentation/].

The remainder of this section describes the steps you need to take to debug using the GNU project debugger.

5.20.1. Set Up the Cross-Development Debugging Environment

Before you can initiate a remote debugging session, you need to be sure you have set up the cross-development environment, toolchain, and sysroot. The "Preparing for Application Development [http://www.yoctoproject.org/docs/1.7.2/adt-manual/adt-manual.html#adt-prepare]" chapter of the Yocto Project Application Developer's Guide describes this process. Be sure you have read that chapter and have set up your environment.

5.20.2. Launch Gdbserver on the Target

Make sure Gdbserver is installed on the target. If it is not, install the package gdbserver, which needs the libthread-db1 package.

Here is an example, that when entered from the host, connects to the target and launches Gdbserver in order to "debug" a binary named helloworld:

```
$ gdbserver localhost:2345 /usr/bin/helloworld
```

Gdbserver should now be listening on port 2345 for debugging commands coming from a remote GDB process that is running on the host computer. Communication between Gdbserver and the host GDB are done using TCP. To use other communication protocols, please refer to the Gdbserver documentation [http://www.gnu.org/software/gdb/].

5.20.3. Launch GDB on the Host Computer

Running GDB on the host computer takes a number of stages, which this section describes.

5.20.3.1. Build the Cross-GDB Package

A suitable GDB cross-binary is required that runs on your host computer but also knows about the the ABI of the remote target. You can get this binary from the Cross-Development Toolchain [15]. Here is an example where the toolchain has been installed in the default directory /opt/poky/1.7.2:

```
/opt/poky/1.7.2/sysroots/i686-pokysdk-linux/usr/bin/armv7a-vfp-neon-poky-linux-gnueabi/ar
```

where arm is the target architecture and linux-gnueabi is the target ABI.

Alternatively, you can use BitBake to build the gdb-cross binary. Here is an example:

```
$ bitbake gdb-cross
```

Once the binary is built, you can find it here:

```
tmp/sysroots/host-arch/usr/bin/target-platform/target-abi-gdb
```

5.20.3.2. Create the GDB Initialization File and Point to Your Root Filesystem

Aside from the GDB cross-binary, you also need a GDB initialization file in the same top directory in which your binary resides. When you start GDB on your host development system, GDB finds this initialization file and executes all the commands within. For information on the .gdbinit, see "Debugging with GDB [http://sourceware.org/gdb/onlinedocs/gdb/]", which is maintained by sourceware.org [http://www.sourceware.org].

You need to add a statement in the ~/.gdbinit file that points to your root filesystem. Here is an example that points to the root filesystem for an ARM-based target device:

```
set sysroot ~/sysroot_arm
```

5.20.3.3. Launch the Host GDB

Before launching the host GDB, you need to be sure you have sourced the cross-debugging environment script, which if you installed the root filesystem in the default location is at / opt/poky/1.7.2 and begins with the string "environment-setup". For more information, see the "Setting Up the Cross-Development Environment [http://www.yoctoproject.org/docs/1.7.2/ adt-manual/adt-manual.html#setting-up-the-cross-development-environment]" section in the Yocto Project Application Developer's Guide.

Finally, switch to the directory where the binary resides and run the cross-gdb binary. Provide the binary file you are going to debug. For example, the following command continues with the example used in the previous section by loading the helloworld binary as well as the debugging information:

```
$ arm-poky-linux-gnuabi-gdb helloworld
```

The commands in your .gdbinit execute and the GDB prompt appears.

5.20.4. Connect to the Remote GDB Server

From the target, you need to connect to the remote GDB server that is running on the host. You need to specify the remote host and port. Here is the command continuing with the example:

```
target remote 192.168.7.2:2345
```

5.20.5. Use the Debugger

You can now proceed with debugging as normal - as if you were debugging on the local machine. For example, to instruct GDB to break in the "main" function and then continue with execution of the inferior binary use the following commands from within GDB:

```
(gdb) break main
(gdb) continue
```

For more information about using GDB, see the project's online documentation at http:// sourceware.org/gdb/download/onlinedocs/.

5.21. Debugging Parallel Make Races

A parallel make race occurs when the build consists of several parts that are run simultaneously and a situation occurs when the output or result of one part is not ready for use with a different part of the build that depends on that output. Parallel make races are annoying and can sometimes be difficult to reproduce and fix. However, some simple tips and tricks exist that can help you debug and fix them. This section presents a real-world example of an error encountered on the Yocto Project autobuilder and the process used to fix it.

5.21.1. The Failure

For this example, assume that you are building an image that depends on the "neard" package. And, during the build, BitBake runs into problems and creates the following output.

Note

This example log file has longer lines artificially broken to make the listing easier to read.

If you examine the output or the log file, you see the failure during make:

```
| DEBUG: SITE files ['endian-little', 'bit-32', 'ix86-common', 'common-linux', 'common-gli
| DEBUG: Executing shell function do_compile
| NOTE: make -j 16
| make ##no-print-directory all-am
| /bin/mkdir -p include/near
| /bin/mkdir -p include/near
| /bin/mkdir -p include/near
| ln -s /home/pokybuild/yocto-autobuilder/yocto-slave/nightly-x86/build/build/tmp/work/i58
  0.14-r0/neard-0.14/include/types.h include/near/types.h
| ln -s /home/pokybuild/yocto-autobuilder/yocto-slave/nightly-x86/build/build/tmp/work/i58
  0.14-r0/neard-0.14/include/log.h include/near/log.h
| ln -s /home/pokybuild/yocto-autobuilder/yocto-slave/nightly-x86/build/build/tmp/work/i58
  0.14-r0/neard-0.14/include/plugin.h include/near/plugin.h
| /bin/mkdir -p include/near
| /bin/mkdir -p include/near
| /bin/mkdir -p include/near
| ln -s /home/pokybuild/yocto-autobuilder/yocto-slave/nightly-x86/build/build/tmp/work/i58
  0.14-r0/neard-0.14/include/tag.h include/near/tag.h
| /bin/mkdir -p include/near
| ln -s /home/pokybuild/yocto-autobuilder/yocto-slave/nightly-x86/build/build/tmp/work/i58
  0.14-r0/neard-0.14/include/adapter.h include/near/adapter.h
| /bin/mkdir -p include/near
| ln -s /home/pokybuild/yocto-autobuilder/yocto-slave/nightly-x86/build/build/tmp/work/i58
  0.14-r0/neard-0.14/include/ndef.h include/near/ndef.h
| ln -s /home/pokybuild/yocto-autobuilder/yocto-slave/nightly-x86/build/build/tmp/work/i58
  0.14-r0/neard-0.14/include/tlv.h include/near/tlv.h
| /bin/mkdir -p include/near
| /bin/mkdir -p include/near
| ln -s /home/pokybuild/yocto-autobuilder/yocto-slave/nightly-x86/build/build/tmp/work/i58
  0.14-r0/neard-0.14/include/setting.h include/near/setting.h
| /bin/mkdir -p include/near
| /bin/mkdir -p include/near
| /bin/mkdir -p include/near
| ln -s /home/pokybuild/yocto-autobuilder/yocto-slave/nightly-x86/build/build/tmp/work/i58
  0.14-r0/neard-0.14/include/device.h include/near/device.h
| ln -s /home/pokybuild/yocto-autobuilder/yocto-slave/nightly-x86/build/build/tmp/work/i58
  0.14-r0/neard-0.14/include/nfc_copy.h include/near/nfc_copy.h
| ln -s /home/pokybuild/yocto-autobuilder/yocto-slave/nightly-x86/build/build/tmp/work/i58
  0.14-r0/neard-0.14/include/snep.h include/near/snep.h
| ln -s /home/pokybuild/yocto-autobuilder/yocto-slave/nightly-x86/build/build/tmp/work/i58
  0.14-r0/neard-0.14/include/version.h include/near/version.h
| ln -s /home/pokybuild/yocto-autobuilder/yocto-slave/nightly-x86/build/build/tmp/work/i58
  0.14-r0/neard-0.14/include/dbus.h include/near/dbus.h
| ./src/genbuiltin nfctype1 nfctype2 nfctype3 nfctype4 p2p > src/builtin.h
```

```
| i586-poky-linux-gcc  -m32 -march=i586 ##sysroot=/home/pokybuild/yocto-autobuilder/yocto-sl
  build/build/tmp/sysroots/qemux86 -DHAVE_CONFIG_H -I. -I./include -I./src -I./gdbus  -I/hon
  yocto-autobuilder/yocto-slave/nightly-x86/build/build/tmp/sysroots/qemux86/usr/include/gli
  -I/home/pokybuild/yocto-autobuilder/yocto-slave/nightly-x86/build/build/tmp/sysroots/qemu>
  lib/glib-2.0/include  -I/home/pokybuild/yocto-autobuilder/yocto-slave/nightly-x86/build/bu
  tmp/sysroots/qemux86/usr/include/dbus-1.0 -I/home/pokybuild/yocto-autobuilder/yocto-slave/
  nightly-x86/build/build/tmp/sysroots/qemux86/usr/lib/dbus-1.0/include  -I/home/pokybuild/y
  yocto-slave/nightly-x86/build/build/tmp/sysroots/qemux86/usr/include/libnl3
  -DNEAR_PLUGIN_BUILTIN -DPLUGINDIR=\""/usr/lib/near/plugins"\"
  -DCONFIGDIR=\""/etc/neard"\" -O2 -pipe -g -feliminate-unused-debug-types -c
  -o tools/snep-send.o tools/snep-send.c
| In file included from tools/snep-send.c:16:0:
| tools/../src/near.h:41:23: fatal error: near/dbus.h: No such file or directory
|  #include <near/dbus.h>
|                        ^
| compilation terminated.
| make[1]: *** [tools/snep-send.o] Error 1
| make[1]: *** Waiting for unfinished jobs....
| make: *** [all] Error 2
| ERROR: oe_runmake failed
```

5.21.2. Reproducing the Error

Because race conditions are intermittent, they do not manifest themselves every time you do the build. In fact, most times the build will complete without problems even though the potential race condition exists. Thus, once the error surfaces, you need a way to reproduce it.

In this example, compiling the "neard" package is causing the problem. So the first thing to do is build "neard" locally. Before you start the build, set the PARALLEL_MAKE [http://www.yoctoproject.org/docs/1.7.2/ref-manual/ref-manual.html#var-PARALLEL_MAKE] variable in your local.conf file to a high number (e.g. "-j 20"). Using a high value for PARALLEL_MAKE increases the chances of the race condition showing up:

```
$ bitbake neard
```

Once the local build for "neard" completes, start a devshell build:

```
$ bitbake neard -c devshell
```

For information on how to use a devshell, see the "Using a Development Shell" section.

In the devshell, do the following:

```
$ make clean
$ make tools/snep-send.o
```

The devshell commands cause the failure to clearly be visible. In this case, a missing dependency exists for the "neard" Makefile target. Here is some abbreviated, sample output with the missing dependency clearly visible at the end:

```
i586-poky-linux-gcc  -m32 -march=i586 ##sysroot=/home/scott-lenovo/......
   .
   .
   .
tools/snep-send.c
In file included from tools/snep-send.c:16:0:
tools/../src/near.h:41:23: fatal error: near/dbus.h: No such file or directory
 #include <near/dbus.h>
```

```
                    ^
compilation terminated.
make: *** [tools/snep-send.o] Error 1
$
```

5.21.3. Creating a Patch for the Fix

Because there is a missing dependency for the Makefile target, you need to patch the Makefile.am file, which is generated from Makefile.in. You can use Quilt to create the patch:

```
$ quilt new parallelmake.patch
Patch patches/parallelmake.patch is now on top
$ quilt add Makefile.am
File Makefile.am added to patch patches/parallelmake.patch
```

For more information on using Quilt, see the "Using a Quilt Workflow" section.

At this point you need to make the edits to Makefile.am to add the missing dependency. For our example, you have to add the following line to the file:

```
tools/snep-send.$(OBJEXT): include/near/dbus.h
```

Once you have edited the file, use the refresh command to create the patch:

```
$ quilt refresh
Refreshed patch patches/parallelmake.patch
```

Once the patch file exists, you need to add it back to the originating recipe folder. Here is an example assuming a top-level Source Directory [16] named poky:

```
$ cp patches/parallelmake.patch poky/meta/recipes-connectivity/neard/neard
```

The final thing you need to do to implement the fix in the build is to update the "neard" recipe (i.e. neard-0.14.bb) so that the SRC_URI [http://www.yoctoproject.org/docs/1.7.2/ref-manual/ref-manual.html#var-SRC_URI] statement includes the patch file. The recipe file is in the folder above the patch. Here is what the edited SRC_URI statement would look like:

```
SRC_URI = "${KERNELORG_MIRROR}/linux/network/nfc/${BPN}-${PV}.tar.xz \
           file://neard.in \
           file://neard.service.in \
           file://parallelmake.patch \
           "
```

With the patch complete and moved to the correct folder and the SRC_URI statement updated, you can exit the devshell:

```
$ exit
```

5.21.4. Testing the Build

With everything in place, you can get back to trying the build again locally:

```
$ bitbake neard
```

This build should succeed.

Now you can open up a devshell again and repeat the clean and make operations as follows:

```
$ bitbake neard -c devshell
$ make clean
$ make tools/snep-send.o
```

The build should work without issue.

As with all solved problems, if they originated upstream, you need to submit the fix for the recipe in OE-Core and upstream so that the problem is taken care of at its source. See the "How to Submit a Change" section for more information.

5.22. Examining Builds Using the Toaster API

Toaster is an Application Programming Interface (API) and web-based interface to the OpenEmbedded build system, which uses BitBake. Both interfaces are based on a Representational State Transfer (REST) API that queries for and returns build information using GET and JSON. These types of search operations retrieve sets of objects from a datastore used to collect build information. The results contain all the data for the objects being returned. You can order the results of the search by key and the search parameters are consistent for all object types.

Using the interfaces you can do the following:

• See information about the tasks executed and reused during the build.

• See what is built (recipes and packages) and what packages were installed into the final image.

• See performance-related information such as build time, CPU usage, and disk I/O.

• Examine error, warning and trace messages to aid in debugging.

Note

This release of Toaster provides you with information about a BitBake run. The tool does not allow you to configure and launch a build. However, future development includes plans to integrate the configuration and build launching capabilities of Hob [http://www.yoctoproject.org/tools-resources/projects/hob].

For more information on using Hob to build an image, see the "Image Development Using Hob" section.

The remainder of this section describes what you need to have in place to use Toaster, how to start it, use it, and stop it. For additional information on installing and running Toaster, see the "Installation and Running [https://wiki.yoctoproject.org/wiki/Toaster#Installation_and_Running]" section of the "Toaster" wiki page. For complete information on the API and its search operation URI, parameters, and responses, see the REST API Contracts [https://wiki.yoctoproject.org/wiki/REST_API_Contracts] Wiki page.

5.22.1. Starting Toaster

Getting set up to use and start Toaster is simple. First, be sure you have met the following requirements:

• You have set up your Source Directory [16] by cloning the upstream poky repository. See the Yocto Project Release item for information on how to set up the Source Directory.

• Be sure your build machine has Django [http://en.wikipedia.org/wiki/Django_%28web_framework %29] version 1.5 installed.

• Make sure that port 8000 and 8200 are free (i.e. they have no servers on them).

Once you have met the requirements, follow these steps to start Toaster running in the background of your shell:

Note

The Toaster must be started and running in order for it to collect data.

1. Set up your build environment: Source a build environment script (i.e. oe-init-build-env [http://www.yoctoproject.org/docs/1.7.2/ref-manual/ref-manual.html#structure-core-script] or oe-init-build-env-memres [http://www.yoctoproject.org/docs/1.7.2/ref-manual/ref-manual.html#structure-memres-core-script]).

2. Start Toaster: Start the Toaster service using this command from within your Build Directory [14]:

```
$ source toaster start
```

When Toaster starts, it creates some additional files in your Build Directory. Deleting these files will cause you to lose data or interrupt Toaster:

• toaster.sqlite: Toaster's database file.

• toaster_web.log: The log file of the web server.

• toaster_ui.log: The log file of the user interface component.

• toastermain.pid: The PID of the web server.

• toasterui.pid: The PID of the DSI data bridge.

• bitbake-cookerdaemon.log: The BitBake server's log file.

5.22.2. Using Toaster

Once Toaster is running, it logs information for any BitBake run from your Build Directory. This logging is automatic. All you need to do is access and use the information.

You access the information one of two ways:

• Open a Browser and enter http://localhost:8000 for the URL.

• Use the xdg-open tool from the shell and pass it the same URL.

Either method opens the home page for the Toaster interface.

Notes

• For information on how to delete information from the Toaster database, see the Deleting a Build from the Toaster Database [https://wiki.yoctoproject.org/wiki/Toaster#Deleting_a_Build_from_the_Toaster_Database] wiki page.

• For information on how to set up an instance of Toaster on a remote host, see the Setting Up a Toaster Instance on a Remote Host [https://wiki.yoctoproject.org/wiki/Toaster#Setting_up_a_Toaster_Instance_on_a_Remote_Host] wiki page.

5.22.3. Examining Toaster Data

The Toaster database is persistent regardless of whether you start or stop the service.

Toaster's interface shows you a list of builds (successful and unsuccessful) for which it has data. You can click on any build to see related information. This information includes configuration details, information about tasks, all recipes and packages built and their dependencies, packages and their directory structure as installed in your final image, execution time, CPU usage and disk I/O per task.

For details on the interface, see the Toaster Manual [https://www.yoctoproject.org/documentation/toaster-manual].

5.22.4. Stopping Toaster

Stop the Toaster service with the following command from with the Build Directory [14]:

```
$ source toaster stop
```

The service stops but the Toaster database remains persistent.

5.23. Profiling with OProfile

OProfile [http://oprofile.sourceforge.net/] is a statistical profiler well suited for finding performance bottlenecks in both user-space software and in the kernel. This profiler provides answers to questions like "Which functions does my application spend the most time in when doing X?" Because the OpenEmbedded build system is well integrated with OProfile, it makes profiling applications on target hardware straight forward.

Note
For more information on how to set up and run OProfile, see the "oprofile [http://www.yoctoproject.org/docs/1.7.2/profile-manual/profile-manual.html#profile-manual-oprofile]" section in the Yocto Project Profiling and Tracing Manual.

To use OProfile, you need an image that has OProfile installed. The easiest way to do this is with "tools-profile" in the IMAGE_FEATURES [http://www.yoctoproject.org/docs/1.7.2/ref-manual/ref-manual.html#var-IMAGE_FEATURES] variable. You also need debugging symbols to be available on the system where the analysis takes place. You can gain access to the symbols by using "dbg-pkgs" in the IMAGE_FEATURES variable or by installing the appropriate debug (-dbg) packages.

For successful call graph analysis, the binaries must preserve the frame pointer register and should also be compiled with the -fno-omit-framepointer flag. You can achieve this by setting the SELECTED_OPTIMIZATION [http://www.yoctoproject.org/docs/1.7.2/ref-manual/ref-manual.html#var-SELECTED_OPTIMIZATION] variable with the following options:

```
-fexpensive-optimizations
-fno-omit-framepointer
-frename-registers
-O2
```

You can also achieve it by setting the DEBUG_BUILD [http://www.yoctoproject.org/docs/1.7.2/ref-manual/ref-manual.html#var-DEBUG_BUILD] variable to "1" in the local.conf configuration file. If you use the DEBUG_BUILD variable, you also add extra debugging information that can make the debug packages large.

5.23.1. Profiling on the Target

Using OProfile, you can perform all the profiling work on the target device. A simple OProfile session might look like the following:

```
# opcontrol ##reset
# opcontrol ##start ##separate=lib ##no-vmlinux -c 5
        .
        .
    [do whatever is being profiled]
        .
        .
# opcontrol ##stop
```

```
$ opreport -cl
```

In this example, the reset command clears any previously profiled data. The next command starts OProfile. The options used when starting the profiler separate dynamic library data within applications, disable kernel profiling, and enable callgraphing up to five levels deep.

Note

To profile the kernel, you would specify the ##vmlinux=/path/to/vmlinux option. The vmlinux file is usually in the source directory in the /boot/ directory and must match the running kernel.

After you perform your profiling tasks, the next command stops the profiler. After that, you can view results with the opreport command with options to see the separate library symbols and callgraph information.

Callgraphing logs information about time spent in functions and about a function's calling function (parent) and called functions (children). The higher the callgraphing depth, the more accurate the results. However, higher depths also increase the logging overhead. Consequently, you should take care when setting the callgraphing depth.

Note

On ARM, binaries need to have the frame pointer enabled for callgraphing to work. To accomplish this use the -fno-omit-framepointer option with gcc.

For more information on using OProfile, see the OProfile online documentation at http://oprofile.sourceforge.net/docs/.

5.23.2. Using OProfileUI

A graphical user interface for OProfile is also available. You can download and build this interface from the Yocto Project at http://git.yoctoproject.org/cgit.cgi/oprofileui/. If the "tools-profile" image feature is selected, all necessary binaries are installed onto the target device for OProfileUI interaction. For a list of image features that ship with the Yocto Project, see the "Image Features [http://www.yoctoproject.org/docs/1.7.2/ref-manual/ref-manual.html#ref-features-image]" section in the Yocto Project Reference Manual.

Even though the source directory usually includes all needed patches on the target device, you might find you need other OProfile patches for recent OProfileUI features. If so, see the OProfileUI README [http://git.yoctoproject.org/cgit.cgi/oprofileui/tree/README] for the most recent information.

5.23.2.1. Online Mode

Using OProfile in online mode assumes a working network connection with the target hardware. With this connection, you just need to run "oprofile-server" on the device. By default, OProfile listens on port 4224.

Note

You can change the port using the ##port command-line option.

The client program is called oprofile-viewer and its UI is relatively straight forward. You access key functionality through the buttons on the toolbar, which are duplicated in the menus. Here are the buttons:

• Connect: Connects to the remote host. You can also supply the IP address or hostname.

• Disconnect: Disconnects from the target.

• Start: Starts profiling on the device.

• Stop: Stops profiling on the device and downloads the data to the local host. Stopping the profiler generates the profile and displays it in the viewer.

• Download: Downloads the data from the target and generates the profile, which appears in the viewer.

- Reset: Resets the sample data on the device. Resetting the data removes sample information collected from previous sampling runs. Be sure you reset the data if you do not want to include old sample information.

- Save: Saves the data downloaded from the target to another directory for later examination.

- Open: Loads previously saved data.

The client downloads the complete profile archive from the target to the host for processing. This archive is a directory that contains the sample data, the object files, and the debug information for the object files. The archive is then converted using the oparchconv script, which is included in this distribution. The script uses opimport to convert the archive from the target to something that can be processed on the host.

Downloaded archives reside in the Build Directory [14] in tmp and are cleared up when they are no longer in use.

If you wish to perform kernel profiling, you need to be sure a vmlinux file that matches the running kernel is available. In the source directory, that file is usually located in /boot/ vmlinux-kernelversion, where kernelversion is the version of the kernel. The OpenEmbedded build system generates separate vmlinux packages for each kernel it builds. Thus, it should just be a question of making sure a matching package is installed (e.g. opkg install kernel-vmlinux). The files are automatically installed into development and profiling images alongside OProfile. A configuration option exists within the OProfileUI settings page that you can use to enter the location of the vmlinux file.

Waiting for debug symbols to transfer from the device can be slow, and it is not always necessary to actually have them on the device for OProfile use. All that is needed is a copy of the filesystem with the debug symbols present on the viewer system. The "Launch GDB on the Host Computer" section covers how to create such a directory within the source directory and how to use the OProfileUI Settings Dialog to specify the location. If you specify the directory, it will be used when the file checksums match those on the system you are profiling.

5.23.2.2. Offline Mode

If network access to the target is unavailable, you can generate an archive for processing in oprofile-viewer as follows:

```
# opcontrol ##reset
# opcontrol ##start ##separate=lib ##no-vmlinux -c 5
     .
     .
     .
[do whatever is being profiled]
     .
     .
     .
# opcontrol ##stop
# oparchive -o my_archive
```

In the above example, my_archive is the name of the archive directory where you would like the profile archive to be kept. After the directory is created, you can copy it to another host and load it using oprofile-viewer open functionality. If necessary, the archive is converted.

5.24. Maintaining Open Source License Compliance During Your Product's Lifecycle

One of the concerns for a development organization using open source software is how to maintain compliance with various open source licensing during the lifecycle of the product. While this section does not provide legal advice or comprehensively cover all scenarios, it does present methods that you can use to assist you in meeting the compliance requirements during a software release.

With hundreds of different open source licenses that the Yocto Project tracks, it is difficult to know the requirements of each and every license. However, the requirements of the major FLOSS licenses can begin to be covered by assuming that three main areas of concern exist:

• Source code must be provided.

• License text for the software must be provided.

• Compilation scripts and modifications to the source code must be provided.

There are other requirements beyond the scope of these three and the methods described in this section (e.g. the mechanism through which source code is distributed).

As different organizations have different methods of complying with open source licensing, this section is not meant to imply that there is only one single way to meet your compliance obligations, but rather to describe one method of achieving compliance. The remainder of this section describes methods supported to meet the previously mentioned three requirements. Once you take steps to meet these requirements, and prior to releasing images, sources, and the build system, you should audit all artifacts to ensure completeness.

Note

The Yocto Project generates a license manifest during image creation that is located in ${DEPLOY_DIR}/licenses/image_name-datestamp to assist with any audits.

5.24.1. Providing the Source Code

Compliance activities should begin before you generate the final image. The first thing you should look at is the requirement that tops the list for most compliance groups - providing the source. The Yocto Project has a few ways of meeting this requirement.

One of the easiest ways to meet this requirement is to provide the entire DL_DIR [http://www.yoctoproject.org/docs/1.7.2/ref-manual/ref-manual.html#var-DL_DIR] used by the build. This method, however, has a few issues. The most obvious is the size of the directory since it includes all sources used in the build and not just the source used in the released image. It will include toolchain source, and other artifacts, which you would not generally release. However, the more serious issue for most companies is accidental release of proprietary software. The Yocto Project provides an archiver [http://www.yoctoproject.org/docs/1.7.2/ref-manual/ref-manual.html#ref-classes-archiver] class to help avoid some of these concerns.

Before you employ DL_DIR or the archiver class, you need to decide how you choose to provide source. The source archiver class can generate tarballs and SRPMs and can create them with various levels of compliance in mind.

One way of doing this (but certainly not the only way) is to release just the source as a tarball. You can do this by adding the following to the local.conf file found in the Build Directory [14]:

```
INHERIT += "archiver"
ARCHIVER_MODE[src] = "original"
```

During the creation of your image, the source from all recipes that deploy packages to the image is placed within subdirectories of DEPLOY_DIR/sources based on the LICENSE [http://www.yoctoproject.org/docs/1.7.2/ref-manual/ref-manual.html#var-LICENSE] for each recipe. Releasing the entire directory enables you to comply with requirements concerning providing the unmodified source. It is important to note that the size of the directory can get large.

A way to help mitigate the size issue is to only release tarballs for licenses that require the release of source. Let us assume you are only concerned with GPL code as identified with the following:

```
$ cd poky/build/tmp/deploy/sources
$ mkdir ~/gpl_source_release
$ for dir in */*GPL*; do cp -r $dir ~/gpl_source_release; done
```

At this point, you could create a tarball from the gpl_source_release directory and provide that to the end user. This method would be a step toward achieving compliance with section 3a of GPLv2 and with section 6 of GPLv3.

5.24.2. Providing License Text

One requirement that is often overlooked is inclusion of license text. This requirement also needs to be dealt with prior to generating the final image. Some licenses require the license text to accompany the binary. You can achieve this by adding the following to your local.conf file:

```
COPY_LIC_MANIFEST = "1"
COPY_LIC_DIRS = "1"
```

Adding these statements to the configuration file ensures that the licenses collected during package generation are included on your image. As the source archiver has already archived the original unmodified source that contains the license files, you would have already met the requirements for inclusion of the license information with source as defined by the GPL and other open source licenses.

5.24.3. Providing Compilation Scripts and Source Code Modifications

At this point, we have addressed all we need to address prior to generating the image. The next two requirements are addressed during the final packaging of the release.

By releasing the version of the OpenEmbedded build system and the layers used during the build, you will be providing both compilation scripts and the source code modifications in one step.

If the deployment team has a BSP layer [http://www.yoctoproject.org/docs/1.7.2/bsp-guide/bsp-guide.html#bsp-layers] and a distro layer, and those those layers are used to patch, compile, package, or modify (in any way) any open source software included in your released images, you might be required to to release those layers under section 3 of GPLv2 or section 1 of GPLv3. One way of doing that is with a clean checkout of the version of the Yocto Project and layers used during your build. Here is an example:

```
# We built using the dizzy branch of the poky repo
$ git clone -b dizzy git://git.yoctoproject.org/poky
$ cd poky
# We built using the release_branch for our layers
$ git clone -b release_branch git://git.mycompany.com/meta-my-bsp-layer
$ git clone -b release_branch git://git.mycompany.com/meta-my-software-layer
# clean up the .git repos
$ find . -name ".git" -type d -exec rm -rf {} \;
```

One thing a development organization might want to consider for end-user convenience is to modify meta-yocto/conf/bblayers.conf.sample to ensure that when the end user utilizes the released build system to build an image, the development organization's layers are included in the bblayers.conf file automatically:

```
# LAYER_CONF_VERSION is increased each time build/conf/bblayers.conf
# changes incompatibly
LCONF_VERSION = "6"

BBPATH = "${TOPDIR}"
BBFILES ?= ""

BBLAYERS ?= " \
  ##OEROOT##/meta \
  ##OEROOT##/meta-yocto \
  ##OEROOT##/meta-yocto-bsp \
  ##OEROOT##/meta-mylayer \
  "

BBLAYERS_NON_REMOVABLE ?= " \
```

```
##OEROOT##/meta \
##OEROOT##/meta-yocto \
"
```

Creating and providing an archive of the Metadata [16] layers (recipes, configuration files, and so forth) enables you to meet your requirements to include the scripts to control compilation as well as any modifications to the original source.

5.25. Using the Error Reporting Tool

The error reporting tool allows you to submit errors encountered during builds to a central database. Outside of the build environment, you can use a web interface to browse errors, view statistics, and query for errors. The tool works using a client-server system where the client portion is integrated with the installed Yocto Project Source Directory [16] (e.g. poky). The server receives the information collected and saves it in a database.

A live instance of the error reporting server exists at http://errors.yoctoproject.org. This server exists so that when you want to get help with build failures, you can submit all of the information on the failure easily and then point to the URL in your bug report or send an email to the mailing list.

Note
If you send error reports to this server, the reports become publicly visible.

5.25.1. Enabling and Using the Tool

By default, the error reporting tool is disabled. You can enable it by inheriting the report-error [http://www.yoctoproject.org/docs/1.7.2/ref-manual/ref-manual.html#ref-classes-report-error] class by adding the following statement to the end of your local.conf file in your Build Directory [14].

```
INHERIT += "report-error"
```

By default, the error reporting feature stores information in ${LOG_DIR [http://www.yoctoproject.org/docs/1.7.2/ref-manual/ref-manual.html#var-LOG_DIR]}/error-report. However, you can specify a directory to use by adding the following to your local.conf file:

```
ERR_REPORT_DIR = "path"
```

Enabling error reporting causes the build process to collect the errors and store them in a file as previously described. When the build system encounters an error, it includes a command as part of the console output. You can run the command to send the error file to the server. For example, the following command sends the errors to an upstream server:

```
send-error-report /home/brandusa/project/poky/build/tmp/log/error-report/error_report_201
```

In the above example, the server parameter is optional. By default, the errors are sent to a database used by the entire community. If you specify a particular server, you can send them to a different database.

When sending the error file, you receive a link that corresponds to your entry in the database. For example, here is a typical link:

```
http://localhost:8000/Errors/Search/1/158
```

Following the link takes you to a web interface where you can browse, query the errors, and view statistics.

5.25.2. Disabling the Tool

To disable the error reporting feature, simply remove or comment out the following statement from the end of your local.conf file in your Build Directory [14].

```
INHERIT += "report-error"
```

5.25.3. Setting Up Your Own Error Reporting Server

If you want to set up your own error reporting server, you can obtain the code from the Git repository at http://git.yoctoproject.org/cgit/cgit.cgi/error-report-web/. Instructions on how to set it up are in the README document.

Chapter 6. Using the Quick EMUlator (QEMU)

Quick EMUlator (QEMU) is an Open Source project the Yocto Project uses as part of its development "tool set". As such, the information in this chapter is limited to the Yocto Project integration of QEMU and not QEMU in general. For official information and documentation on QEMU, see the following references:

- QEMU Website [http://wiki.qemu.org/Main_Page]: The official website for the QEMU Open Source project.

- Documentation [http://wiki.qemu.org/Manual]: The QEMU user manual.

This chapter provides an overview of the Yocto Project's integration of QEMU, a description of how you use QEMU and its various options, running under a Network File System (NFS) server, and a few tips and tricks you might find helpful when using QEMU.

6.1. Overview

Within the context of the Yocto Project, QEMU is an emulator and virtualization machine that allows you to run a complete image you have built using the Yocto Project as just another task on your build system. QEMU is useful for running and testing images and applications on supported Yocto Project architectures without having actual hardware. Among other things, the Yocto Project uses QEMU to run automated Quality Assurance (QA) tests on final images shipped with each release.

QEMU is made available with the Yocto Project a number of ways. The easiest and recommended method for getting QEMU is to run the ADT installer. For more information on how to make sure you have QEMU available, see the "The QEMU Emulator [http://www.yoctoproject.org/docs/1.7.2/adt-manual/adt-manual.html#the-qemu-emulator]" section in the Yocto Project Application Developer's Guide.

6.2. Running QEMU

Running QEMU involves having your build environment set up, having the right artifacts available, and understanding how to use the many options that are available to you when you start QEMU using the runqemu command.

6.2.1. Setting Up the Environment

You run QEMU in the same environment from which you run BitBake. This means you need to source a build environment script (i.e. oe-init-build-env [http://www.yoctoproject.org/docs/1.7.2/ref-manual/ref-manual.html#structure-core-script] or oe-init-build-env-memres [http://www.yoctoproject.org/docs/1.7.2/ref-manual/ref-manual.html#structure-memres-core-script]).

6.2.2. Using the runqemu Command

The basic runqemu command syntax is as follows:

```
$ runqemu [option ] [...]
```

Based on what you provide on the command line, runqemu does a good job of figuring out what you are trying to do. For example, by default, QEMU looks for the most recently built image according to the timestamp when it needs to look for an image. Minimally, through the use of options, you must provide either a machine name, a virtual machine image (*.vmdk), or a kernel image (*.bin).

Following is a description of runqemu options you can provide on the command line:

Tip

If you do provide some "illegal" option combination or perhaps you do not provide enough in the way of options, runqemu provides appropriate error messaging to help you correct the problem.

- QEMUARCH: The QEMU machine architecture, which must be "qemux86", "qemux86-64", "qemuarm", "qemumips", "qemumipsel", "qemumips64", "qemush4", "qemuppc", "qemumicroblaze", or "qemuzynq".

- VM: The virtual machine image, which must be a .vmdk file. Use this option when you want to boot a .vmdk image. The image filename you provide must contain one of the following strings: "qemux86-64", "qemux86", "qemuarm", "qemumips64", "qemumips", "qemuppc", or "qemush4".

- ROOTFS: A root filesystem that has one of the following filetype extensions: "ext2", "ext3", "ext4", "jffs2", "nfs", or "btrfs". If the filename you provide for this option uses "nfs", it must provide an explicit root filesystem path.

- KERNEL: A kernel image, which is a .bin file. When you provide a .bin file, runqemu detects it and assumes the file is a kernel image.

- MACHINE: The architecture of the QEMU machine, which must be one of the following: "qemux86", "qemux86-64", "qemuarm", "qemumips", "qemumipsel", "qemumips64", "qemush4", "qemuppc", "qemumicroblaze", or "qemuzynq". The MACHINE and QEMUARCH options are basically identical. If you do not provide a MACHINE option, runqemu tries to determine it based on other options.

- ramfs: Indicates you are booting an initial RAM disk (initramfs) image, which means the FSTYPE is cpio.gz.

- iso: Indicates you are booting an ISO image, which means the FSTYPE is .iso.

- nographic: Disables the video console, which sets the console to "ttyS0".

- serial: Enables a serial console on /dev/ttyS0.

- biosdir: Establishes a custom directory for BIOS, VGA BIOS and keymaps.

- qemuparams=\"xyz\": Specifies custom QEMU parameters. Use this option to pass options other than the simple "kvm" and "serial" options.

- bootparams=\"xyz\": Specifies custom boot parameters for the kernel.

- audio: Enables audio in QEMU. The MACHINE option must be either "qemux86" or "qemux86-64" in order for audio to be enabled. Additionally, the snd_intel8x0 or snd_ens1370 driver must be installed in linux guest.

- slirp: Enables "slirp" networking, which is a different way of networking that does not need root access but also is not as easy to use or comprehensive as the default.

- kvm: Enables KVM when running "qemux86" or "qemux86-64" QEMU architectures. For KVM to work, all the following conditions must be met:

  - Your MACHINE must be either "qemux86" or "qemux86-64".

  - Your build host has to have the KVM modules installed, which are /dev/kvm.

  - Your build host has to have virtio net device, which are /dev/vhost-net.

  - The build host /dev/kvm directory has to be both writable and readable.

  - The build host /dev/vhost-net directory has to be either readable or writable and "slirp-enabled".

- publicvnc: Enables a VNC server open to all hosts.

For further understanding regarding option use with runqemu, consider some examples.

This example starts QEMU with MACHINE set to "qemux86". Assuming a standard Build Directory [14], runqemu automatically finds the bzImage-qemux86.bin image file and the core-image-minimalqemux86-20140707074611.rootfs.ext3 (assuming the current build created a core-image-minimal image).

Note

When more than one image with the same name exists, QEMU finds and uses the most recently built image according to the timestamp.

```
$ runqemu qemux86
```

This example produces the exact same results as the previous example. This command, however, specifically provides the image and root filesystem type.

```
$ runqemu qemux86 core-image-minimal ext3
```

This example specifies to boot an initial RAM disk image and to enable audio in QEMU. For this case, runqemu set the internal variable FSTYPE to "cpio.gz". Also, for audio to be enabled, an appropriate driver must be installed (see the previous description for the audio option for more information).

```
$ runqemu qemux86 ramfs audio
```

This example does not provide enough information for QEMU to launch. While the command does provide a root filesystem type, it must also minimally provide a MACHINE, KERNEL, or VM option.

```
$ runqemu ext3
```

This example specifies to boot a virtual machine image (.vmdk file). From the .vmdk, runqemu determines the QEMU architecture (MACHINE) to be "qemux86" and the root filesystem type to be "vmdk".

```
$ runqemu /home/scott-lenovo/vm/core-image-minimal-qemux86.vmdk
```

6.3. Running Under a Network File System (NFS) Server

One method for running QEMU is to run it on an NFS server. This is useful when you need to access the same file system from both the build and the emulated system at the same time. It is also worth noting that the system does not need root privileges to run. It uses a user space NFS server to avoid that. This section describes how to set up for running QEMU using an NFS server and then how you can start and stop the server.

6.3.1. Setting Up to Use NFS

Once you are able to run QEMU in your environment, you can use the runqemu-extract-sdk script, which is located in the scripts directory along with runqemu script. The runqemu-extract-sdk takes a root file system tarball and extracts it into a location that you specify. Then, when you run runqemu, you can specify the location that has the file system to pass it to QEMU. Here is an example that takes a file system and extracts it to a directory named test-nfs:

```
runqemu-extract-sdk ./tmp/deploy/images/qemux86/core-image-sato-qemux86.tar.bz2 test-nfs
```

Once you have extracted the file system, you can run runqemu normally with the additional location of the file system. You can then also make changes to the files within ./test-nfs and see those changes appear in the image in real time. Here is an example using the qemux86 image:

```
runqemu qemux86 ./test-nfs
```

6.3.2. Starting and Stopping NFS

You can manually start and stop the NFS share using these commands:

• start: Starts the NFS share:

```
runqemu-export-rootfs start file-system-location
```

• stop: Stops the NFS share:

```
runqemu-export-rootfs stop file-system-location
```

• restart: Restarts the NFS share:

```
runqemu-export-rootfs restart file-system-location
```

6.4. Tips and Tricks

The following list describes things you can do to make running QEMU in the context of the Yocto Project a better experience:

• Switching Between Consoles: When booting or running QEMU, you can switch between supported consoles by using Ctrl+Alt+number. For example, Ctrl+Alt+3 switches you to the serial console as long as that console is enabled. Being able to switch consoles is helpful, for example, if the main QEMU console breaks for some reason.

Note
Usually, "2" gets you to the main console and "3" gets you to the serial console.

• Removing the Splash Screen: You can remove the splash screen when QEMU is booting by using Alt+left. Removing the splash screen allows you to see what is happening in the background.

• Disabling the Cursor Grab: The default QEMU integration captures the cursor within the main window. It does this since standard mouse devices only provide relative input and not absolute coordinates. You then have to break out of the grab using the "Ctrl+Alt" key combination. However, the Yocto Project's integration of QEMU enables the wacom USB touch pad driver by default to allow input of absolute coordinates. This default means that the mouse can enter and leave the main window without the grab taking effect leading to a better user experience.